Violence and Society:
Toward a New Sociology

The Sociological Review Monographs

Since 1958, *The Sociological Review* has established a tradition of publishing one or two Monographs a year on issues of general sociological interest. The Monograph is an edited book length collection of refereed research papers which is published and distributed in association with Wiley Blackwell. We are keen to receive innovative collections of work in sociology and related disciplines with a particular emphasis on exploring empirical materials and theoretical frameworks which are currently under-developed.

If you wish to discuss ideas for a Monograph then please contact the Monographs Editor, Chris Shilling, School of Social Policy, Sociology and Social Research, Cornwallis North East, University of Kent, Canterbury, Kent CT2 7NF, C.Shilling@kent.ac.uk

Our latest Monographs include:

Disasters and Politics: Materials, Experiments, Preparedness (edited by Manuel Tironi, Israel Rodriguez-Giralt and Michael Guggenheim)
Urban Rhythms: Mobilities, Space and Interation in the Contemporary City (edited by Robin James Smith and Kevin Hetherington)
Waste Matters (edited by David Evans, Hugh Campbell and Anne Murcott)
Live Methods (edited by Les Back and Nirmal Puwar)
Measure and Value (edited by Lisa Adkins and Celia Lury)
Norbert Elias and Figurational Research: Processual Thinking in Sociology (edited by Norman Gabriel and Stephen Mennell)
Sociological Routes and Political Roots (edited by Michaela Benson and Rolland Munro)
Nature, Society and Environmental Crisis (edited by Bob Carter and Nickie Charles)
Space Travel & Culture: From Apollo to Space Tourism (edited by David Bell and Martin Parker)
Un/Knowing Bodies (edited by Joanna Latimer and Michael Schillmeier)
Remembering Elites (edited by Mike Savage and Karel Williams)
Market Devices (edited by Michel Callon, Yuval Millo and Fabian Muniesa)
Embodying Sociology: Retrospect, Progress and Prospects (edited by Chris Shilling)
Sports Mega-Events: Social Scientific Analyses of a Global Phenomenon (edited by John Horne and Wolfram Manzenreiter)
Against Automobility (edited by Steffen Böhm, Campbell Jones, Chris Land and Matthew Paterson)
A New Sociology of Work (edited by Lynne Pettinger, Jane Parry, Rebecca Taylor and Miriam Glucksmann)

Other Monographs have been published on consumption; museums; culture and computing; death; gender and bureaucracy; sport plus many other areas. For further information about the Monograph Series, please visit: www.sociologicalreviewmonographs.com

Violence and Society:
Toward a New Sociology

Edited by Jane Kilby and Larry Ray

Wiley Blackwell/The Sociological Review

This edition first published 2014
© 2014 The Editorial Board of the Sociological Review
Chapters © 2014 by the chapter author

ISBN 9781118942017 and The Sociological Review, 62:S2.

All articles published within this monograph are included within
the ISI Journal Citation Reports® Social Science Citation Index.
Please quote the article DOI when citing monograph content.

Registered Office
John Wiley & Sons Ltd, The Atrium, Southern Gate, Chichester, West Sussex, PO19 8SQ, UK

Editorial Offices
350 Main Street, Malden, MA 02148-5020, USA
9600 Garsington Road, Oxford, OX4 2DQ, UK
The Atrium, Southern Gate, Chichester, West Sussex, PO19 8SQ, UK

For details of our global editorial offices, for customer services, and for information about how
to apply for permission to reuse the copyright material in this book please see our website at
www.wiley.com/wiley-blackwell.

The right of Jane Kilby and Larry Ray to be identified as the editors of this work has been
asserted in accordance with the UK Copyright, Designs and Patents Act 1988.

First published in 2014 by John Wiley & Sons

Library of Congress Cataloging-in-Publication Data

Violence and society : toward a new sociology / Jane Kilby, Larry Ray.
   pages cm. – (Sociological review monographs)
     ISBN 978-1-118-94201-7 (paperback)
1. Violence–Social aspects. 2. Violence. 3. Violence–Psychological
aspects. I. Ray, Larry J. II. Title.
  HM1116.K5295 2014
  303.6–dc23

                                                                    2014037262

A catalogue record for this title is available from the British Library

Set in TimesNRMT 10/12pt by Toppan Best-set Premedia Limited

Printed and bound in the United Kingdom

1   2014

Contents

Series editor's acknowledgements

The Sociological Review Monograph series publishes special supplements of the journal in collections of original refereed papers that are included within the ISI Journal Citation Reports and the Social Science Citation Index.

In existence for over fifty years, the series has developed a reputation for publishing innovative projects that reflect the work of senior but also emerging academic figures from around the globe.

These collections could not continue without the considerable goodwill, advice and guidance of members of the Board of *The Sociological Review*, and of those anonymous referees who assess and report on the papers submitted for consideration for these collections. I would like to thank all of those involved in this process, especially Professor David Smith for his very considerable input into the collection as a whole, all of the referees, and also the editors of *Violence and Society: Toward a New Sociology* for having produced such a stimulating volume.

Chris Shilling, SSPSSR, University of Kent, UK.

Introduction

Jane Kilby and Larry Ray

Abstract: After many decades of neglect, sociologists have in recent years been giving renewed attention to violence and the problem of how to develop theoretically informed approaches to questions of definition, understanding and explanation. This volume is part of this ongoing project, which has an urgency generated both by the reality of violence and suffering and the need to address previous lack of sociological engagement. Violence is a complex phenomenon that involves violation, trauma and loss, which requires sociologists to contemplate the antithesis of the social, which is not anything as simple as 'antisocial behaviour'. While violence is a negative phenomenon that has no obvious antonym, it is clearly part of social life, social structures and institutions. It is at times also an agent of social and political change. In many ways confrontation with violence takes sociology to its limits and as both literary writers and sociologists have claimed, the attempt to understand it will ultimately lead us into the dark. A new sociology is one committed to imaginative, innovative ways of exploring violence, with inspiration sought from cognate disciplines and from art and literature.

Keywords: violence, sociology, new theoretical approaches, trauma, subjectivity

In recent years sociologists have made a concerted effort to develop our thinking about violence (Collins, 2008; Kilby, 2013a; Malešević, 2010; Ray, 2011; Walby, 2013; Wieviorka, 2009, 2012).[1] This volume is part of that project, rendered urgent both by the ongoing reality of violence and suffering, no matter how contested its relative status (as we discuss below); and by the need to address a perceived lack of sociological engagement. However, as the subtitle makes clear, this issue promises more. Violence is a complex, slippery phenomenon, but rather than repeat this insight, the authors in this volume are helping to develop a new agenda for sociology, one adequate to its complexity. To claim complexity as the imperative for new forms of sociological engagement is, of course, a common if possibly redundant ruse: the social is complex per se. But violence is uniquely so in that it also requires sociologists to contemplate the antithesis of the social, which is not anything as simple as 'antisocial behaviour'. Violence is a singularly negative phenomenon (and hence it has no obvious antonym, for example). This is not to deny that violence is

The Sociological Review, 62:S2, pp. 1–12 (2014), DOI: 10.1111/1467-954X.12188
© 2014 The Authors. Editorial organisation © 2014 The Editorial Board of the Sociological Review. Published by John Wiley & Sons Ltd, 9600 Garsington Road, Oxford OX4 2DQ, UK and 350 Main Street, Malden, MA 02148, USA

clearly part of social life, part also of social structures and institutions; and at times also an agent of social and political change, as Karl von Holdt and Glenn Bowman make clear in this volume. Rather it is to argue that violence takes sociology to its limits: from Joseph Conrad to Randall Collins there is recognition that the attempt to understand violence will ultimately lead us into the dark. Minimally, then, a new sociology is one committed to imaginative, innovative ways of exploring violence, with inspiration sought not only from cognate disciplines, such as anthropology, history and psychoanalysis, but from art and literature.[2]

Whether sociologists are willing to employ the concept of 'evil' to help us imagine violence is the provocation made by Steve Hall in his contribution, as it is made by Michel Wieviorka in his recent book *Evil*. The problems of doing so are easily rehearsed: sociology is not moral philosophy, psychology or theology; violence is not a metaphysical or individual problem. It is a social problem, a question, that is, of social injustice. And yet disciplinary borders should not allow sociologists to shy away from the difficulties posed by violence. Violence requires engagement with the question of human nature and subjectivity. What makes some people act violently is a function of historical, cultural and social variables, but it is not determined as such. There are questions of biography to be accounted for, and a need also 'to capture the moment of decision which is the real impetus for violent action. For without this decision there will be no violent act, not even in circumstances which potentially permit it. It is the decision to violate, not just the act itself, which makes a person a perpetrator of violence' (Kappeler, 1995: 5). For the most part, and despite living in situations which would nevertheless permit it, people do not choose to act violently so knowing why some make that decision, and how, is vital.

Making the subject central to a new sociology of violence is, then, a key challenge, as Michel Wieviorka, and Simon Winlow make clear in their papers. Their argument is not for a psychological profiling of the violent subject, as those vested in a psychosocial approach more broadly also make clear; nor is it an attempt to pathologize the violent subject. But rather it is a commitment to listening carefully to the perpetrator, and learning how to listen beyond the excuses and justifications perpetrators are nearly always compelled to give. This will yield among other things knowledge of shame and trauma and hence sociologists will have to explore how, why and when some affects make violence a possibility for some subjects. The question of gender will remain crucial on this count, as will the need for critical patience as we seek to decipher the logic dictating the instability of perpetrator and victim categories. Listening carefully will also yield an understanding of the plurality of violent subjects: the decision to act violently is taken for complex reasons by a range of subjects, some of whom will struggle also to know why they act as they do. Perpetrators may not be monsters, but nor do they necessarily have insight into why they choose violence. At times their answers will appear inadequate, and perhaps should never be held to be adequate. Thus our desire to make up for the perceived lack

The Sociological Review, 62:S2, pp. 1–12 (2014), DOI: 10.1111/1467-954X.12188

of meaning, to speculate, will have to be checked. In addition to critical imagination and patience, sociologists will have to learn a tolerance for not knowing all the answers.

This is the case also if listening to those who inflict violence on themselves, as Patricia A. Adler and Peter Adler illustrate in their *The Tender Cut: Inside the Hidden World of Self-Injury* (2011). Like any criminologist or sociologist committed to researching 'hidden' worlds, Adler and Adler have to solve the problem of access, of how, when and where to listen to those who self-harm. Indeed, in this respect, the study is especially impressive, with a total of 135 in-depth interviews, many years of Internet participant-observation as well as 30,000–40,000 e-messages. However, there is a second problem, which separates the study of self-inflicted violence from the study of other criminal or deviant behaviour: self-harm is not only stigmatized but counterintuitive, rendering it a seemingly pathological behaviour. In order to study it sociologically, Adler and Adler are compelled to impose a social logic, which they do by stressing its therapeutic function: it is a way of tending to the self, hence the book title. The integrity of Alder and Adler is not in question, the testimony of self-harmers support their reading of self-cutting as a survival, self-sustaining strategy. But by insisting on its social value, Adler and Adler must downplay the extent to which self-injury is irrational: they hear what they can and want to hear. Self-injury is normed off, such that readers are less likely to find it as 'gruesome, morbid and depressing' as Adler and Adler suggest they might (2011: ix). In keeping, then, with the 'stories of self-understanding, triumph and redemption' (2011: ix) they collected, Adler and Adler redeem self-inflicted injury in such a manner that it can be placed on a continuum with other body practices such as tattooing or body-piercing. Self-harm thus becomes an endorsed, violent self-fashioning.

To avoid this sanitization, sociologists such as Adler and Adler must find a way of confronting the issue of stigmatization (which given the harsh treatment self-harmers receive is a necessary project), such that it is possible to strike a balance between expressions of incomprehensibility ('The horror! The horror!') and phobic sterilization. To be fair, Adler and Adler were most likely overwhelmed if not depressed by the project (they could only hear what they could bear to hear), and thus a more sympathetic reading of their study would consider their neglect of the rampant contradictions thrown up by the accounts as evidence of a struggle on their part to make sense of self-harm. Indeed, in a recent, insightful article which explores the biographical context of Zygmunt Bauman's *Holocaust and Modernity*; and Max Horkheimer and Theordor Adorno's *Dialectic of Enlightenment*, Ron Eyerman, with a debt to recent developments in trauma and testimony studies, argues that social theory (and it is guessed other types of sociological writing) can be read as trauma texts. This is an important methodological innovation which licenses us to read sociological texts 'as literature' (2013: 47), and in an 'aesthetic mode' (2013: 50). Read differently, Adler and Adler's *The Tender Cut* is likely to produce additional insights, as might many other sociological texts about violence. Alternatively put, making the subject central to our analysis means also making ourselves central, which in conventional socio-logical parlance is to insist on greater reflexivity.

Listening carefully to the violent subject is not easy, though, especially also when perpetrator accounts remain steeped in the language of rationalization. This challenge is illustrated by Philippe Bourgois (2004), who having spent years living among Puerto Rican crack dealers, is thrown into a research crisis when listening to the young men talk about their violence, which includes brutally graphic accounts of gang 'sex' (the young men insist that the girls, ranging, it is said, from 12 to 17, enjoy the experience of group 'sex' despite also acknowl-edging that they were imprisoned, beaten about and held down by gangs of 5–6 men). Bourgois is tempted to omit the accounts from his study, fearing that 'readers would become too disgusted and angry with the protagonists and deny them a human face', or worse that the young Puerto Rican men would become the face of the rape, when as Bourgois rightly points out gang rape is not unique to them. Yet the violence of their language is such that it is difficult not to censor it in our writing (as we have opted to do so here; see Kilby, 2013b for an uncensored analysis): as Joanna Bourke argues in her impressive study of rape, the words of rapists 'try to harm women', hence 'No amount of distancing oneself from their comments can negate the fact that simply repeating their distortions threatens to construct a female body that (once again) becomes little more than property, the object of trespass' (2007: 7). The risk that we will become complicit in reproducing the language that helps perpetrators to ration-alize their violence, if not practise it, is one that sociologists will have to address.

It is important to remember, in other words, that rationalizations are not simply retrospective defences, as Stanley Cohen argues in his already classic *States of Denial: Knowing about Atrocities and Suffering*: justificatory accounts, which include, for example, that 'women ask for it', 'prepare the ground for the offence to take place' (2001: 61). Myths and rumouring making are proactive, scapegoating mechanisms. Indeed, despite the importance of Collins's *Violence: A Micro-sociological Theory* (2008), his lack of attention to the role of language in circumventing the emotional barrier perpetuates the idea that violence is an impassioned yet silent phenomenon. The tunnel of violence which the perpetra-tor enters may be a dark fog but it is rarely quiet. Monsters grunt, men talk. What perpetrators say before and during the act of violence requires closer attention, and while this poses significant challenges, victim testimony is one useful starting point.

While many of the contributors here are looking to ask new questions and start new debates, others return to existing, pertinent ones, including whether we live in more or less violent times. The idea that we live in a 'violent age' is widespread and the view is hardly surprising after the world wars and genocides of the twentieth century. But there is also wide disagreement about global trends. On the one hand Ungar *et al.* (2002) argue that as 'the new century opens, violence has been growing within many countries [. . .] Fragile govern-ments in Africa, Asia and Europe are being weakened by civil wars [. . .] in every region [. . .] rapid economic change and reform has been associated with rising

The Sociological Review, 62:S2, pp. 1–12 (2014), DOI: 10.1111/1467-954X.12188

levels of violence'. Again, predicting a bifurcation in the world system, Wallerstein (2005: 87) claims that a 'high degree of violence [. . .] erupts everywhere in smaller and larger doses and over relatively long periods'. Such views have been challenged recently by Steven Pinker who famously claims that 'The most important thing that has ever happened in human history' is that 'violence has declined over long stretches of time, and today we may be living in the most peaceable era in our species existence' (2012: xix). And finally, Norberg (2003) points to rising living standards for many millions, the spread of democracy and the decline in wars, conflict and violence towards the end of the twentieth century, particularly following the end of the cold war.

The long-running debate over historical trends in the prevalence of violence raises critical issues about the human condition. There are familiar though rather simplified lines of debate that fracture around 'pessimists' and 'optimists'. The former include Hobbes and Freud, for whom predilection to violence and other forms of destructiveness is rooted in the human condition, whether bio-psychologically or socially, and therefore requires constant vigilance exercised by institutional and internalized processes of control in order to maintain social peace. 'Optimists', on the other hand, point to the exceptional nature of violence in the *longue durée* of human history and early critics of Hobbes, such as Locke, claimed that the state of nature was not terrifying but naturally sociable, while a real threat came from the state that could make subjects slaves and destroy them when it had 'a fancy to it' (Locke, 1980: 278). Similarly, some archaeologists, anthropologists and sociologists claim that pre-state human societies were largely egalitarian and peaceful prior to a cataclysmic change that occurred after the Neolithic and the subsequent emergence of state societies (eg Fromm, 1974; Sahlins, 1974; and Knauft, 1991). While evidence can be assembled for both narratives (Ray, 2011) there are now also what one might call 'ameliorationists' who argue that while there are bio-psychological bases for human violence, the historical trend is in the direction of greater impulse control, increased inter-human empathy and declining interpersonal and global violence. Pinker is one of the leading contemporary exponents of this view and draws heavily on Elias's project of historicizing the Freudian understanding of the relationship between instincts and social process. However, whereas Elias was very aware of the fragility of this process, in Pinker's hands it is a classical liberal-Enlightenment story of progress. Moreover, as Sinisa Malešević, argues in this volume, Pinker's theory is informed by an idealist epistemology in which the modern 'Humanitarian Revolution' significantly reduced violence on all levels – interpersonal, collective, and civil and inter-state conflicts.

It is true that the ameliorationist thesis can (as does Pinker) draw on an impressive range of evidence ranging from historical criminology to conflict studies. For example, Eisner (2001) documents the long-range decline in European homicide rates and Spierenburg (2013) elaborates Elias to analyse declining violence and punishment from the early modern period onwards. Data from Human Security Brief (2006: 6) suggests that with the decline in inter-state wars in the later twentieth century, average battle deaths per armed conflict fell from 50,000–70,000 in mid-century to under 5,000 during the 1990s and 2000s, making this the *least* violent period in human history. Further, Human Security data on how conflicts end points to the decline in the number of victories and 'a fairly steady increase in negotiated settlements' (2012: 176). A case can be made, then, for the decline of violence thesis.

However, the contributions to this volume offer innovative and more nuanced ways of addressing these issues. Understanding violence is subject to state policy and social meanings and hence the question of whether 'it' is rising or falling is difficult to judge. Moreover, in many theorizations of violence ambivalence is central – for Freud after all the constraint of the superego is aggression against oneself, Elias's pacification is dependent on state centralization of violence and in Girard chaotic violence is contained by an act of violence: scapegoating-sacrifice. Further, as Mark Cooney argues here, violence has its own particular geometry and movement through time. Violence is dynamic and episodic rather than a single event and is embedded in inequalities and movements of social time. Identifying linear trends in the statistical register then risks overlooking the way 'violence' is subject to shifting definitions and changing social context. The pacification thesis, addressing the reduction of interpersonal violence, largely documents a shift from predominantly male face-to-face impulsive violence conducted in public to more 'private' and gendered violence that takes place in intimate spaces. Further, as Cooney argues, the survival of masculine honour (an example of an Eliasian figuration that is reconstituted within modern society) points to the ways in which the enactment of violence remains highly gendered.

While Spierenburg (2013) associates the decline in violence in Western Europe with a concomitant decline in the brutality of punishment, in this volume Hall argues that the pacification process is receding as we see an increase in carceral discipline and a proportionate growth in prison populations in many developed countries, notably the US and UK. According to the International Centre for Prison Studies, between 1992 and 2013 the prison population in the UK rose from 90 to 163 per 100,000 of the population (Walmsley, 2013). Further, Hall argues that the growth of poverty, sociospatial segregation and lack of opportunities generate increased levels of stress, depression, anger. Reflecting the turn to the subject in other papers in this volume, such as Winlow and Wieviorka, Hall discusses criminogenic sublimated aggressive competition and how the apparent 'crime drop' conceals a 'retreat into subjectivity'. These arguments resonate with Parker (2008) who emphasizes the spatiality of the distribution of crime and how violence changed significantly in American urban areas between 1980 and 2000. She emphasizes the uneven nature of trends in urban violence – so while national rates in the US (and the same can be said of the UK) declined from the mid-1990s there were localities in which the rates have remained higher. The latter localities are those that experienced the worst effects of neoliberal economic restructuring in the late twentieth century (Parker, 2008).

The Sociological Review, 62:S2, pp. 1–12 (2014), DOI: 10.1111/1467-954X.12188
© 2014 The Authors. Editorial organisation © 2014 The Editorial Board of the Sociological Review

These arguments in turn signal the importance of widening analysis of violence from Europe and addressing global trends, which is represented in papers by Kevin McSorley and Karl von Holdt. Bourdieu commented that one 'cannot cheat with the law of conservation of violence: all violence is paid for, and [. . .] the structural violence exerted by the financial markets, in the form of layoffs, loss of security, etc., is matched sooner or later in the form of suicides, crime and major everyday acts of violence' (Bourdieu, 1998: 39–40). An illustration of this can been seen by examining the global consequences of the 2008 financial crisis, following which there have been rising levels of violence, and especially gendered violence, in developing countries that runs against the 'crime decline' trend in developed countries. Food and fuel crises have been exacerbated by investment collapse and increased unemployment which has especially affected women in the informal economy. At the same time, reduced access to credit combined with women's lack of financial autonomy have led to diminished social capital and increased risk of domestic violence. The World Bank predicted excess infant mortality of 700,000 in Africa as a result of the 2008 crash, of which mortality would be five times higher among girls than boys (Sabarwal *et al.*, 2009). It is reasonable to conclude, then, that it is difficult to identify any linear trend in the incidence of violence, the patterns of which are highly differentiated and are embedded in multiple inequalities and cultural formations.

Equally difficult to assess is the relationship between war, the state and nationality. Sociologists have generally focused predominantly on interpersonal violence and left questions of war, the state and genocide to other disciplines, especially political science and international relations. There have been notable exceptions, such as Zygmunt Bauman, Michael Mann and Martin Shaw, as well as Bowman, Malešević, von Holdt and McSorley in this volume. We explore the sociological analysis of war and the state since the process of state formation is closely imbricated with the formation of patterns of violence. Indeed, as Malešević argues, 'one of the significant recent developments in the new sociological focus on violence is the rethinking of the relationship between war and society'. There are wide differences in processes of state formation and violence between, for example, Europe and the US and the colonizing and postcolonial states. The US, for instance, has a homicide rate over three times higher than that of other 'established market economies', a situation that Monkkonen (2006) argues is based on the inability of the post-independence federal state to achieve a monopoly of force. At the same time, in the slave plantations of the anti-bellum South, social relations were more akin to the unpacified Middle Ages where honour violence was widespread, a culture that persisted into the twentieth century. The upshot of this was a less embedded civilizational process than in Western Europe. In relation to postcolonial societies von Holdt shows, with reference to South Africa, how democratization has created 'violent democracies' characterized by deep inequalities and legacies of violent rule. There are then 'violent multiplicities of violent actors in civil society', a phenomenon that requires rethinking the notions of power and violence that have been developed in relation to Western modernity.

Violence carries the power of enforcement and has been effective historically. Violence has naissance – it is productive as well as destructive and most nations were founded by violent acts of rebellion or exclusion. Bowman examines how communities are 'addressed' by an act of violence which can create integrities as well as being a force that violates, pollutes and destroys already existing entities. Drawing on Ariella Azoulay's concept of the 'political imaginary' he suggests that a perceived antagonism stimulates the emergence of an identity constituted precisely by the need to defend itself against an enemy. This resonates with understandings of ethnonational conflicts drawing on René Girard's concept of 'mimetic violence' and 'violent doubles' in which the perceived violence, or threat of violence, from one side is mimed by the mutual hostility of the other – so two parties are bound together into cycles of violence in which 'peace' involves the destruction of the other. This often makes negotiated peace processes elusive. Although the Human Security (2012) data noted above records an increasing trend towards negotiated settlements to conflicts, more pessimistically the report also notes that conflicts ending in a 'victory' are less likely than negotiated conflicts to resume within five years (2012: 175). Understanding the dynamics and cycles of conflict is thus essential to understanding the possibilities for conflict resolution.

Unlike writers for whom humans are 'hard wired' for violence, Malešević regards war as a novel form of human action that emerges with stratified societies, sedentary lifestyles, agriculture and social hierarchies. In the modern period it has become a stimulus for state development and social change culminating with the total war of the twentieth century. In the process war undermined traditional and patriarchal relationships with a lasting impact on post-war societies. Indeed this process is ongoing and will continue in a context of heightening environmental pressures and shortages, an argument developed too by John Urry (2013). By contrast to Pinker, the level of human causalities might not be a barometer of war's destructiveness as the use of technologies such as robots in warfare increases. With these come mass dispossession and forced displacement and as Hannah Arendt argued several decades ago, the modern age brings a huge increase in 'superfluous' and 'rightless' peoples. While we still live in the age of the nation state there are increasingly millions of victims of local conflicts, mass dispossession and environmental degradation, who are forced into vulnerable and potentially violent spaces beyond the institutional protections of the legal state.

With the decline in inter-state warfare in the later twentieth century, civil conflicts become more visible although the scale of civilian casualties is difficult to calculate, as seen in the Iraq war and subsequent conflicts. The sociology of violence needs an understanding of the dynamics of civil conflicts involving mass participation. Preferring the term 'extremely violent societies' to that of 'genocide' Gerlach (2010) argues that mass violence depends on broad and diverse support but offers an explanatory multicausal process linked to a wide range of aspects of social mobility. He lists as factors predisposing to the eruption of mass violence: a temporary state of crisis, drastic drop in living standards, new groups

The Sociological Review, 62:S2, pp. 1–12 (2014), DOI: 10.1111/1467-954X.12188
© 2014 The Authors. Editorial organisation © 2014 The Editorial Board of the Sociological Review

ascended to elites, transformation of the countryside, forced decline of middle-men minorities who are accused of being linked to foreign interests, and loss of monopoly of state violence. Violence then comes from both 'above' from state agents, and 'below' from local militias. Further, foreign armies induce violence in societies that were often already ridden with ethnic, religious and class conflicts (Gerlach, 2010). Seen in these terms, mass violence is a social event of crisis and panic in which ethical norms and values are devalidated, while polarization offers perpetrators new solidarity through participation in atrocities. Evidence from atrocities and mass violence indicates that members of victimized groups are murdered routinely but also with spectacles of sadistic violence, such as shooting children in front of and before their mothers and days of gang-rape and torture before death (Grabowski, 2013). Such public spectacles of violence serve to constitute and dramatize a new moral hegemony and power of the social order. Moreover, as Kalyvas (2006) notes, selective violence gives individuals an incentive to cooperate, since it requires non-combatant informants rendering rule a joint process created by political actors and civilians. From the point of view of these broader sociological and historical studies, mass violence can be a consequence of multiple factors that need to be understood in particular historical contexts but nonetheless permit comparisons between different instances.

Finally, the definition of violence is absolutely central to how we measure and understand it, and hence key to our hopes for change. It is not our intention to rehearse the debates over adopting a narrow or broad definition (see Bufacchi, 2007; and Schinkel, 2010 for extensive discussion of the debates). The task instead is to keep debate open, as the papers in this volume by Curtis Jackson-Jacobs, and Sylvia Walby, Jude Towers and Brian Francis do. Indeed, Walby *et al.*'s paper is likely to provoke intense debate given that as a consequence of refusing the Crime Survey of England and Wales' separate definition – and hence counting – of 'sexual violence' and 'violence against the person', they show how radically our understanding of the gendered pattern of violence and victimization changes. Indeed, their bold conclusion that 'there is almost as much violence against women as there is against men' (as opposed to the conventional wisdom which has men as primary perpetrators and victims) will demand a radical rethink of the nature of violence, both for left-leaning and feminist sociologists (it appears also that violence against women is more often perpetrated by acquaintances than intimates).

While endorsing the challenge presented by Walby *et al.*, we would add that it is always important to keep our definitions open, sensitive to how the picture of violence changes as we move from interpersonal to mass violence, from self-inflicted to revolutionary violence for as Elizabeth Stanko argues 'it is only through fluidity of definition that we can think creatively about disrupting violence as a social phenomenon' (2003: 3) (see also de Haan, 2009, for an excellent defence of the importance of violence as an essentially contested concept). That said, we would also argue that it is always important to define violence as a process, meaning, as Willem Schinkel argues (2010: 35), that violence 'consists of actions that recursively follow each other and that cannot be wholly singled out without losing the identity ("violence") of the process as a whole'. This emphasis on the temporal character of violence makes isolating causes and consequences difficult, but not impossible.

Violence is, of course, a normative concept: it is a word that denotes a wrong; and hence the definition of violence is (implicitly and normally) a matter of judgement and politics. This will always make the task of defining violence tricky, especially for those committed to a value-free science of violence. Importantly, though, we do not read this struggle to define violence as a refusal on the part of sociologists to acknowledge a common capacity for violence, as thinkers as diverse as Jack Katz and Pinker would have us believe. The issue is not a denial of the monster in us all, of recognizing as Katz puts it 'the piercing reflection we catch when we steady our glance at those evil men' (1988: 324). Indeed, somewhat perversely to claim a glimpse of our own image in the eyes of those who commit acts of violence serves to deny the humanity of the violent subject, which is the point of such argument. If we content ourselves with imagining our own reflection, we fail, that is, to acknowledge their difference, of how and why they acted out a desire to be violent. We fail, in other words, to be sociologists. The distinctly theological 'know thyself' thesis serves also to negate the humanity of the victim, whose suffering is a function of having to look into the eyes of somebody in particular, and *not* seeing themselves reflected. Thus we fail on two counts.

Notes

1 In addition, and following 9/11, a wide-range of critics have also taken up the question of violence, resulting in a plethora of monographs, edited collections and special issues; see Bernstein, 2013; Bernstein *et al.*, 2008; Bufacchi, 2009, 2011; Butler, 2004, 2009; Eckstrand and Yates, 2011; Oksala, 2012; Pinker, 2012; Sarat *et al.*, 2011; Žižek, 2008.
2 See Mariam Fraser (2009, 2012), and Alberto Toscano (2012) for highly suggestive arguments for how sociologists might use art and literature as methods for sociological analysis and theorizing.

References

Adler, P. A. and Adler, P., (2011), *The Tender Cut: Inside the Hidden World of Self-Injury*, New York: New York University Press.
Bernstein, H., Leys, C. and Panitch, L. (eds), (2008), 'Reflections on violence today', *Socialist Register 2009*, Pontypool: The Merlin Press.
Bernstein, R. J., (2013), *Violence: Thinking without Bannisters*, Cambridge: Polity Press.
Bourdieu, P., (1998), *Acts of Resistance: Against the Tyranny of the Market* (trans. R. Nice), New York: The New Press and Polity Press.
Bourgois, P., (2004), 'Gang rape', in N. Scheper-Hughes and P. Bourgois (eds), *Violence in Times of War and Peace: An Anthology*, London and New York: Blackwell Publishing.
Bourke, J., (2007), *Rape: A History from 1860 to the Present*, London: Virago.
Bufacchi, V., (2007), *Violence and Social Justice*, London: Palgrave.
Bufacchi, V. (ed.), (2009), *Violence: A Philosophical Anthology*, London: Palgrave.

The Sociological Review, 62:S2, pp. 1–12 (2014), DOI: 10.1111/1467-954X.12188

Bufacchi, V. (ed.), (2011), *Rethinking Violence*, London: Routledge.

Butler, J., (2004), *Precarious Life: The Powers of Mourning and Violence*, London and New York: Verso.

Butler, J., (2009), *Frames of War: When Is Life Grievable?*, London and New York: Verso.

Cohen, S., (2001), *States of Denial: Knowing about Atrocities and Suffering*, Cambridge: Polity Press.

Collins, R., (2008), *Violence: A Micro-sociological Theory*, Princeton, NJ: Princeton University Press.

de Haan, W., (2009), 'Violence as an essentially contested concept', in S. Body-Gendrot and P. Spierenburg (eds), *Violence in Europe: Historical and Contemporary Perspectives*, New York: Springer.

Eckstrand, N. and Yates, S. C. (eds), (2011), *Philosophy and the Return of Violence: Studies from this Widening Gyre*, London: Continuum.

Eisner, M., (2001), 'Modernization, self-control and lethal violence: the long-term dynamics of European homicide rates in theoretical perspective', *British Journal of Criminology*, 41 (4): 618–638.

Eyerman, R., (2013), 'Social theory and trauma', *Acta Sociologica*, 56 (1): 41–53.

Fraser, M., (2009), 'Experiencing sociology', *European Journal of Social Theory*, 12 (1): 63–81.

Fraser, M., (2012), 'Once upon a problem', *The Sociological Review*, 60 (1): 84–107.

Fromm, E., (1974), *Anatomy of Human Destructiveness*, New York: Holt, Rinehart & Winston.

Gerlach, C., (2010), *Extremely Violent Societies: Mass Violence in the Twentieth Century World*, Cambridge: Cambridge University Press.

Grabowski, J., (2013), *The Hunt for the Jews: Betrayal and Murder in German-Occupied Poland*, Bloomington and Indianapolis: Indiana University Press.

Human Security Brief, (2006), Simon Fraser University, Vancouver, Canada, available at: http://www.humansecuritybrief.info/2006/index.html

Human Security Report, (2012), *Sexual Violence, Education, and War: Beyond the Mainstream Narrative*, Vancouver: Human Security Press, available at: http://www.hsrgroup.org/human-security-reports/2012/text.aspx

Kalyvas, S. N., (2006), *The Logic of Violence in Civil War*, Cambridge: Cambridge University Press.

Kappeler, S., (1995), *The Will to Violence: The Politics of Personal Behaviour*, Cambridge: Polity Press.

Katz, J., (1988), *Seductions of Crime*, London and New York: Basic Books.

Kilby, J. (ed.), (2013a), 'Theorizing violence', *European Journal of Social Theory*, 16 (3) Special Issue.

Kilby, J., (2013b), 'In letting the perpetrator speak: sexual violence and classroom politics', in M. T. Segal and V. Demos (eds), *Gendered Perspectives on Conflict and Violence (Advances in Gender Research, Volume 18)*, Bingley: Emerald Group Publishing Limited.

Knauft, B. M., (1991), 'Violence and sociality in human evolution', *Current Anthropology*, 32 (4): 391–409.

Locke, J., (1980), *Second Treatise on Civil Government* (ed. C. B. Macpherson), Indianapolis: Hackett (first published 1681–3).

Malešević, S., (2010), *The Sociology of War and Violence*, Cambridge: Cambridge University Press.

Monkkonen, E., (2006), 'Homicide: explaining America's exceptionalism', *The American Historical Review*, 111 (1): 76–94.

Norberg J., (2003), *In Defence of Global Capitalism*, Lagos: Cato Institute.

Oksala, J., (2012), *Foucault, Politics and Violence*, Evanston, IL: Northwestern University Press.

Parker, K. F., (2008), *Unequal Crime Decline*, New York: New York University Press.

Pinker, S., (2012), *The Better Angels of our Nature: A History of Violence and Humanity*, London: Penguin.

Ray, L. J., (2011), *Violence and Society*, London: Sage.

Sabarwal, S., Sinha, N. and Buvinic, M., (2009), *The Global Financial Crisis: Assessing Vulnerability for Women and Children*, Washington, DC: World Bank, available at: http://worldbank.org/financialcrisis/pdf/Women-Children-Vulnerability-March09.pdf

Sahlins, M., (1974), *Stone Age Economics*, London: Tavistock.

Sarat, A., Basler, C. R. and Dumm, T. L. (eds), (2011), *Performances of Violence*, Amherst, MA: University of Massachusetts Press.

Schinkel, W., (2010), *Aspects of Violence*, Farnham: Ashgate.

Spierenburg, P., (2013), *Violence and Punishment: Civilizing the Body through Time*, Cambridge: Polity Press.

Stanko, E. (ed.), (2003), *Meanings of Violence*, London: Routledge.

Toscano, A., (2012), 'Seeing it whole: staging totality in social theory and art', *The Sociological Review*, 60 (1): 64–83.

Ungar, M., Bermanzohn, S. A. and Worcester, K., (2002), 'Introduction' to *Violence and Politics*, 1–12, London: Routledge.

Urry, J., (2013), *Societies beyond Oil*, London: Zed Books.

Walby, S. (ed.), (2013), 'Violence and society', *Current Sociology*, 61 (2) Special Issue.

Wallerstein, I., (2005), *World-Systems Analysis: An Introduction*, London: Duke University Press.

Walmsley, R., (2013), *World Prison Population List*, International Centre for Prison Studies, available at: http://www.prisonstudies.org/sites/prisonstudies.org/files/resources/downloads/wppl_10.pdf

Wieviorka, M., (2009), *Violence: A New Approach*, London: Sage.

Wieviorka, M., (2012), *Evil*, Cambridge: Polity Press.

Žižek, S., (2008), *Violence: Six Sideways Reflections*, London: Profile Books.

The Sociological Review, 62:S2, pp. 1–12 (2014), DOI: 10.1111/1467-954X.12188

The socioeconomic function of evil

Steve Hall

Abstract: This article challenges various theories that depict the capitalist epoch as a process of civilization to posit a new theoretical framework built around the concept of pseudo-pacification. Principal indicators of civilizing momentum, such as the decline in homicide and brutal punishment, are relocated in a new perspective that juxtaposes them with the concomitant proliferation of non-violent crimes and the types of aggressive sociosymbolic competition that energize and structure consumer culture. What seems to have occurred is not the repression or dissipation of aggressive libidinal energy but its conversion into a dynamic yet largely pacified form that performs the dual function of protecting property and expanding production and trade by intensifying and democratizing sociosymbolic competition. The pseudo-pacification process does not counteract but stimulates and reproduces aggressive drives in sublimated forms to create a fragile social peace whose potential disintegrative forces are manufactured at the very core of its own socioeconomic and cultural systems.

Keywords: capitalism, history, evil, violence, pseudo-pacification, consumer culture, libidinal energy

Introduction

Statistical evidence supports the Whiggish claim that from its nascence in the Late Middle Ages in Europe the Western liberal-capitalist era has been characterized by a decline in rates of homicide and serious violence in the public sphere (Eisner, 2001). This decline seems to have occurred alongside progress in economic productivity and individual rights. However, it was also accompanied by a notable, if rather undulating, rise in the rate of acquisitive property crime (Sharpe, 1996), committed increasingly for the purpose of obtaining and displaying symbols of conspicuous consumption (Hallsworth, 2005; Hall *et al.*, 2008). This suggests not a diminution but a conversion of aggressive libidinal energy into a more pacified yet more expansive form. Thus we must consider the possibility that the liberal-capitalist epoch has not been characterized by a *civilizing process* but a *pseudo-pacification process*. This process seems to have evolved to perform the complementary tasks of sublimating libidinal energy into a form that fuels aggressive competition in the sociosymbolic field, whilst

The Sociological Review, 62:S2, pp. 13–31 (2014), DOI: 10.1111/1467-954X.12189

simultaneously reducing the physical violence that hampers the protection and trading of property. Therefore the pseudo-pacification process supplied the liberal-capitalist project with the invaluable combination of psychosocial momentum alongside a pacified environment conducive to the project of economic expansion. In essence, the primary purpose behind reducing and sublimating physical violence was not to establish a peaceful, sociable existence for human beings but to maintain a safer environment for the intensification and democratic expansion of aggressive yet rule-bound sociosymbolic competition. This chapter charts the process from its beginnings in the later Middle Ages and analyses its psychosocial dynamics. At its core, the process is reliant on the stimulation and pacified acting-out of obscene drives and object-related desires, whose generative bases are in anxiety, torment and dissociation. Acting out these drives and desires would have once attracted the label 'evil'. The aim of this chapter is not to reduce explanations of diverse manifestations of human violence to the singular effect of pseudo-pacification, but to reveal this process as a pervasive and fragile cultural current in which eruptions of various forms of violence are likely to occur as long as it continues to be a mainstay of cultural and socioeconomic life.

Pseudo-pacification as a historical process

In England, the homicide rate entered a long period of decline from the late 14th century. From the mid-16th century, mainland Western Europe also experienced a similar decline. Although unknown rates of violence remained hidden in the family, the workplace and other private spaces, and there were many undulations and complexities, the general long-term historical trend in the world's first market-capitalist societies seems to have been a decline in homicide and life-threatening physical violence in the public sphere (Eisner, 2001). This seems to lend empirical weight to Elias's (1994) claim that the continent underwent a 'civilizing process'. According to Elias, the process's three mainstays are the state's monopolization of physical violence, the diffusion of behavioural codes throughout the social body, and the expansion of 'figurational' social interdependencies that drew individuals together in relations of mutual benefit and respect. The vital cultural product of this triptych of civilizing forces was the inculcation and reproduction of embodied sensibilities in the majority of individuals, who, as the subjects of new processes of sociogenesis and psychogenesis, began to react with repugnance to the gruesome consequences of physical violence and cruel punishments.

However, Elias's theory glosses over important aspects of the general field of crime, harm and violence. Apart from numerous problems associated with the relation between culture and nature, and the lack of a clear explanation of the relation between sociogenesis and psychogenesis, it understates the continuation of brutality in the punishment system and the reproduction of exploitative social relations in the economic system. Elias understood that the 'civilizing

The Sociological Review, 62:S2, pp. 13–31 (2014), DOI: 10.1111/1467-954X.12189
© 2014 The Author. Editorial organisation © 2014 The Editorial Board of the Sociological Review

process' was not an attempt to eliminate violence from human life, but to relocate and store it 'behind the scenes' to unleash in practices of punishment (Garland, 1990) or military violence (Fletcher, 1997). However, because he overstates the functional efficacy, neutrality and legitimacy of the state he therefore understates the violent social conflict frequently precipitated by the ineffectiveness and politicization of its control apparatus. The thesis's explanatory framework also fails to incorporate the fragile pacifying effect of the institutionalization of social conflict, as organized labour developed practices of negotiation with capital in the industrial capitalist era from the late 19th century (Wieviorka, 2009). This established temporary and partial solidarity amongst the working classes and pacified what had frequently been violent social conflict over inequality, oppression and various single issues such as religious rights and food prices. Elias's rather simplified tripartite structure of civilizing forces also fails to incorporate the developing bureaucratic organization of welfare and education systems (Mucchielli, 2010), and his rather transcendent conceptualization of 'social' interdependencies ignores the incorporation of subjects and their fears, passions and associations into productive work; direct participation in stable forms of organized labour itself, not just the social figurations it underpins, has a vital civilizing effect based on the daily affirmation of the knowledge that the individual cannot survive alone (Dejours, 2003).

Constant eruptions of state violence, organized criminal violence, political violence and privatized violence in the domestic sphere and the workplace throughout the liberal-capitalist epoch, and the recent riots and the rise of violent crime in the West since the 1980s, all suggest that the so-called civilizing process is in its form and function actually a rather fragile and unstable pacification process, whose tripartite structure is unable to reproduce itself in a coherent and stable form, and whose ability to inculcate durable civilized emotions in subjects must be questioned. This inherent instability suggests that the process is ultimately dependent on the maintenance of a stable and supportive politico-economic environment and the constant gratification of social ambitions and private fantasy-desires inculcated in subjects by mass-mediated consumer culture (Hall *et al.*, 2008). The tendency for individual and group violence incessantly to burst through the restraints supposedly provided by Elias's cultivated sensibilities suggests that violence was not simply concealed and 'stored up' behind physical and metaphorical walls, but that it was also 'stored up' behind the sensibilities and cultural codes that restrained its physical form and converted it to an aggressive yet pacified sociosymbolic form that displayed a tendency to revert to physicality in specific circumstances.

However, Wieviorka (2009) warns us that we cannot understand violent subjectivities as a singular undifferentiated category produced by a process of social evolution. He provides us with a typology: hypersubjectivity, the product of an overload or a plethora of meanings; desubjectivated non-subjectivity capable of surrender to the banality of evil; socially liberated antisubjectivity orientated to cruelty, sadism and violence as an end in itself; and subjectivity aimed at conserving its being or its foundation. He also reminds us that these subjectivities are the products of heterogeneous circumstances and experiences at the micro-level. However, we do not have to disagree with this pluralistic analysis and descend to crude forms of reductionism and essentialism to acknowledge the copious evidence of both long-term and short-term spatial and historical patterns of serious violence, ranging from homicide and serial killing to riots, which are quite easy to identify (Dorling, 2004; Wilson, 2007; Parker, 2008). The long-term decline in the homicide rate in Europe over the course of modernity holds true (Eisner, 2001), and a number of decades characterized by disruptive socioeconomic change – for instance, neoliberal Britain and the USA in the 1980s – have suffered from abrupt rises in rates of most forms of crime and public violence (Reiner, 2007; Hall and McLean, 2009; Marktanner and Noiset, 2013). In other words, we can identify long-term periods, short-term periods and specific social spaces in which there is some degree of synchronization in both the generative constitution and acting out of Wieviorka's differentiated categories of violent subjectivity. The following argument will show how tendencies towards these various forms of subjectivity and modes of acting them out are rooted in a long-term process of cultural change that cannot be described as a 'civilizing process', and why these differentiated forms are interrelated variants with a common root in generative conditions associated with an underlying historical process.

Mucchielli (2010) reminds us that Elias's thesis also ignores the destructive effects of socio-spatial segregation and consumer culture's anti-social psychological stimulations and distractions. The ubiquity and durability of these socially disintegrative conditions and tendencies suggest that they are not simply the products of latent regressive forces released from some unknown source by temporal lapses in the maintenance of Elias's triangular framework. Mucchielli argues that the social effects of disintegrative forces – poverty, segregation, lack of opportunity – produce corresponding psychological effects: stress, depression, frustration, resentment, anger and so on. However, as prescient as it is, this analysis offers no answer to the question of why psychological life in these adverse conditions manifests itself in bouts of competitive consumption and violence rather than articulate political protest or rebellion. Why resort to acting out the ideologically disavowed 'dark heart' of the system – violence, looting, exploitation, infantile hedonism – rather than seek solidarity and articulate politics in the face of adversity? Throughout the industrial era of institutionalized conflict the European working class consistently demonstrated the drive to seek and occasionally find solidarity and unifying politics in three primary forms – communism, socialism and reformist social democracy – despite these conditions (Winlow and Hall, 2013).

We can agree with Mucchielli's critique of Elias's thesis and his useful additions to the explanatory framework, and with Wieviorka's (2009) appeal to abandon Elias's evolutionary approach because it simply cannot explain the conflict, heterogeneous forms of violence and violent subjectivity we have witnessed throughout the 20th century. However, both Mucchielli and Wieviorka have trouble explaining why the post-war social democratic system of institutionalized and politicized conflict fell apart so easily in the 1980s (see Dean, 2009) to be displaced by sporadic eruptions of violent pre-political crime and rioting (Bauman, 2012; Stiegler, 2013; Treadwell *et al.*, 2013). Although we must acknowledge and attempt to incorporate Wieviorka's formal plurality, the existence of identifiable patterns of violence suggests that our understanding is best advanced by continuing to conceptualize the types we are seeing in Europe today as the products of some sort of underlying process.

Before we investigate this process we must begin with a de-romanticizing correction. The popular revisionist notion of ethnic groups peacefully accommodating each other in the intervallic Dark Age between the fall of the Roman Empire and the Late Middle Ages has been challenged by Ward-Perkins's (2005) revealing study. The decline of material production, culture and ethnic relations to prehistoric levels – the latter resulting in the death of huge proportions of European populations by blows to the head and vital organs – suggests that this period was every bit as violent as traditional historians once thought it was (see Žižek, 2010). It looks like the 'grand narrative' that from the Late Middle Ages Europe experienced a broad shift away from a notably violent period in its history – characterized by the acquisition and defence of land, treasure and bodily honour – towards the less violent acquisition of more diverse sociosymbolic resources has some purchase on reality (Hall, 2012a). The signs also point to the probability that although regions in southern Europe began to develop market economies earlier, this mutative process first took hold more firmly in England on the back of unique legal and sociocultural changes (see Macfarlane, 1978), which we will now investigate in further detail.

After the Norman invasion disrupted the island's socio-political fabric, violent gangs took advantage of the Norman warlords' lax administration (Hibbert, 2003). By the late Middle Ages, violence structured and reproduced a rigid class-based social order whose weak legitimacy and institutional framework were in constant danger of collapsing (Maddern, 1992). In such a hostile and lawless environment the population felt safer entrenched in defensive familial and communal units. However, this lax administration also created a broader deregulated space in which wealthier peasants and merchants could accelerate the commercial development of land and urban markets. These newcomers into the economic fold realized that both authorized structural violence and unauthorized criminal violence were impeding the growth of markets (Hall, 2012a). This proto-bourgeoisie, initially attempting to ascend the social order by convincing monarchs that they could increase the wealth of the nation, sought a middle way. It quickly became apparent that if property is to be safely and efficiently traded it must be protected by the rule of law. Yet, paradoxically, it also became apparent that if the expansion of this trade can be accelerated in unregulated spaces beneath the law, wealth creation can be more efficiently developed in a 'third space' created by the tension between order and disorder. Hence, in order to create this third space, the new and ambitious social group sought pacified variants of order and disorder to operate in a more stable form of dynamic tension. To protect property and allow trade the embryonic market-capitalist system required the rule of law to evacuate previously normalized physical violence from nascent commercial nodes and arteries (market towns, roads etc.). Simultaneously, the law had to sever its relation to existing customs of fair trading, yet deter violent retribution when moral judgements were cast onto the more dubious emerging practices – especially when they went awry – such as usury, cheating on weights and measures, bad debts or undercutting prices (Hall, 2012a). Physical violence was to be displaced by pacified yet aggressive, competitive and exploitative practices, which were destructive to existing customs but could also be freely encouraged and acted out as they were protected by law. The overall shift was dependent on the dual pacification of the forces of social *order* and *disorder*.

First, a concerted attempt was made to gradually and partially pacify violent modes of maintaining social order. In the 12th to 13th centuries, under the misgovernment of Henry III, order could not be imposed as violent gangs monopolized trading nodes and arteries, including valuable ports and market towns, and controlled the trade in precious metals (Hibbert, 2003). The ruling aristocracy's violent control methods often proved ineffective, escalating conflict as they confronted these heavily armed gangs. This palpable failure reduced public confidence in the ability of government to deal with privatized violence and protect property. Edward I, crowned in 1274, reorganized the militias and the whole criminal justice system in ways that involved the delegation of everyday citizens as agents in practices of crime control. This democratization of control set in motion the gradual diminution of violence, to be displaced by diffused surveillance and 'social pressure' as the primary social structuring and regulatory forces. This allowed more effective control of violent gangs, which created a space of reduced physical violence in which the early bourgeoisie could increase trade and the commercialization of land in relative safety. In this environment the richer and more enterprising peasants and merchants could become more confident and active as they built the nascent market economy.

Secondly, the violent forces of social disorder were not only more efficiently repressed but significantly reconstructed. The presence of physically violent gangs, whose practices maintained brutal forms of order only at the nodal micro-level, limited market-driven economic growth at the broader level. Methods were sought to simultaneously stimulate individualized desire for new commodities yet increase pacification in civil society. The introduction of the laws of primogeniture and entail throughout the social structure in England – which were applied solely to the ruling class across the rest of Europe – from the 12th century made families less secure places for children. This was the first step in the gradual dissolution of the family, community and land as the principal sites of honour, protection, identification and solidarity (Macfarlane, 1978), creating sibling rivalry on a new enhanced scale and extending it from the internal affective-relational dimension to the external economic dimension. This major cultural shift also significantly increased siblings' mistrust and potential hatred of parents, who from that point onwards had total arbitrary rights to property and its distribution amongst family members. The legally driven split-

The Sociological Review, 62:S2, pp. 13–31 (2014), DOI: 10.1111/1467-954X.12189
© 2014 The Author. Editorial organisation © 2014 The Editorial Board of the Sociological Review

ting of the family, and with it the geographically bound ethnic community, corresponds with the splitting of the individual ego and the redirection of its identification processes, from the family and community outward to the world of the commercial market in which offspring were forced to engage in pacified economic competition against each other as their traditional mode of security and status was disrupted. The psychosocial process was analogous to biological cell-splitting and growth, creating a sort of socioeconomic tumour as anxious individuals were cast out into competitive markets to seek wealth and establish their own domains. The overall process weakened the family as the legitimate unit of 'righteous violence' (Hall, 2012a). It risked the continued formation of violent gangs as substitute families, but as the complementary pacification and individualization processes were gradually normalized this risk was significantly reduced.

This new insecure and competitive subjectivity became functional to the developing market economy, advantaging those who more fully embodied and practised it; it was unprotected, vulnerable, anxious, ambitious and resentful of community and its multiple obligations. The process resembles Deleuze and Guattari's (1984) deterritorialization, but it was more dialectical in the sense that the desire to deterritorialize and reterritorialize in a constant, circular dynamic process of expansion and proliferation was, after the initial disintegrative legal force had been applied, internally driven and reproduced rather than imposed exclusively by some extraneous political force. The process intensified, systematized and harnessed to the developing market economy the relational-subjective contradictions and hostile relations that Jameson (2010) points out as the norm in family units in the ancient world, the origin of the social dialectic. In this more recent period, however, the subject was forced to seek new security, status and identity not in the ancient cycle of Odyssey and Anabasis – the outward journey to adventure and the difficult return home to receive accolades (see Badiou, 2007) – but in the rapidly developing commercial economy, with its proliferation of symbolic objects. Many parents attempted to compensate for their legally grounded role in this process and recover affection by doing everything they could to equip children to compete effectively in an increasingly pacified, rule-bound mode, the new measure of 'successful parenting' which persists today.

Between the Norman invasion and the Industrial Revolution, England ceased to be a standard European peasant society; it became highly individualized, competitive and oriented to small business (Bloch, 1967; Macfarlane, 1978). The individualization process spawned a huge literature concerned with the expression of private dreams, ideals and life-projects (Thomas, 2009; Eagleton, 2009). The private pursuit of *jouissance* and the non-violent competition to monopolize trade displaced the traditional culturo-economic mode that had been maintained and reproduced by violence, redirecting libidinal energy to the pursuit of money and commercially distributed symbols of social distinction. The mode of acquiring material wealth and social status gradually shifted from 'somewhere', the violent defence of bodily honour and the monopolization of trade, precious metals and land, to 'everywhere and nowhere', the pacified acquisition of the abstract values of money and social symbolism (Hall, 2012a).

Individualist culture, beginning in England and gathering tributaries from elsewhere in Europe, spread across the developing capitalist world (Dumont, 1986). The vital psychosocial element was rooted in the Lacanian principle that absence creates desire; the loss of protective, reproductive community with its durable identity became the great *objet petit a*, the unnameable lost object (see Lacan, 2006; Žižek, 2006). The replacement – the competitive individual seeking personal wealth and security in the market – became the master signifier of the new fundamental fantasy, the dream in which amorphous libidinal energy assumes its initial imaginary and symbolic shape to forge the individual's basic identity. In both the fundamental fantasy and the economic practice of the competitive, acquisitive entrepreneur, successful performance in the market became the principal form of combined cultural and symbolic capital, and thus, in the absence of traditional brethren, the source of ego-ideal figures in the shape of the new masters of sublimated aggressive competition (Winlow and Hall, 2009). England, the first fully industrialized imperial capitalist nation, invented a disproportionate number of the world's sports and games (see Holt, 1990) in order to encourage subjectivity – particularly male subjectivity in the shape of the 'muscular Christian' (see Whitehead, 2002) – to forge itself in an environment of rule-bound aggression.

It's important to note that both poles of the human emotional spectrum were truncated for the purpose of domestication and socioeconomic utilization. Violence was repressed and sublimated along with the impulse to concrete altruism. As the market-capitalist project developed and expanded its territorial scope from the 15th century, the eternally difficult ethico-social task of diffusing the ideals and protocols of the community outwards to the general society and economy was abandoned (Eagleton, 2009), and laws regulating usury, wages and prices were relaxed. In many respects the opposite process prevailed as competitive market practices were introduced into communities and all social institutions; in the current neoliberal era we witness an attempt to totalize this process and bring economic history to a close. Concrete altruism was transposed into the diluted form of *post hoc* sentimentalism and benevolentism, which constituted Pocock's (1989) 'commercial humanism'. In a remarkable process of defeat and subjugation, capitalism confronted, sublimated, incorporated and put to work in a relation of dynamic tension its two main psychosocial threats, violence and altruism; it cannot reproduce itself in an environment dominated by either. Our culture exists in a fragile pseudo-pacified *third space* compressed and propelled beyond these two potent but repressed social forces and their volatile sublimatory relation; forward momentum is generated by the constant movement beyond the violence and altruism that always seek to return to their traditional places.

The process that activated and controlled the stimulation and pacification of aggressive libidinal energy in England, and, later, Europe and North America, was quite unique. Many societies disarmed and pacified their populations –

indeed some might have been more civilized in the true sense of the word – but none developed with so much success the specific amalgam of pacification and sublimation required to establish *la doceur du commerce* (see Hirschman, 1977) and simultaneously stimulate the libidinal energy that feeds the consumer-driven market economy. The old rigid class relation had to be made more permeable and meritocratic – but only under the strict criterion of market performance – to boost individual ambition, energize markets and quell dissent and social conflict to a manageable level. The accepted route for educated and enterprising members of the lower classes was upwards through the loose and permeable class structure, which constantly released the political pressure that can build up from below.

The role of consumer culture in the pseudo-pacification process

Social science still tends to underestimate the importance of consumer culture, as both a primary driver in early capitalist history and the dominant cultural form in the neoliberal era (Campbell, 1987; Smart, 2010). It developed as a potent dynamic force and pre-existed full industrialization. In 14th century Europe, when the population reduction caused by the Plague made the expansion of production and trade vital, consumer culture was propagated first amongst the courtly and gentrified classes as a means of increasing demand. The ascent of these groups was the first step in the gradual shift to a more permeable social structure which eased social climbing by economic means. Consumer symbolism was certainly regarded as a serious social issue; in England, as the aristocracy were troubled by the rapidity of social change, Edward III enacted secular 'sumptuary laws' to prevent the potential reversal of the sociosymbolic violence that has always played an important part in the reproduction of elite rule (Sassatelli, 2008).

The explosion of consumer culture rapidly expanded demand for luxury goods industries across Europe. By the 15th century, entrepreneurial peasants became wealthier as navigation and superior ships opened up new sea lanes and markets began to expand. Defying the sumptuary laws and often marrying into the aristocracy to enable their social ascent, the new gentrified class started dressing in ways that imitated or in some cases outshone an aristocracy that could already sense its own decline. As consumer culture permeated social life it provided actors with a crucial sociosymbolic infrastructure whose almost unlimited ability to change its cultural codes at an increasing velocity over time (see Appadurai, 1996) combined rule-bound pacification with ruthless forms of individualized socioeconomic struggle. The heightened anxiety in England caused by familial and communal disruption drove enterprising individuals to compete harder than their European counterparts.

This dynamic movement seemed irrepressible; as the early capitalists moved into urban centres to expand trading activities and develop 'sumptuary' tastes, many began to by-pass legal restrictions on trade. They developed informal markets outside towns to avoid rents, tolls and taxes, and struck up relations with illegal traders to secure cheaper commodities and undercut prices. As many criminologists suggest, throughout this long period the distinction Max Weber (2002) made between good and bad business practice was in reality far more blurred (Hobbs, 1989). Protestant asceticism was a latecomer to a socioeconomic process already well established, acting largely as a restraint rather than a driver. Protestantism's public distaste for excess masked the underlying and very active drives for luxury and decadence, which were acted out in private aristophiliac games (Hall *et al.*, 2008). The often rather amusing hypocrisy that resulted from this tension between private desires and public correctness was the focus of some of the best bourgeois literature (Moretti, 2013). Neither can the Weberian view of capitalism as 'ethically driven' account for Protestant asceticism as the 'vanishing mediator' in the capitalist project (Jameson, 2010). This, and the standard Marxist notion that it is simply 'the system' and its drive for profits that damages our lives, have both obstructed intellectual enquiry into the ways in which individuals ritually by-pass ethical injunctions to perform yet simultaneously disavow their vital roles in the system's reproduction (Hall, 2012a).

As the capitalist project developed, the pseudo-pacification process became more successful in its primary task of evacuating ethical and communal values from their position as core drivers and relocating them to a new position in the socioeconomic system to meld with norms and laws and function as a strategic device to guide both action and restraint (Hall *et al.*, 2008; Moxon, 2011). Concerned members of the bourgeoisie developed a rather schizoid and fearful attitude to the socioeconomic change they were actively promoting and, indeed, often regarded as historically inevitable. Henry Fielding, for instance, condemned moral decline and the drive for 'luxury amongst the vulgar' as he also paradoxically recognized competitive individualism and the controlled seeking of status symbols as essential for economic development (Hall, 2012a).

As the middle classes became wealthier they also became victims of a new form of 'objectless anxiety' (Hall, 2012a, 2012b) as the socioeconomic system they promoted hollowed out social life and introduced novel, subtle and clandestine forms of 'little evils' as myriad drive-fuelled unethical practices in everyday life (Badiou, 2002). However, this anxiety – objectless because its foundation in social dissolution and the ethical and political problems it caused were ideologically disavowed and banished from everyday discourse – was also the system's primary energy source. As we have seen, anxiety creates desire (Lacan, 2006; see also Roudinesco, 2014), but this amorphous, multi-purpose objectless anxiety was reproduced by the constant denial of its own objective causal condition – hollowed-out ethical and social life and the unstable economy – to become the primary stimulant in capitalism's productive and consumerized cultural life. It was highly effective because it could both create and utilize human drives to produce a new range of objective desires that constantly promise and fail to compensate for the constitutive lack that lies at the heart of subjectivity. The diversity of objective desires was limited only to the number of

The Sociological Review, 62:S2, pp. 13–31 (2014), DOI: 10.1111/1467-954X.12189

symbolically laden commodities the production system could produce and circulate in markets. If we emphasize the distinction between drive and desire, here we can see clearly that the foundations of Wieviorka's (2009) typology – the *loss* of meaning (as fragile solidarity is constantly dissolved), the *liberation* of substitute meanings (as drive-fuelled desires are stimulated), and the *overload* of substitute meanings (as drives are repressed and sublimated to proliferate desires) – are interconnected dynamic aspects of the pseudo-pacification process.

As industrialization brought affordable luxuries to the majority, the developing consumer-capitalist system continued to expand the compensatory comforts in the system of sign-objects that mass-mediated consumer culture now presents as a surrogate social world (Hall *et al.*, 2008). The individual is beckoned towards painful, socially destructive and unachievable *jouissance*, but also restricted to a domesticated mode of *acting out* ambition and frustration (see Stiegler, 2009) as it declares a victory each time a fragile, temporary position of sociosymbolic distinction is achieved by pacified means (Hall *et al.*, 2008). In Lacanian terms, the consumer-capitalist system retained its proximity to the obscene Real, stimulating envy and anxiety (Žižek, 2010) and reworking in a pseudo-pacified form the barbaric, wasteful and violently competitive drives for the pecuniary reward, status and honour that were political currency in the Dark Ages (Veblen, 1994). The obscene drives located in the Lacanian Real were not transcended but stimulated and subsequently sublimated in a complex culturo-legal system to be rule-bound and harnessed to the economy. In the neoliberal era we are experiencing the restoration and global diffusion of this process in a borderless, minimally regulated and technologically enhanced form.

The pseudo-pacification process falters and recovers

The libidinal energy generated by the unstable pseudo-pacification process is highly criminogenic. It is the principal force behind the expansion of property crime over the course of capitalist history. The criminogenic effect is restrained at its boundary by an expansive and intrusive public/private control system. We have little choice but to make a concession to the Right and admit that the 'crime drop' the West experienced in the 1990s after the 'crime explosion' in the 1980s is largely the product of advances in the control system – smart policing, expansive social programmes, increased surveillance, mass imprisonment, DNA testing, environmental securitization and so on operating in a context shored up by huge welfare budgets. This explanation must be combined with additional criminological factors, which include the continuation of a large realm of unrecorded 'crimes of the powerful' and the mutation of crime into new and only partially recorded forms such as cyber-crime, the reduction in the number of young adults in the population and the appearance of a remarkable lethargy amongst many young people (Hall, 2012a). Reflecting on his experience of teaching young people in Britain's Further Education system, Fisher (2009: 23) notes their tendency to fall into 'depressive hedonia', the 'soft narcosis, the comfort food oblivion of Playstation, all-night TV and marijuana'. We now see culture and economy working in harmony in a post-political world to constitute and reproduce the perfectly anxious yet docile consumer (Winlow and Hall, 2013).

None of these factors signifies an improvement in social relations or a reduction in the subjective motivation to crime and the competitive individualism that pervades Western societies. Rather, the crime-drop signifies a retreat into subjectivity (Winlow and Hall, 2013) and the successful adaptation of the pseudo-pacification process as it adjusts its mode of operation to new circumstances laid down by neoliberalism's global economy. The dual system of pacification and control has been advanced as the techniques of stimulation were intensified to release more energy into a culturally driven economy that offers significantly expanded opportunities for the gratification of *jouissance* via the consumption of important symbolic objects and forms of entertainment in its advanced digital media systems. After a brief period of instability in the 1980s and 1990s as the neoliberal political and business elite decided to combat economic stagnation by performing the dangerous operation of downscaling social democracy's old economic regulatory system at the same time as increasing consumer pressure on the individual, the pseudo-pacification process fought back to return to operational duties in its most advanced form. Put simply, the key to the reduction in crime and violence was the expansion and improved efficiency of both 'soft' and 'hard' dimensions of the control system at the same time as the significant expansion of opportunities for even the poorer service workers and welfare recipients to *act out* non-violently the drives that were stimulated further by a culture dominated by competitive individualism and consumer hedonism.

The psychosocial basis of evil

A crucial factor currently hampering social science's investigation into today's harmful forms of crime and violence is that the main philosophical schools from which it draws offer no conception of evil as *drive*. Only the temporary departure from prevailing ethical standards, the lust for domination amongst powerful elites, or the social reaction to 'otherness' receive critical attention. To speak of evil is condemned as pathologization, a vestige of obsolete theological paradigms (Wieviorka, 2012). However, Jameson (2010) and Todorov and Brown (2010) argue that the good/evil duality is universal in human ethical discourse, and remind us that it is not really 'evil' as a concept that the liberal establishment worries about but the social structuring of the idea as it is used to construct a pathologized 'other' on the social margins. Social science textbooks often begin with grim warnings that pathologization was behind the evil regimes of the past – most importantly Nazism. Evil has been excised from the discourse because of the fear that it could be used to legitimize the politics of violent social reaction, which we all hope we can one day consign to the dustbin of history. Conse-

The Sociological Review, 62:S2, pp. 13–31 (2014), DOI: 10.1111/1467-954X.12189
© 2014 The Author. Editorial organisation © 2014 The Editorial Board of the Sociological Review

quently, liberal thought in general has been able to replace the idea of evil as an eternal force against which we must constantly struggle with a highly diluted, temporal and individualized substitute; individuals simply 'err' as they fail to live up to cultural standards, often through no fault of their own. Thus liberalism acts as an avuncular patrician, like 'a headmaster signing off the end-of-year report' (Dews, 2008: 11) on individuals who tried but perhaps, with understanding and guidance, could have done a little better.

This intellectual ban prevents us from even considering the possibility that some restrained and reworked form of 'evil' might exist at the very core of the socioeconomic system. The idea was certainly shared by some traditional Marxists and conservatives, such as Adorno and Eliot (see Shusterman, 1993), and it is regaining traction amongst their current equivalent pairings, such as Žižek and Sloterdijk (see Winlow and Hall, 2013), who agree on problems such as the evaporation of solidarity and public space in the heat generated by the individual competition for endless superficial novelties. Because it offends a central injunction, the idea proposed here – that the 'evil' of Dark Age violence was gradually sublimated, democratized and harnessed via sociosymbolic competition to drive the economy – risks outright rejection in the post-war liberal social-scientific establishment. However, in defence of the idea, it must be noted that very similar types of politico-cultural opportunism cropped up regularly in the discourses that accompanied most of the more economically successful civilizations. For instance, as the Chinese Legalists displaced Confucians they were quite open about their commitment to retain 'evil' and harness it to the expansion of empire with the aid of a bureaucratic state (Žižek, 2010). It was also common in political and economic circles across modern Europe; classical liberalism's economic first principle was simply an adoption of the Mandevillean notion of stimulating specific 'refined private vices' orientated to a more pacified and efficient form of economic growth, the principal 'public good' that the early bourgeoisie were interested in promoting. This method of invoking and employing the potent and volatile drives that Keynes (1935) called 'animal spirits' – drives that never learn from their consequential errors – is acknowledged with few misgivings in economic literature across the political spectrum from Adam Smith to the present day (see also Akerloff and Shiller, 2009).

European and American liberal-capitalist discourse has always displayed a fear of naturalism, the collapse of the autonomous individual's ability to withstand natural drives and forces (Dews, 2008). However, what this prevailing discourse neglects is that, with the constant accent on novelty, sensation and positive freedom, consumer culture systematically taps into drives to stimulate desires, which constantly propels the individual too close to the obscene Real, the psyche's natural core of conflicting and unnameable drives, the primal source of objectless anxiety (Hall *et al.*, 2008; Hall, 2012b). Liberal-capitalist discourse facilitates the process negatively by deflecting critique away from consumer culture and its constantly expanding space for desire in the system of symbolic objects (Baudrillard, 2005), a space in which unleashed drives can spill out to be captured and transformed as yearnings for various commodities.

When liberal-capitalism replaced various cultures based on collective orientation to the Good with a system of minimal rights (Badiou, 2002), drives were no longer directed by cultivated desires towards the transcendental Ideal, but unleashed to be harnessed by the economy. Any overspill acted out as violent or acquisitive crime is simply dissipated in a brief ritual of moral outrage and fielded on the boundary by bureaucratic institutions, which punish or try to reform or rehabilitate the individual rule-breaker. Thus liberal-capitalism has been moderately successful in its attempts to transcend the 'big evils' that can be committed in the service of the transcendental Ideal. However, because it refuses to engage intellectually or politically with drive, desire and consumer culture's techniques of stimulation and capture, it remains trapped in the tension between the constant effervescence of atomized 'little evils' and the constant recourse to the potential 'big evil' of repressive, authoritarian governance (Hall, 2012a).

What is the psychosocial source of what we have in times past called 'evil'? For many psychoanalysts it is associated with social interaction during early stages of the life-course:

> Psychoanalysts, even from widely differing traditions, have concurred that evil is best understood as the attempt to inflict one's own experience of the evacuation of meaning on others. In his study of serial killers, for example, Christopher Bollas [1995] has suggested that such individuals seek to induce in others their own early experience of a total, traumatic breakdown of trust in the benignity of the adult world. (Dews, 2008: 133; see also Winlow, this volume)

This formulation casts doubt on Wieviorka's (2012) claim that evil tends to be invoked to restore meaning and control. In extreme cases trauma prevents initial formative experiences of meaning and control and is thus unable to be accepted, symbolized or explained by the child; meaning and control are never established in the first place. Such fundamental terror invokes recourse to drive, the impulse to *act out* without first delaying and considering the broader causes and potential consequences through ethical and rational-communicative filters. However, acting out the stimulated impulse to defend the self is impossible in such an imbalanced power relation. Constant exposure to traumatic abuse with no effective means of defence or escape represses and embodies the impulse to act in the neurological system as a latent but volatile force in the individual's plastic, adaptable pre-symbolic system of affects and emotions, which comes to the fore when exposed to symbolic actions that represent and thus trigger the memory of trauma (Winlow and Hall, 2009). Associated with the unleashing of the impulse is a primal embodied ethic, one of justifiable revenge sought to redress the original trauma and defend the self from a world populated by untrustworthy, violent others (Winlow, this volume).

However, if the subject's drive to act out extreme revenge risks being compromised by even the slightest inkling that the selected victim is not in reality the source of the original trauma, the subject enters another dimension beyond ethical justification. For Sullivan (1953), where the 'good me' is a product of

The Sociological Review, 62:S2, pp. 13–31 (2014), DOI: 10.1111/1467-954X.12189

love, warmth and nurturing and the 'bad me' is a product of anxiety, the psychopathic 'not me' – the dissociated self – is a product of its own ethically and intellectually unrestrained acting out of the initially repressed impulse to violence in the face of symbols of extreme threat, and the subsequent denial of the action and the impulse behind it in order to protect the self from both its own residual moral judgement and the further threat of social retribution. The 'not me' is born of absolute denial. Indeed, the threatening other can be constructed ideologically to induce fear for political purposes – the central thesis behind the standard 'fear of crime' discourse – but this can provide only a secondary aetiological analysis because the primary cause *and* the mechanism of denial are already established in the affective-emotional system of the subject, before violent actions can be justified and excused in socio-cultural systems of knowledge and communication. The denial of the violence of the self and its perceived identity-group is a product of the symbolic reproduction of the conditions in which trauma was experienced and the subject created itself in its fundamental fantasy (see Žižek, 2006) of the victim seeking revenge on the force that destroyed the original 'lost object' of love, trust and security, a force that can be represented by a broad spectrum of ideological symbols.

We cannot simply extend this explanation of the source of violence in extreme individual trauma to the study of violence in its broad and complex social context. Although there is little doubt that liberal-capitalism, like other unequal yet enduringly successful socioeconomic systems, was founded on traumatizing episodes of violence in its founding phases and punctuated by similar episodes in periods of crisis (Lusordo, 2011), it certainly does not want public life to be overrun by hordes of psychopathic serial killers. However, what the liberal-capitalist socioeconomic project *does* require, as we have seen, is a hegemonic culture of measured aggression to fuel the dynamic force of social competition in the economy. As well as eager consumers, the system's logic also requires leading subjects to act as role-models and 'movers and shakers' at the cutting edge of its unforgivingly competitive economy, occasionally ruthless 'undertakers' who are willing to risk harm to others in order to 'get things done' in their functional business lives in a sublimated, rule-bound mode of action that constantly pushes against ethical boundaries (see Hall, 2012a).

The question we must ask in future theory and research is whether an attenuated, modified variant of the potentially violent dissociated self has throughout the capitalist-modernist era been cultivated as an everyday form of subjectivity that combines the ability to exist as a normal law-abiding citizen yet retain and act out ruthlessly aggressive impulses in non-violent modes in the interconnected realms of consumerism, business and politics. As we have already seen in the legally induced disruption of the family unit and the casting out of the individual into a competitive outland, 'breakdown of trust' was a traumatic formative event in the formation of English bourgeois culture. This is of course trauma of a far more subtle and variable type, but over the course of the capitalist project it has nonetheless been sustained and systematically applied to working individuals who, because they have rarely achieved a high degree of political solidarity, have only the flimsiest means of defence. In today's post-political climate (see Mouffe, 2000) the fundamental breakdown of trust in the benignity of the world has been diffused outwards from the micro-relations of the family to be reflected in broad social attitudes, which, over recent decades, seem to be harshening, not just towards the global business class and the bureaucratized and supine political class, but, more crucially, in the absence of political solidarity, towards fellow citizens (Winlow and Hall, 2013). As the majority lose sight of alternative visions of the future and become increasingly affected by negative feelings of cynicism and nihilism, anxiety is intensified and drives are reactivated. The atomized individual must compete in some way or face crushing failure in life, but in doing so risks a movement too close to the obscene Real, a possible descent into the natural uncontrolled drives that to liberal discourse is the one true evil that still exists in a latent form, currently restrained by relocated ethics acting as 'strategic normative practices' (Hall *et al.*, 2008: 62) backed up on the boundary by a repressive external system of control.

Concluding remarks

Liberal-capitalism was an experiment with the length of the libidinal leash, to see how far it could be released and in which ways drives could be stimulated, sublimated, restrained and disciplined before they became socially toxic. The culture that accompanied this epoch cannot be seen as a 'civilizing process' or a 'disciplinary society', except insofar as it acted as a restraining mechanism on pre-existing drives that had been systematically stimulated for specific political and economic purposes. Rather, the simultaneous functional stimulation and control of libidinal drives constitutes a *pseudo-pacification process*. This process generates immense undialectical tension between stimulated obscene drives and a complex system of desire-formation, repression, sublimation and economic utilization. This is not simply desire manipulated to serve control, as Marcuse (1991) suggested; desire is genuinely free to seek its objects, but the media-marketing system monopolizes the communicative space in which objects are socially valued and sought. Control – unwieldy, expensive and anathema to neoliberalism's core ethos of cost-cutting and downsizing public institutions – is the reluctant means, not the end, in a process that serves stimulation, pacification, economic growth and profitability.

In a process that constantly and systematically stimulates a pervasive sense of loss and trauma, the meaning and control that Wieviorka (2012) claims the subject seeks to 'restore' has never been fully experienced. Social peace became dependent on the constant expansion of the arena in which the majority can compete over economic opportunities and sociosymbolic status by pseudo-pacified means. We all need to consume, but deep incorporation into consumerism's culture of *jouissance* distracts the mass of working-class individuals from fully committed involvement in the politics of solidarity (Winlow and Hall, 2012, 2013). If 'evil' is the product of the breakdown of solidarity and trust and the subsequent activation of the malignant will in an unmediated connection to death drive, which seeks its enjoyment in the destruction of all meaning and morality and the infliction of this painful experience on the other, it is not difficult to understand how this force can be invoked and repressed in an attenuated form that is quite easily sublimated by the indiscriminately competitive sociosymbolic world of consumer culture and harnessed to capitalist production. However, first it must be stimulated as drive, and this is the danger. People are not immutably 'evil', but our culture rests on a bedrock of overstimulated drives that can cut through systems of ethico-rational mediation and external control to fuel anti-social and violent actions when the promise of an endless supply of opportunities for economic prosperity and sociosymbolic ascendance begins to look empty.

References

Akerloff, G. and Shiller, R., (2009), *Animal Spirits: How Human Psychology Drives the Economy, and Why it Matters for Global Capitalism*, Princeton, NJ: Princeton University Press.

Appadurai, A., (1996), *Modernity at Large: Cultural Dimensions of Globalization*, Minneapolis, MN: University of Minnesota Press.

Badiou, A., (2002), *Ethics: An Essay on the Understanding of Evil*, London: Verso.

Badiou, A., (2007), *The Century*, Cambridge: Polity Press.

Baudrillard, J., (2005 [1968]), *The System of Objects*, London: Verso.

Bauman, Z., (2012), 'Fuels, sparks and fires: on taking to the streets', *Thesis Eleven*, 109: 11–16.

Bloch, M., (1967), *Land and Work in Mediaeval Europe*, London: Routledge and Kegan Paul.

Bollas, C., (1995), *Cracking Up*, London: Routledge.

Campbell, C., (1987), *The Romantic Ethic and the Spirit of Modern Consumerism*, Oxford: Blackwell.

Dean, J., (2009), *Democracy and Other Neoliberal Fantasies: Communicative Capitalism and Left Politics*, Durham, NC: Duke University Press.

Dejours, C., (2003), *L'Evaluation du travail à l'épreuve du reel*, Paris: INRA Editions.

Deleuze, G. and Guattari, F., (1984), *Anti-Oedipus: Capitalism and Schizophrenia*, London: Athlone.

Dews, P., (2008), *The Idea of Evil*, Oxford: Blackwell.

Dorling, D., (2004), 'Prime suspect: homicide in Britain', in P. Hillyard, C. Pantazis, S. Tombs and D. Gordon (eds.), *Beyond Criminology: Taking Harm Seriously*, London: Pluto.

Dumont, L., (1986), *Essays on Individualism: Modern Ideology in Anthropological Perspective*, Chicago, IL: University of Chicago Press.

Eagleton, T., (2009), *Trouble with Strangers: A Study of Ethics*, Chichester: Wiley-Blackwell.

Eisner, M., (2001), 'Modernization, self-control and lethal violence: the long-term dynamics of European homicide rates in theoretical perspective', *British Journal of Criminology*, 41: 618–638.

Elias, N., (1994), *The Civilizing Process*, Oxford: Blackwell.

Fisher, M., (2009), *Capitalist Realism: Is There No Alternative?*, Alresford: Zero Books.

Fletcher, J., (1997), *Violence and Civilization*, Cambridge: Polity Press.

Garland, D., (1990), *Punishment and Modern Society*, Oxford: Clarendon.

Hall, S., (2012a), *Theorizing Crime and Deviance: A New Perspective*, London: Sage.

Hall, S., (2012b), 'The solicitation of the trap: on transcendence and transcendental materialism in advanced consumer-capitalism', *Human Studies: Special Issue on Transcendence and Transgression*, 35 (3): 365–381.

Hall, S. and McLean, C., (2009), 'A tale of two capitalisms: preliminary spatial and historical comparisons of homicide rates in Western Europe and the USA', *Theoretical Criminology*, 13 (3): 313–339.

Hall, S., Winlow, S. and Ancrum, C., (2008), *Criminal Identities and Consumer Culture: Crime, Exclusion and the New Culture of Narcissism*, Cullompton: Willan.

Hallsworth, S., (2005), *Street Crime*, Cullompton: Willan.

Hibbert, C., (2003), *The Roots of Evil*, Stroud: Sutton.

Hirschman, A., (1977), *The Passions and the Interests*, Princeton, NJ: Princeton University Press.

Hobbs, D., (1989), *Doing the Business: Entrepreneurship, the Working Class, and Detectives in the East End of London*, Oxford: Oxford University Press.

Holt, R., (1990) *Sport and the British: A Modern History*, Oxford: Clarendon Press.

Jameson, F., (2010), *Valences of the Dialectic*, London: Verso.

Keynes, J. M., (1935), *The General Theory of Employment, Interest and Money*, New York: Harcourt, Brace and Co.

Lacan, J., (2006), *Ecrits*, New York: Norton.

Lusordo D., (2011), *Liberalism: A Counter History*, London: Verso.

Macfarlane, A., (1978), *The Origins of English Individualism: The Family, Property and Social Transition*, Oxford: Blackwell.

Maddern, P., (1992), *Violence and Social Order: East Anglia 1422–1442*, Oxford: Oxford University Press.

Marcuse, H., (1991 [1964]), *One-Dimensional Man: Studies in Ideology of Advanced Industrial Society*, 2nd edn, London: Routledge.

Marktanner, M. and Noiset, L., (2013), 'Social versus conservative democracies and homicide rates', *International Journal of Social Economics*, 40 (4): 292–310.

Moretti, F., (2013), *The Bourgeois: Between History and Literature*, London: Verso.

Mouffe, C., (2000), *The Democratic Paradox*, London: Verso.

Moxon, D., (2011), 'Consumer culture and the 2011 "riots" ', *Sociological Research Online*, 16 (4): 19.

Mucchielli, L., (2010), 'Are we living in a more violent society? A socio-historical analysis of interpersonal violence in France, 1970s–present', *British Journal of Criminology*, 50 (5): 808–829.

Parker, K. F., (2008), *Unequal Crime Decline: Theorizing Race, Urban Inequality and Criminal Violence*, New York: New York University Press.

Pocock, J., (1989), 'Civic humanism and its role in Anglo-American political thought', in J. Pocock (ed.), *Politics, Language and Time: Essays on Political Thought and History*, Chicago, IL: University of Chicago Press.

Reiner, R., (2007) *Law and Order: An Honest Citizen's Guide to Crime and Control*, Cambridge: Polity.

Roudinesco, É., (2014), *Lacan: In Spite of Everything*, London: Verso.

Sassatelli, R., (2008), *Consumer Culture: History, Theory and Politics*, London: Sage.

Sharpe, J., (1996), *Crime in Early Modern England 1550–1750*, Harlow: Longman.

Shusterman, R., (1993), 'Eliot and Adorno on the critique of culture', *Theory, Culture and Society*, 10: 25–52.

Smart, B., (2010), *Consumer Society: Critical Issues and Environmental Consequences*, London: Sage.

Stiegler, B., (2009), *Acting Out* (trans. D. Barison, D. Ross and P. Crogan), Stanford, CA: Stanford University Press.

Stiegler, B., (2013), *Uncontrollable Societies of Disaffected Individuals*, Cambridge: Polity Press.

Sullivan, H. S., (1953), *Conceptions of Modern Psychiatry*, New York: W.W. Norton.

Thomas, K., (2009), *The Ends of Life: Roads to Fulfilment in Early Modern England*, Oxford: Oxford University Press.

Todorov, T. and Brown, A., (2010), *The Fear of Barbarians*, Cambridge: Polity Press.

Treadwell, J., Briggs, D., Winlow, S. and Hall, S., (2013), 'Shopocalypse now: consumer culture and the English riots of 2011', *British Journal of Criminology*, 53 (1): 1–17.

Veblen, T., (1994 [1899]), *The Theory of the Leisure Class*, London: Penguin.

Ward-Perkins, B., (2005), *The Fall of Rome and the End of Civilization*, Oxford: Oxford University Press.

The Sociological Review, 62:S2, pp. 13–31 (2014), DOI: 10.1111/1467-954X.12189

Weber, M., (2002), *The Protestant Ethic and the Spirit of Capitalism* (trans. S. Kalberg), Oxford: Blackwell.

Whitehead, S., (2002), *Men and Masculinities: Key Themes and New Directions*, Cambridge: Polity.

Wieviorka, M., (2009), *Violence: A New Approach*, London: Sage.

Wieviorka, M., (2012), *Evil*, Cambridge: Polity.

Wilson, D., (2007), *Serial Killers: Hunting Britons and their Victims 1960–2006*, Sherfield-on-Loddon: Waterside Press.

Winlow, S. and Hall, S., (2009), 'Retaliate first: memory humiliation and male violence', *Crime, Media, Culture*, 5 (3): 285–304.

Winlow, S. and Hall, S., (2012), 'A predictably obedient riot: postpolitics, consumer culture, and the English riots of 2011', *Cultural Politics*, 8 (3): 465–488.

Winlow, S. and Hall, S., (2013), *Rethinking Social Exclusion: The End of the Social?*, London: Sage.

Žižek, S., (2006), *How to Read Lacan*, London: Granta.

Žižek, S., (2010), *Living in the End Times*, London: Verso.

Trauma, guilt and the unconscious: some theoretical notes on violent subjectivity

Simon Winlow

Abstract: This paper draws together elements of cultural sociology and theoretical psychoanalysis in order to address the creation and enactment of a particular form of violent subjectivity. Its primary concern is the experience of traumatic events and prolonged periods of insecurity during childhood. The paper argues that the experience of trauma, when set against a particular cultural background, can act to create a subjectivity characterized by a deep commitment to physical violence. The principal original contribution of this paper is to claim that guilt and shame play a crucial role in the creation of this violent subjectivity, and that these affects are, for the most part, unconscious.

Keywords: psychoanalysis, trauma, unconscious affects, masculinity, habitus

Introduction

In this paper I hope to offer a basic analysis of what I will call 'violent subjectivity'. That is, a form of subjectivity that understands itself principally in relation to violence, and its own violence in particular. During my ethnographic work in urban spaces in northern England, given their character by economic redundancy and loss (eg Winlow, 2001; Hobbs *et al.*, 2003; Winlow and Hall, 2006; Hall *et al.*, 2008; Winlow and Hall, 2009), I encountered many men who placed violence and a willingness to fight close to the centre of self-identity. I spent many hours discussing violence with them, and the theoretical framework I outline here has grown from those conversations.

Before I begin it is worth discussing in a little more detail whose violence I intend to analyse. On Britain's low-income estates it is clear that there exists a population of men willing to use physical violence. These men tend to be highly conversant with the rich symbolism of violence and attuned to the syncopated rhythms of its enactment. In the sociological sense, they occupy a culture of enclassed masculinity that has evolved in relation to the shifting mode of production and the vicissitudes of capital accumulation. This post-working class culture has taken at least part of its character from the toughness, fortitude, physicality and stoicism that were obvious characteristics of male working class

The Sociological Review, 62:S2, pp. 32–49 (2014), DOI: 10.1111/1467-954X.12190
© 2014 The Author. Editorial organisation © 2014 The Editorial Board of the Sociological Review. Published by John Wiley & Sons Ltd, 9600 Garsington Road, Oxford OX4 2DQ, UK and 350 Main Street, Malden, MA 02148, USA

cultures during the industrial age (Hobbs, 1994, 1995; Winlow and Hall, 2006; Hall, 2012). In turn, the characteristics of the industrial-modern visceral habitus of the working-class male (see Hall, 1997; 2002) developed in relation to the competition for scarce resources and the expectation of exploitation in the economic sphere. Of course, not all working-class men fully subscribed to this habitus. What Connell calls 'subordinate masculinities' (2005) existed throughout the industrial-modern period, and deviation from the cultural norm ensured marginalization and a reduction in social status.

In a very practical way, men born into this class experienced, to varying degrees, a socialization, often by both parents and reinforced by extended family members, that encouraged a toughening of the psycho-somatic disposition (see Hall, 1997). Industrial working-class men often depended upon their very physicality to provide for themselves and their families, but perhaps more importantly, they had to absorb the hardships of the working week and continue to return, ready to take those hardships again. The very significant physical and psychological pressures borne by this class of men eased somewhat with the dawning of the social democratic age as working conditions in some industries improved, but by then the die was cast; capitalism remained in place and key features of the working-class male habitus were reproduced as a resilient norm, with subtle variations, across the generations. The quiet solemnity of this submission, this grudging acceptance of the pressures and hardships of economic exploitation, informed 20th-century class formation and shaped the male working-class habitus and the way that working-class men understood themselves and acted in relation to the world around them. The pressures borne by the male worker, and the conscious and unconscious toughening of the body and mind as a practical defence against these pressures, tended to mean that they were not given to the peaceable expression of their internal emotional life.

During early childhood these men were taught to expect that physical conflict would find them at some stage, and that it was in their own best interests to rise to the challenge and acquit themselves in a way that would discourage others keen to seize upon and exploit any suggestion of weakness. While violent skill was, and continues to be, a highly prized characteristic, for most working-class men the crucial consideration was to retain dignity when encountering potential violence. That is, to come through the violent event with one's integrity, symbolic identity and reputation pretty much intact. For the vast majority of industrial working-class men, 'winning' the physical conflict was less important than standing one's ground and proving to themselves and their peers that they would not meekly submit to the violent will of others (Anderson, 2001; Bourgois, 2002; Winlow and Hall, 2006).

In modern working-class male cultures, violent skill and a willingness to fight became characteristics that elicited a degree of appreciation and respect. For many young men violence was a topic of wonder and gossip. It inspired schoolboys to construct mythical match-ups and neighbourhood hierarchies of violent capacity. Even adult and ostensibly respectable men treated violence itself as something truly awesome, the return of an incomprehensible Real that should be treated with a degree of reverence, something brutally powerful that existed beyond language, something that could be at once horrible and beautiful and could condemn or elevate the protagonist beyond the realm of the mundane. As numerous urban ethnographers have acknowledged, in a world in which virtually all battles are lost in advance, the symbolic importance of 'respect' gained through fighting ability and the willingness to fight can become a central cultural concern for men marginalized from the legitimate economy (for example, Patrick, 1973; Anderson, 2001; Bourgois, 2002; Mullins, 2006; Ayres and Treadwell, 2012; Treadwell and Garland, 2012; Densley, 2012; Bengtsson, 2012, 2013). Again, this is not simply a matter of raw brutality or an unsocialized, domineering masculinity. There exist many non-violent escape routes that enable the individual to retain dignity and the basic coordinates of symbolic identity. The point to bear in mind as we move forward is that, in such spaces, individuals know that violence is real, that it can and will happen and that its physical and symbolic consequences can be hugely disruptive and damaging. As a consequence of the painful reality of violence, which those who occupy this cultural field know to be real and capable of radically destabilizing the normal run of things, violence itself is treated with a degree of solemnity, a raw brutality that lurks just beneath the surface, its return inevitable.

The end of industrialism changed things for Britain's working class. I will not discuss these changes at length other than to say that, in my view, the relatively organized, anti-utilitarian and politicized cultures of the social democratic era's industrial working class were unable to withstand the concerted assault of global neoliberalism and the movement of production to the developing world. The individualized and demoralized consumer, locked in an interminable and perilous battle for social significance, occupies the field on which the industrial working class once stood (see Baudrillard, 2007; Winlow and Hall, 2013). The return of a discourse of class struggle has the capacity to change this dour outlook, but, it seems to me, the undiluted romanticism of the Thompsonite liberal left – which imagines the poor to be 'naturally' concerned with equality and fairness, refusing to acknowledge just how problematic low income areas have become – only hinders the politics of the social group whose interests they purport to represent.

By the time I arrived in the neighbourhoods in which I conducted my fieldwork, the old world of industrialism was gone. All that remained was its shadow, a ghostly reminder of what once was. However, many of the cultural characteristics of the old working-class habitus continued to linger on. They were essentially *hauntological* (Derrida, 2006): spectral apparitions that refused to countenance their own immateriality, trying as much as they could to impose their will upon unfolding social reality. Those cultural characteristics that were forged in industry continued to shape the social engagement of post-industrial 'working-class' men even though the world of the factory and the organized and politicized working class was at an end (Baudrillard, 2007; Winlow and Hall, 2013). This world, in which the occupants of the cultural field take violence seriously in full recognition that it can in fact move beyond language to become

The Sociological Review, 62:S2, pp. 32–49 (2014), DOI: 10.1111/1467-954X.12190

real, that it is not just a mediatized spectacle, exists as a constant background for those men who are the focus of this paper.

Many of the men I observed during my research were socialized with the basic expectations I outlined above. My work has mostly focused on committed criminals, but the vast majority of those criminals I spoke to did not display the characteristics I apply to 'violent subjectivity'. Many had a clear capacity for and appreciation of violence, but their violence tended not to be all-consuming. A much smaller proportion of my research sample was quite different in this regard, and in the rest of this paper I offer a basic guideline to their all-consuming violence.

Before commencing I should perhaps make one point explicit: in my view, if sociology is to develop a more penetrating analysis of the forces that drive individuals to violence it must return to an analysis of subjectivity and once again borrow from cognate fields. With only a few exceptions (see, for example, Wieviorka, 2009; Hall, 2012) sociology has yet to take the complexities of subjective violence seriously. What I am trying to do here is to move beyond a meta-psychology of psychopathy and sociopathy. I hope to connect the deep traumas of internal life to the social field that shapes those traumas and determines the context of their return. The sociology of violence is at the moment quite poorly developed, and there are certainly productive seams still to be mined. When sociologists have attempted to address subjective violence they have tended to utilize the tools of symbolic interactionism and other forms of micro analysis. This means that we have a number of detailed accounts of the interactional scene, the violent encounter, violence as performance, and so on, but there only now appears to be a growing recognition that sociology must attempt to think through the complexities of the inner life of the subject and its relation to the objective world that surrounds it. The reduction of violence to communicative interaction marginalizes analyses of power and fails to address the crucial background issues that shape violence and the subject's attitude towards it. It underplays the internal life of the agent who draws upon violence when encountering frustration or when plagued by memories of humiliation and shame, and it fails to teach us anything new about the journey one must take in order to be willing to harm another. If theoretical sociology is to advance its understanding of violence, it must abandon its attachment to Cartesian rationality and make room for an analysis of the unconscious. So, that said, my analysis will draw upon one or two basic ideas from theoretical psychoanalysis and put them to work alongside a more traditional assessment of culture and socialization.

What are the characteristics of violent subjectivity?

The 'violent subject' is quite distinct from those men who have a basic appreciation of violence, and their psychopathology is quite different from that displayed by serial killers. We are talking about a very small sample of men, but their place in the social life of marginalized neighbourhoods is often quite significant. Those I spoke to all had substantial criminal records, mostly for violent offences. Not all had been in custody, although those that had not appeared inevitably to be heading along this path. I have often been accused of pathologizing the working class by the 'beautiful souls' (Hegel, 1977) of the liberal left (O'Brien, 2007; Ilan, 2010; Cooper, 2012). While this accusation is entirely baseless, in this instance I concede that I am attempting to outline the pathologies that drive a small number of individuals from a research sample of ex-working-class men involved in criminal markets. I do so because the violence of this small group of violent offenders is pathological. Their violence is like a sickness that takes over and determines the subject and inflicts serious harm on victims and the shared social environment. Violence is never far from their thoughts, and in their more contemplative and analytical moments they often appear to possess some vague comprehension of the structure that enslaves them and the fate that awaits them.

The feature of this determinative psychical structure that appears most comprehensible to the violent subject is a sense of daemonic repetition and entrapment. Basically, they keep finding themselves in the same situations, situations that necessitate a violent response. They keep encountering the same types of people, people who will undermine or challenge their symbolic identity. They must continually face down bullies and tormentors in the same way they did during their youth. They are surrounded by those they see as brainless idiots who do not understand the reality of the world and who appear incapable of reading the signs that clearly indicate their willingness to use violence. In verbal accounts of their own violence, the ultimate victim of the violent subject's wrath is often poorly developed, and the victim's character, demeanour and offence tend to descend into crude stereotypes. In Lacanian terms, the victim of the violent subject's violence exists only as a *signifier of lack*, and it is quite easy to identify how the violent subject can come to believe, in very basic and rather hazy terms, that they have essentially been fighting the same opponent since their earliest youthful encounters.

It is certainly true that not all those who fit my description of the violent subject hail from the post working class. Both men and women who pass through a range of biographical experiences that reinforce a sense of existential insecurity can take up the key characteristics of violent subjectivity that I outline here. However, I persevere with an analysis of ex-working-class men because that is where the norm seems to reproduce itself with most vigour and where my research experience lies, and my data clearly suggest that the visceral habitus of such men patterns their violent social engagement as they seek to assuage their inner torment (see Stein, 2006; Winlow and Hall, 2009; Ellis and Wykes, 2013; Ellis, 2013).

The violent subject responds quickly to any suggestion that an attempt is being made to reduce his symbolic identity. They sift through conversations for words or phrases that might suggest that the other is trying to undermine them in some way, attempting to get one over on them. The assumption that the other

The Sociological Review, 62:S2, pp. 32–49 (2014), DOI: 10.1111/1467-954X.12190

is engaged in such a practice reflects the basic principles and parameters established during socialization. Often the violent subject has been told over and over again during childhood, in a cultural form of *realpolitik*, that the world is a hostile place populated by nakedly instrumental others engaged in ceaseless competition for supremacy and recognition. It is the childlike innocence of the unworldly that condemns them to forever be subject to the will of more driven 'realist' adversaries; idealism, trust and unguarded sociability are simply unwise and potentially dangerous. By extension, the social bonds formed by violent subjects always exist in a weakened state. The violent subject rarely experiences genuine repose among friends and must always remain attentive to attempts to undermine his symbolic identity. The tendency is to adopt a domineering social bearing and to force others to accept this basic social arrangement. Those who call the violent subject a friend must structure their relationships with him around an acknowledgement of his propensity toward what often seems like irrational violence. Of course, the violent subject is sure in his conviction that all of his violence is perfectly rational and, in most cases, absolutely necessary and justified. If he were to walk away from an insult he knows that he would be plagued by disturbing memories that would be far more injurious than the mere physical injuries suffered in a violent encounter (Winlow and Hall, 2009). He has passed through this process too often to let an insult pass. He knows that he must respond with immediate aggression if he is to free himself from the emotional disturbances that follow a conscious recognition that the other has attempted to humiliate him or challenge aspects of his social identity.

The violent subject oscillates between two modes of self-analysis. The first is a coldly prescient acknowledgement of the pathological structure that binds him to a particularly combative form of social engagement. They have a vague awareness that they are unable to control their hyper-sensitivity to insults and masculine status-competition. In the quote below, Ray, who was 29 at the time of our interview and has an established reputation for violence, talks about his inability to control his own violence. He has numerous convictions for violent offences and he is trying as much as he can to avoid a violent encounter that might see him returned to prison:

> I get in situations where I'll just get so angry, I just can't, there's just nothing I can do . . . I get the 'red mist' and that's it, I'm off, I can't be stopped. I go proper mental and people will say, you know, what happened there? They won't recognise me cos I've gone fucking mental and lost it totally. Now I know I've just got to keep out of them situations, keep away from certain types of people, keep out of certain types of places. I just fuck everything up if I put myself next to people who's going to rile me. That's what I've got to do or they'll lock me up for good. (taken from Ellis and Winlow, forthcoming)

These men know the destructive power they possess, and they know that this power has the capacity to destroy sources of nourishment and value in their everyday lives. They see others engage with the social in a quite different manner and wonder what it would be like to inhabit that life, free from their all-consuming commitment to violence. Above all, this mode of self-analysis is suggestive of an acknowledgement of their own destructive impotence, their inability to free themselves from a pathological form of psychical enclosure. Occasionally the violent subject will catch sight of the horror of their own violence yet their attachment to a particular form of self-annihilation remains in place. The violent subject often asks, why did I have to commit that act of violence? In asking this question they display a dissociative form of subjective disjuncture in which the violence they have committed is enacted by another part of themselves over which they have minimal control. For example, when reflecting on their own violence such men (like Ray, above), often talk of a 'red mist' descending, or some equivalent. What they are identifying is a psychical framework that allows them to hold their own violence at a distance. Here they are not fully accountable for their own violence as the energy of the violent moment itself prevents rational social engagement, rendering them merely a conduit for a blind inner rage that overcomes them. Some are keen to impress upon the interviewer that they routinely attempt to avoid situations likely to prompt the descent of the red mist, but again this indicates a framework in which the violence that takes place is never really theirs, always existing in the 'not me' of their violent subjectivity (see Stein, 2006; Hall, 2012).

The counterpoint to this position is one of narcissistic justification and celebration, in which they see themselves as equivalent to a Nietzschean Übermensch, free from the parochial restrictions of community life, free from the interminable myopic moralizing of the herd. They have overcome all normative social constraints in order to take their fated place among the elite group of farsighted realists who, seeing the enslavement of the herd, forge their own path and determine the ethical structure of their lives for themselves. They believe they see the stupidity of normative rules relating to violence. For example, they are aware that the cultural field disapproves of violence against women. Such violence would erode the basis of the fragile hypermasculinity that is the main constituent of their social identity. However, they also see these conventions as overly restrictive and blind to the reality of the world. For them, women can occasionally act in ways that fully justify violence and, in such instances, why should a woman be allowed to walk away unscathed? The violent subject sees the limitations of cultural conventions relating to violence against women and, while occasionally giving lip-service to such conventions, and without ever fully committing to them, believes he should be given licence to decide for himself when violence is justified. For the violent subject context is crucial. They accept, when asked directly, that violence against women is wrong, but they then follow this with an analysis of the contextual factors that make the rule against violence towards women inapplicable. Sure, they say, men shouldn't hit women, but on this occasion I had no choice but to hit this woman. In this respect the violent subject appears disturbingly similar to the archetypal postmodern subject who disavows god, science, politics and any immaterial force that might determine what is good and what is bad (Winlow and Hall, 2013), a product of what has become the 'dark side' of liberal individualism, a narcissistic product of the ancient recourse to drive given free-rein by

The Sociological Review, 62:S2, pp. 32–49 (2014), DOI: 10.1111/1467-954X.12190
© 2014 The Author. Editorial organisation © 2014 The Editorial Board of the Sociological Review

hyper-modern ethical freedom (Dews, 2012; Hall, 2012). Any force that might seek to impose a moral or ethical framework that seeks to mark out boundaries of acceptable action is terrorizing the postmodern subject with parochial restrictions. Now that god is dead, now that we are all incredulous to metanarratives, who or what is to say what is right or wrong? Nine years ago I interviewed Robert at length about his violent career. Below he discusses an incident in which he assaulted a young woman:

> Probably what everyone else thinks is the worst is I knocked a lass out. I can't remember what started it . . . she starts shouting and bawling, getting right up in my face . . . it's a bad spot to be in because you don't know what to do right? . . . She's right up in my face, and she's screaming and . . . I'm thinking, this isn't funny anymore and I can feel me mood changing. I've telt her to pack in, telt her it wasn't me [who grabbed her arse], so I tell her, you know, fuck off, like, whatever . . . She just starts swinging. The first one caught me a bit around the ear . . . I mean, I've told her to pack in, but she's just gone nuts. So I've tried to push her away, and then I've just lost my rag and given her a clip . . . She's gone over and then the bouncers have come. You feel a bit bad after but really there's nothing else I could do I don't think. You shouldn't hit women I know that but what could I do? I'm not standing there getting slapped about by anybody. It's her fault: . . . she should've left it when I told her. She was right out of order going on like that. It pisses me off thinking back cos she's started wacking me, and she must be thinking, he wouldn't dare hit me back. If she had anything about her she would've walked away. And now see what happens, right? I feel like a twat for hitting her, she obviously isn't too happy and it's a bad situation all around . . . I had to do something; she's taking the piss. I mean I still feel a bit bad about it but really there was nowt else for it.

Here we can see Robert's acceptance of the cultural frame and his acknowledgement of the rules that forbid violence against women. However, he is determined to convince his audience and himself that, in the context he describes, these rules should be considered inapplicable.

The violent subject's narcissism reflects both engagement with the cultural field and separation from it. A reputation for violence can attract a significant measure of respect, and those who move in the same milieu become wary of the violent subject. They tread carefully in conversations, keen to avoid conflict. All those who form close bonds with the violent subject must accept the latter's supremacy and the insecurity that accompanies and typifies the relationship. This reflection of the subject from the social mirror bolsters the narcissistic self-image and reassures him that his commitment to violence elicits approval and envy from those others who occupy the cultural field. He is the one who dares to act, who won't let an insult pass. He is the one willing to risk serious body harm and even death to preserve a pathological self-image that reflects a complex combination of traumatic subjective experience and the cultural conventions of the masculine visceral habitus. This narcissism encourages the violent subject to form a transcendent self-image that flickers in and out of consciousness. This self-image first identifies the unworldly stupidity of the herd so that the subject's own battle against convention might appear heroic. Where other men meekly follow merely conventional rules relating to social conduct and violent action, the violent subject imagines himself to be transcendent, occupying a position of *special liberty* above the social (see Hall, 2012), free to make a life on his own terms, and free to punish all those who incur his wrath.

Anger rises quickly and is slow to dissipate. There is no staged progression towards violent conflict. No taking off of coats, no offers to step outside. Beneath what can appear to be a rather tranquil surface, the violent subject often remains in a state of almost perpetual agitation, wary never to let his guard down, forever vigilant of others attempting to usurp his social status and condemn him to a life of worthless and permanent humiliation. For him, virtually every social encounter has the potential to end in violence. He is sure of this, and he can take a measure of comfort when violence does occur and the waiting is over. Amid the tumult of the conflict itself, he experiences a kind of peace, engaging in a social practice that makes immediate sense to him. It is crucial that we do not take his violent confidence at face value. Beneath this exterior lies a tangled web of insecurities, and his structuring anxiety resides mostly in the unconscious.

In order to enact serious violence the subject must experience rage. He must feel angered, humiliated or forced to act by external circumstances beyond his control. When offering retrospective justifications for their own violence, repeated violent offenders often utilize the narrative of the 'stupid adversaries' who brought it on themselves. In such a narrative, the violent offender is merely a conduit, an educator delivering a memorable lesson to all on the boundaries of acceptable social conduct when encountering men of violence. Again, this rage is closely related to unconscious anxiety. When the rage is made social it represents an attempt to address the complexity of emotional disturbances and enduring anxiety. The violent subject is responsive to events as they unfold in social reality, but for him the meaning of violence cannot be reduced to a culturally informed 'rational' response to social triggers. In order to engage with the social world in such a violently distrustful manner, the individual who becomes the violent subject must have first experienced deep trauma and its various psychical accompaniments.

Becoming a violent subject

The most obvious stereotype here is of a domineering and egocentric father plagued by a powerfully perverse super-ego that ensures over-attention to the 'hegemonic' masculine hierarchies of the cultural field. The domineering father, by simply being himself and making social his own unresolved traumas, begins a process that will transform the innocent boy into a tough, no-nonsense adult male worthy of status and respect, able to stand up for himself, and ready for the depressing reality of a world evacuated of all human warmth. The violent and domineering father is perfectly positioned to assist the boy in this journey towards an encultured image of the *ego ideal*, of a man who forges his own path,

The Sociological Review, 62:S2, pp. 32–49 (2014), DOI: 10.1111/1467-954X.12190

blithely unconcerned about the social world and its petty rules. The father imagines himself to be a confirmed and indefatigable realist who sees the world as it is, able to identify the brutal reality of structural instrumentalism, envy and competition, perfectly capable of detecting the stupid lies that constitute the moral order and its weak inducements and protocols. He smirks at the world, convinced that all kindness is weakness, that all charity masks selfishness, and that all righteousness is irreparably corrupted. It is his paternal responsibility to communicate this knowledge to the boy, and to do this he draws upon the standard rubric of 'toughening the boy up'.

Many entirely normative and functional men also expose their charges to a process of 'toughening up'. The basic essence of this process is to encourage the boy to move away from childish things and to separate themselves from maternal comfort so that they might be better equipped to engage with the ceaseless aggressive competition of the social field, and to prepare them for the inevitable disappointments and frustrations that await those who don't fight hard and dirty, who don't display a daemonic drive to win at all costs. Of course, this is not simply a matter for the working classes. It is a characteristic of all social classes in contemporary Western societies, as anyone who has ever seen *The Apprentice* will know. What the historical evolution of capitalism reveals to us is that successful socio-economic groups no longer need to manifest thymotic drives in actual physical violence. Internal drives to secure the interests of the self and to have one's successes acknowledged by the social field require a 'pseudo-pacified' (Hall, 2007, 2012) form of *symbolic* violence that underpins the inherent aggressivity of profit-seeking and claims to social distinction. The rich have little need to become directly involved in the grubby business of interpersonal violence. Unlike the violent subjects who are the focus of this piece, they were not, during their childhood, firmly ensconced in the visceral habitus of the working class or subject to its combative behavioural regimes. Instead, their violence is sublimated and manifested in an economically functional form (Hall, 2007, 2012). This symbolically violent pseudo-pacified subject supplies the raw human energy needed to drive new markets as it engages in a constant battle to gain the recognition that might assuage the anxieties and constitutive lack that lies at the core of subjectivity (Lacan, 2007). Was the rise of neoliberalism not accompanied by a process that sought to institutionalise envy, competition and insecurity (Žižek, 2010; Hall, 2012)? Was the outcome of this process not the erosion of community sentiments and the rise of a symbolically aggressive form of possessive individualism? And after 35 years of neoliberalism, might we now begin to speculate that this individualism has metamorphized into a retreat into subjectivity, reflective of the decline of symbolic efficiency as we approach the death of the social (Winlow and Hall, 2013)?

The 'toughening up' of the child by parents who truly believe themselves to be acting in the child's best interests is deeply suggestive of the transformation of civil society and helps us to see what the continuation of liberal capitalism further into the 21st century will mean for collective life. This expectation of perpetual struggle and competition is closely related to the elevation of money –

and the social recognition and envy it brings – to the primary source of value these days. I will not labour this point any further, other than to say processes of toughening up the child, and equipping that child with the wherewithal to engage in *symbolic* forms of violence, both reflects and extends trends towards anti-sociality, and reduces the potential for Aristotelian 'human flourishing' (see Dews, 2012).

Of course, this paper is primarily concerned with those family situations where the process of toughening up is a more direct physical and emotional process. In the cultural field I am addressing in this paper, the child that develops an all-encompassing commitment to violence often comes from a family environment characterized by pronounced conflict and insecurity. They are exposed to violence and threats to their physical security, and the emotional intensity of these events tends to ensure the family milieu is pervaded by a more general atmosphere of wariness and insecurity. The uncultured child quickly learns that violence is real and that it possesses a raw interactional utility. Violence gets things done (see Hall, 2012 on 'the undertaker'). With time, the child absorbs the father's assessment of the threats posed by the social field. He imagines social reality to be an aggressive competition with only notional rules. He learns that even in places of social excision a sudden burst of entirely unrestrained violence can inspire fear in others. By the time he enters early adulthood he believes he sees a truth that the rest of the world cannot. Violence for him is stripped of its usual civilized associations. Violence exists. It is real, and it is best to face up to this fact. To spend one's life running away from it is no life at all.

The child who is socialized in a micro-climate of insecurity and fear, and subject to an external cultural field that encourages tough masculinity, will often encounter deeply traumatic events that resonate throughout his adult life. The subject will return to these events countless times as the psyche attempts to deal with the emotional pain they inspire. In many cases the actuality of traumatic events cannot be revisited in a straightforward manner. The events themselves were so injurious that conscious recollection would be far too painful for the psyche to bear. In such cases they are disguised by the psyche's various defence systems. The 'memory' of the traumatic event takes a different form, or it is shut away, disavowed or repressed. However, the repressed memory inevitably returns as the psyche attempts to cathartically release the disturbing energy of the traumatic event. I have addressed these processes at length elsewhere (eg Winlow and Hall, 2009; Winlow, 2012) and it makes little sense to do so again. Instead, in the remainder of the paper, I would like to explore some of the experiences and consequences of traumatic humiliation, and the guilt that often accompanies it.

Humiliation and guilt

Christopher Bollas (1997) claims that most of the men who go on to become serial killers experience an emotional death during childhood. Importantly, he

The Sociological Review, 62:S2, pp. 32–49 (2014), DOI: 10.1111/1467-954X.12190

acknowledges that some men who have experienced deep trauma during their youth can be 'brought back to life' with love, care and support. However, the most damaged subjectivities appear to experience a 'recurrent killing of the self throughout [their] childhood as the destruction of their own personally determined self state' (1997: 188). He speculates that the now dead inner self of the serial killer often develops a companionship with the dead, and 'in the place of the once-live self, a new being emerges, identified with the killing of what is good, the destruction of trust, love, and reparation' (1997: 189). For Bollas, the serial killer transports his victims through the terms of his 'own childhood, ritualizing their extinction by sacrificing them to a killing trauma' (1997: 192). Here it is worth quoting Bollas at length:

> The person who has been killed in his childhood is in unwilling identification with his own premature mortality, and by finding a victim whom he puts through the structure of evil, he transcends his own killing, psychically overcoming his own endless deaths by sacrificing to the malignant gods that overlooked his childhood. (1997: 193)

Bollas also identifies the importance of the victim's innocence in the 'economics of this primal scene' (1997: 197). For Bollas, the 'empty-headed other' is erotically exciting for the killer.

> The victim's seeming gullibility, stupidity, and lack of foresight are attractive. So far as the killer is concerned he deserves what he has coming to him. And . . . when the killer announces his intent to kill the victim, his speech empties the other's head, creating a vacuum from mute incomprehension. Bollas (1997: 197)

Bollas's point is to equate the empty-headedness of the victim to the killer's childlike former self, a form of 'unconscious transference' through which the killer's child-self lives through the victim, and the ultimate death of the victim 'renders the self mute and empty' (1997: 197). While my focus is on excessively violent men and not on serial killers specifically, there is much here to draw from. What is it about the experience of trauma that has the potential to be so catastrophically damaging, to totally transform the lifecourse, forcing the individual to live forever in the shadow of a long-past event?

Bollas suggests that there exists a kind of elemental trust that acts as the foundation of human relations. This trust is so basic that it becomes a thoughtless assumption, and it appears to be one that stems from the care that is offered to the child by the parent. The child 'trusts' the parent to defend and nurture it, to overlook its simple-minded narcissism, and it is the breaking of this trust that appears to be so detrimental for the child's psychic well-being. Of course, in the midst of the harmful act, the child is stupefied at the fracturing of this trust. In Lacanian terms, the child is thrust into an unspeakable Real. He can find no words, no way to make sense of what is happening. When the horror is complete, when the parent's rage is spent, in most cases the child remains dependent upon this pathological adult. However, even in those cases where the child grows distant from the oppressive parent, he feels secretly bonded to him, 'brought closer to the very object which has betrayed him' (Bollas, 1997: 200; see also Gadd, 2003).

We can see elements of this in the accounts offered by violent men of their childhood relationship with their fathers. In a number of instances, there is what seems to be a pathological over-identification with the father, especially in light of the victimization of the child at the hands of this man. Such violent men often trivialize their own victimhood and instead talk of a process of self-becoming, in which they learnt during their childhood important lessons about being a man in a heartless world (see Winlow and Hall, 2006, 2009; Winlow, 2012). In turn they portray their fathers as tough, no-nonsense men who dutifully cleansed the child of its innocence, revealing to them the truths that other men seem entirely unable to appreciate. In the violent subject's self-narrative, the experience of his own victimhood toughened him up and set him on a path toward an enviable masculinity entirely free from affective bonds, willing to fight and destroy and cleanse others of their stupid innocence. Of course, the narrative of self-becoming obfuscates the deep harms of such events and their tendency to reverberate through the life course. These events inevitably shape social identity and one's engagement with the world. Despite the protestations of such men, nothing positive comes from the experience of such brutality. It is the context of the cultural field that is crucial in ensuring that the effects of such abuse result in destructive hyper-masculine violence. While there is clearly a self-destructive tendency to their social engagement, a tendency displayed in other forms of traumatic life, the effects of trauma do not result in a conscious adoption of a narrative of victimhood. Their rage at the world reflects their own inner torment, and the principal effects of the trauma are harboured in the unconscious.

Before taking this argument further it is worth briefly recapping and making clear the connection that exists between the violent subject's inner torment and the social field that contextualizes subjective harm. Of course, my claim is not that the experience of trauma tends to result in a deep commitment to violence in adult life. In order for the initial trauma to return in the form of externalized violence there must be significant forms of social and cultural experience in place to encourage trauma to take this specific form upon its return. Of course, when particular forms of hyper-masculinity are less apparent, or entirely absent, the experience of deep trauma frequently leads to the internalization of violence, often seen in forms of non-violent self-sabotage and self-annihilation. Of course, pathological over-attachment to a violent social identity is closely related to other manifestations of death drive, but the drive to continually seek out violent encounters in the manner I describe here is reflective of a quite specific social frame. Without the presence of particular adults during socialization, and with the context of the visceral habitus and its expectations entirely withdrawn, it is not difficult to imagine these men, as Stein's (2006) research reveals, as serious drug or alcohol abusers or involved in other forms of petty

The Sociological Review, 62:S2, pp. 32–49 (2014), DOI: 10.1111/1467-954X.12190

crime. Without this specific social context in place, their childhood trauma might have driven them into a series of abusive social relationships, or to other forms of socially or sexually problematic behaviour. If their early family life had not been typified by violence, abuse, insecurity and an almost total lack of trust, and the boys had instead been surrounded by supportive individuals keen to encourage him to overcome his traumatic experiences and form nourishing social bonds with others, it is entirely possible that these men might have led reasonably rewarding and productive lives. The horrors of childhood might have been overcome and positive experiences might have taken their place. I am speculating of course, but the point is to identify the importance of developing an analysis of the social field when attempting to explain the outcomes of childhood trauma. My point here is simply that an analysis of the social field can give us some insight into the possible outcomes of traumatic experience. For those individuals who are the subjects of this paper, the narrative of cold realism and the background of a particular form of visceral habitus frame the experience of childhood trauma and help us to understand why the traumatized boy grows into a violent adult offender. It is not that the offender 'had no other option'. Rather it is that, living in the cultural climate and being subject to the upbringing I describe here, the chances of the traumatized boy drawing upon aggressive violence as a means of addressing his own inner torment are greatly increased.

So, that said, let me try to advance my argument a little further by looking more closely at the experience of guilt. I claim that the fracturing of what Bollas calls 'elemental trust' and the prolonged insecurity of childhood experience produces trauma. But what are the principal emotional components of this trauma? How should we conceptualize the affective consequences of trauma in the biographies of excessively violent men? First, in continuation of the point raised above, and following Žižek (2000: 256), we must note that guilt is 'ultimately unconscious'. There are two straightforward ways of understanding guilt in this way. First, 'the subject is unaware of his or her guilt', and second, 'he or she, while experiencing the pressure of guilt, is unaware of what he or she is guilty of' (2000: 256). Consciously, the violent subject feels no sense of shame or guilt in relation to his own victimhood, but unconsciously these feelings are a crucial aspect of the violent subject's psychopathology. We can immediately understand why a violent subject should feel guilty about his own violence, but why should he feel guilty about his own childhood victimization? He was simply a defenceless child subject to the barbarity of an abusive parent. Johnston's most recent work (see Johnston and Malabou, 2013) is particularly instructive. Žižek's (2000: 256) articulation of what can be basically described as 'unfelt feelings' and 'misfelt feelings' helps us to understand the shape and impact of unconscious affects. For example, the 'unfelt feeling' appears to suggest the total absence of guilt from consciousness, but despite this, the guilt works behind the scenes in the unconscious, shaping the social bearing of the violent subject. Johnston and Malabou (2013: 162) suggest that the misfelt feeling can be understood as follows:

[I]n the absence of an explicit cognizance of culpability apropos a misdeed relative to a certain rule, the feeling that might otherwise be self-interpretively felt as guilt is consciously registered as some other affective tonality (such as anxiety, nervousness, vague discomfort, or even physical illness).

The uncultured child, yet to become fully integrated into the moral and symbolic orders, has no available means of understanding the behaviour of the pathological parent who abuses. The child grasps around helplessly for some structure that might allow him to address the fundamental shock that accompanies the rupturing of basic trust. No answers are to be found, and the search continues unconsciously throughout the life course.

For Lacan (2007), shame is inevitably connected to *jouissance*. In Lacanian psychoanalysis *jouissance* references those forms of pleasure-seeking that result in pain, tend to sabotage the interests of the subject, or reveal to the subject something that it would prefer to remain hidden. This connection between shame and *jouissance* is suggestive of the role played by fantasy in structuring our experience of shame. Our shame does not spring from the actuality of the event. Of course, consciously there is nothing for the child to feel ashamed of. They have done nothing wrong whatsoever. So from where does shame come? Following Lacan, we might claim that our experience of shame references the ways that the event relates to unconscious fantasy. As one might expect, Žižek (2005: 147) goes right to the heart of the matter with a troubling example: 'shame is not simply passivity, but an actively assumed passivity: if I am raped, then I have nothing to be ashamed of; but if I enjoy being raped, then I deserve to feel ashamed'. Žižek's analysis is prefaced on the belief that our internal fantasy space is never fully rational. A gap always exists between our external social identity and the complexities of our internal fantasy space, but when the gap is closed, when aspects of the fantasy space are effectively 'realized', then the result can be profoundly traumatic. Žižek (2005: 178) suggests that being compelled to live out a hidden fantasy in a passive mode, a fantasy that we are not consciously aware of and over which we feel no sense of ownership, in which one is reduced to a mere body to be used by the other, is 'perhaps, the worst, most humiliating kind of violence, a violence that undermines the very basis of my identity . . . by exposing me to an unbearable shame'.

So, my admittedly disturbing thesis is that shame is an unconscious affect of the childhood trauma that I briefly outlined above. The child is 'ashamed' not because he has been victimized, but because the manner of the child's victimization indirectly references the content of his fantasy space. We can begin to see how this might work if we imagine the child as he begins to enter the symbolic order. He is exposed to transgression/punishment narratives, especially in the home, which is an environment characterized by insecurity and threat. His unconscious searches for ways to explain his victimhood at the hands of the abusive father. His psyche is desperate to understand the violent event and cathect its disturbing energy. My claim is that the male child retrospectively comes to experience his victimhood as shameful because, in the unconscious, the child feels he must have done something to provoke the violence of the abusive parent, and the 'something' done by the child that provoked this violence must have been truly awful to drive the parent to such unspeakable abuse. During times of repose the violent subject trawls through images and mythical scenarios that might have compelled the parent to enact such violence. The never fully conscious 'why did they do it?' becomes an unconscious 'what did I do to deserve it?' It is impossible to attempt to understand the violent event – the rupturing of elemental trust – rationally and consciously because the event was so injurious that intense pain accompanies any attempt to return to the memory of its actuality. It is impossible to understand why another would break this elemental trust. Why would a parent behave in such a way? The irrationality of the unconscious arrives at the conclusion that the child has done something to inspire such a violent intervention.

This is not an attempt to pathologize the victim. The shame I am talking about here takes the form of an unfelt (or misfelt) feeling. There is no rational reason for the victim to feel ashamed, and in their everyday life there is no conscious feeling of shame. Rather, as I have attempted to describe above, shame is an unconscious affect created by traumatic experience. Shame exists in the unconscious, working behind the scenes to shape the ways in which the violent subject engages with social life. In the violent subject's constant edginess, in his sensitivity to threats, and in his desire to rise immediately to any challenge; in his very attempt to disguise shame, we catch sight of it.

Conclusion

In this paper I have attempted to connect an analysis of the unconscious affects of traumatic experience to a sociological analysis of culture and socialization. My goal is to encourage sociologists interested in violence to think again about the complexities of our internal emotional life and the crucial impact trauma can have upon social behaviour and biographical development. Of course, as I stress above, the framework I have developed here is conceptual, although it draws upon considerable empirical data. Children who experience trauma are not inevitably thrust along a path that leads to sustained aggressivity in adult life. Many individuals who experience deeply problematic childhoods will overcome these events to lead reasonably 'normal' lives, especially when they are able to cultivate supportive relationships. For other individuals, the traumas of childhood will encourage very different forms of self-sabotaging behaviour. Similarly, the role of 'toughening the boy up' need not be taken by a male parent (see Stein, 2006). Any significant figure in the life of the child can take it upon themselves to destroy innocence and trust. My point is simply this: childhood trauma and parenting that stresses functional asociality, when combined with a surrounding culture that stresses tough masculinity, tends to produce an adult identity dependent upon violent action. In the sociological sense, the framework I outline here is something akin to an ideal type rather than a hard and fast rule, and it is certainly not my intention to deny the uniqueness of individual experience. I have also attempted to advance a psychoanalytic thesis that repudiates simple Cartesian rationality and identifies the deep complexities of affective life. Following Johnston (in Johnston and Malabou, 2013), and contra Lacan, I claim that feelings can be 'misfelt'. With regard to violent subjectivity, the narcissism of the hyper-aggressive violent offender is a reflection of deep insecurity, and the original contribution of my paper is to draw sociological attention to the ways in which the social bearing of the violent offender often reflects unconscious shame and guilt related to childhood victimization.

References

Anderson, E., (2001), *Code of the Street*, New York: Norton.

Ayres, T. and Treadwell, J., (2012), 'Bars, drugs and football thugs: alcohol, cocaine use and violence in the night time economy among English football firms', *Criminology and Criminal Justice*, 12 (1): 83–100.

Baudrillard, J., (2007), *In the Shadow of the Silent Majorities*, Los Angeles, CA: Semiotext(e).

Bengtsson, T. T., (2012), 'Learning to become a "gangster"?', *Journal of Youth Studies*, 15 (6): 677–692.

Bengtsson, T. T., (2013), 'It's what you have to do!': exploring the role of high-risk edgework and advanced marginality in a young man's motivation for crime', *Criminology and Criminal Justice*, 13 (1): 99–115.

Bollas, C., (1997), *Cracking Up: The Work of Unconscious Experience*, London: Routledge.

Bourgois, P., (2002), *In Search of Respect*, Cambridge: Cambridge University Press.

Connell, R. W., (2005), *Masculinities*, Berkeley, CA: University of California Press.

Cooper, C., (2012), 'Understanding the English "riots" of 2011: "mindless criminality" or youth "Mekin Histri" in austerity Britain?' *Youth and Policy*, 109: 6.

Densley, J. A., (2012), 'It's gang life, but not as we know it: the evolution of gang business', *Crime and Delinquency*, doi: 10.1177/0011128712437912.

Derrida, J., (2006), *Spectres of Marx*, London: Routledge.

Dews, P., (2012), *The Idea of Evil*, Oxford: Wiley-Blackwell.

Ellis, A. J., (2013), *'Handy Lads': An Ethnographic Research Study of Men and Violence in Northern England*, PhD thesis, University of Sheffield.

Ellis, A. and Wykes, M., (2013), 'Bringing the boys back home: re-engendering criminology' in M. Cowburn, M. Duggan, A. Robinson and P. Senior (eds), *Values in Criminology and Community Justice*, Bristol: Policy Press.

Ellis, A. and Winlow, S., (forthcoming), '"Throughout my life I've had people walk all over me": trauma, identity and subjective violence'.

Gadd, D., (2003), 'Reading between the lines: subjectivity and men's violence', *Men and Masculinities*, 5 (4): 333–354.

Hall, S., (1997), 'Visceral cultures and criminal practices', *Theoretical Criminology*, 1 (4): 453–478.

Hall, S., (2002), 'Daubing the drudges of fury: men, violence and the piety of the "hegemonic masculinity thesis"', *Theoretical Criminology*, 6 (1): 35–61.

Hall, S., (2007), 'The emergence and breakdown of the pseudo-pacification process', in K. Watson (ed.), *Assaulting the Past: Violence and Civilization in Historical Context*, Cambridge: Cambridge Scholars Publishing.

Hall, S., (2012), *Theorizing Crime and Deviance: A New Perspective*, London: Sage.

Hall, S., Winlow, S. and Ancrum, C., (2008), *Criminal Identities and Consumer Culture: Crime, Exclusion and the New Culture of Narcissism*, Cullompton: Willan.

Hegel, G. W. F., (1977), *Phenomenology of Spirit*, Oxford: Oxford University Press.

Hobbs, D., (1994), ' "Mannish boys": Danny, Chris, crime, masculinity and business', in E. Stanko (ed.), *Just Boys Doing Business*, London: Routledge.

The Sociological Review, 62:S2, pp. 32–49 (2014), DOI: 10.1111/1467-954X.12190

Hobbs, D., (1995), *Bad Business*, Oxford: Oxford University Press.

Hobbs, D., Hadfield, P., Lister, S. and Winlow, S., (2003), *Bouncers: Violence and Governance in the Night-time Economy*, Oxford: Oxford University Press.

Ilan, J., (2010), 'Book review: *Criminal Identities and Consumer Culture: Crime, Exclusion and the New Culture of Narcissism* by S. Hall, S. Winlow and C. Ancrum', *Urban Studies*, 47 (5): 1151–1154.

Johnston, A. and Malabou, C., (2013), *Self and Emotional Life*, New York: Columbia University Press.

Lacan, J., (2007), *Ecrits*, New York: Norton.

Mullins, C., (2006), *Holding your Square*, Cullompton: Willan.

O'Brien, M., (2007), 'Book review: *Violent Night: Urban Leisure and Contemporary Culture* Simon Winlow and Steve Hall Oxford: Berg, 2006', *Crime, Media, Culture*, 3 (3): 398–401.

Patrick, J., (1973), *A Glasgow Gang Observed*, London: Eyre Methuen.

Stein, A., (2006), *Prologue to Violence: Child Abuse, Dissociation and Crime*, London: Routledge.

Treadwell, J. and Garland, J., (2012), 'Masculinity, marginalization and violence: a case study of the English Defence League', *British Journal of Criminology*, 51 (4): 621–634.

Wieviorka, M., (2009), *Violence: A New Approach*, London: Sage.

Winlow, S., (2001), *Badfellas: Crime, Tradition and New Masculinities*, Oxford: Berg.

Winlow, S., (2012), 'All that is scared is profaned: towards a theory of subjective violence', in S. Hall and S. Winlow (eds), *New Directions in Criminological Theory*, London: Routledge.

Winlow, S. and Hall, S., (2006), *Violent Night: Urban Leisure and Contemporary Culture*, Oxford: Berg.

Winlow, S. and Hall, S., (2009), 'Retaliate first: memory humiliation and male violence', *Crime, Media, Culture*, 5 (3): 285–304.

Winlow, S. and Hall, S., (2013), *Rethinking Social Exclusion: The End of the Social*, London: Sage.

Žižek, S., (2000), 'Da Capo senza Fine', in J. Butler, E. Laclau and S. Žižek, *Contingency, Hegemony, Universality: Contemporary Dialogues on the Left*, London: Verso.

Žižek, S., (2005), 'Neighbors and other monsters: a plea for ethical violence', in S. Žižek, E. Santner and K. Reinhard, *The Neighbor: Three Inquiries in Political Theology*, Chicago: University of Chicago Press.

Žižek, S., (2010), *Living in the End Times*, London: Verso.

The sociological analysis of violence: new perspectives

Michel Wieviorka

Abstract: Violence has been a central preoccupation for political and social scientists, and this paper begins with a critical appraisal of the classical approaches to the phenomenon of violence, showing how despite their considerable differences, they are not necessarily contradictory. Via engagement with the recent work of Randall Collins, the paper pays particular attention to the limits of symbolic interactionism. The paper then places the subject central to sociological analysis, showing how it is possible to avoid the determinism of classical sociology by exploring the meaning of violence for the subjects who use it, and how these meanings relate to the processes of subjectivation and desubjectivation.

Keywords: violence, Randall Collins, subject, subjectivation, desubjectivation, meaning

Introduction

There is no shortage of sociological theories of violence or historical, ethnological or political science approaches to the subject. Despite their considerable differences, however, they are not necessarily contradictory. In a first approximation, they can be regarded as belonging to three large families or three types of paradigm. Surprisingly none of these are particularly interested in the *subjectivity* of the protagonists of violence, or in the meeting of *subjectivities* in a pre-violent situation. Nor do any focus on the meaning and loss of meaning which leads to violence, and to the processes of subjectivation and desubjectivation which make it possible. This text, after having stressed these shortcomings in classical approaches to the phenomenon, begins to address and correct these deficiencies.

The classical social sciences and violence

Some theories of violence are concerned with the instrumental dimensions of the phenomenon, the calculations of the actors and their strategy. In these instances,

The Sociological Review, 62:S2, pp. 50–64 (2014), DOI: 10.1111/1467-954X.12191

violence is a resource used to obtain a result; it is a means to an end. The analysis here can apply equally well to individual actors who resemble the *Homo Oeconomicus* of economic theory, or to groups and collective action, as in the so-called resource mobilization theories.[1] The limits of this type of approach are to be found in what historical or empirical observation teaches us: instrumental violence is always liable to get out of hand, or be carried away by other than purely strategical approaches and of being overtaken by meanings other than those which come under rational calculation.

Other theories attribute violence to a reaction to a situation, and in particular, a crisis situation. Violence, there again both individual and collective, is then explained by the events which determine it but which are external to it, by a context which has become unbearable, evolutions arousing frustrations which have become intolerable.[2] In this perspective, it is the behaviour which constitutes the response to, for example, sudden economic difficulties, the threat of closure of a firm, unemployment or destitution.

Finally, a third set of analyses, equally classical, insists on the idea of a culture of violence, which is said to predispose the members of a family, a group, a community or an entire society, more than others, to act out their violence. There are numerous variations of these approaches which may possibly propose to make a link between culture and personality, violence here and now finding its sources, for example, in a form of education or a primary socialization which predisposes thereto.[3] Thus, criminology sometimes explains sexual crimes of violence to children by the fact that the perpetrators themselves were subjected to horrors of this type during their childhood.

Whether they are utilitarian, impelled by the idea of a response to a fairly broadly defined situation, or concern a culture shaping predispositions, the most classical approaches in the social sciences and the humanities do not entirely avoid the determinist failing which postulates a causality or a range of causes to explain violence. Determinism is sometimes pushed to extremes, and from social or cultural, it may even in some approaches become natural, or biological. For example there are proposals[4] today which, in their way, update the old theories of Cesare Lombroso by seeking the sources of crime, terrorism or sexual violence in the genetic heritage of individuals – a theme for journalists as well as for those in the sciences.

Determinist approaches, particularly when they include biological-type dimensions, are always suspect in the eyes of social science researchers who rightly distrust determinism in general, and naturalization of the social sciences in particular. These approaches are increasingly alarming from the perspective of human rights and democratic and humanist values which they rapidly admit with abusing. From their point of view, should prisoners who have served their sentences but have a genetic and social profile considered to be liable to make them reoffend be kept in detention? Should travellers who wish to enter a country but whose profile is considered pre- or proto-terrorist be refused entry or not? In this respect, the move to the 'Big Data' era where data of genetic type and social and cultural data may possibly be merged is extremely disturbing for those who are concerned with the fundamental rights of the individual. This is why when the social sciences and the humanities see fit to resist the idea of causality and pure determinism they seem more qualified to shed light on the conditions which make violence possible than on the violence itself.

The main point is that the approaches which have just been outlined all to some extent leave to one side the most mysterious aspect, and therefore what is most characteristic of violent behaviour: the fact that almost always, if the behaviour is of some significance, or tends to continue or to become repetitive, *the meaning of this violence may differ from that assigned by the theory which claims to explain it.* There is a rapid tendency to exaggerate, or to minimize, in relation to the type of explanation marshalled. For example, when actors sacrifice their lives how can we be satisfied with an explanation which reduces a terrorist action to the idea of a calculation and therefore of rational instrumentality? What cost/advantage calculation can be made here? How can we claim that a crisis situation wholly explains violent political protests, when gratuitous cruelty is incurred, violence for violence's sake or violence as an end in itself? Why do some protagonists of violence, in addition to their actions, feel the need to make ideological or religious speeches, which at times are simply floods of words? Why are others, or the same, sadistic?

The reply to this type of question often depends on the idea that as far as violence is concerned, it is the 'micro-macro problem' which has to be solved; this also applies to other issues being analysed. Since violence can be observed, empirically, at 'micro' level, where it occurs, or spreads, where individuals or groups are wounding and killing others, does this not primarily call for a 'micro' approach? But since it is central to history, shaping and destroying whole societies, do we not in the first instance require a 'macro' perspective? Violence is localized; it is a form of action which refers, materially, to specific human beings defined by a given situation to the extent that, in the last resort, it seems to fall under psychology. At the same time, it is part of the work of society on itself, its functioning and dysfunctioning, or its relations with other societies, for example in times of war, in which case it comes under sociology. In the face of violence, the social sciences cannot simply distinguish these two levels – the micro-level and the macro-level. They have to attempt, if appropriate, to articulate them and to envisage, if possible, an integrated approach to the phenomenon. This would put an end to the 'micro-macro' gap which is central to many discussions and endeavours in the social sciences, as shown, for example, by David Gadd and Tony Jefferson's (2007) studies in criminology.

The social sciences can also try and introduce other levels. This is one of the features which strikes the reader of the special section in the journal *Sociologica,* featuring Randall Collins in discussion with other researchers including myself.[5] Collins insists on distinguishing three levels: that of 'macro-history', that of individual consciousness and, between the two, the one which he prioritizes, as we shall see, that of immediate interactions. Stathis Kalyvas requests that consideration be given to what he calls the *meso* level, 'where both measurement and testing especially when it comes to the study of violence, are often easier to achieve

The Sociological Review, 62:S2, pp. 50–64 (2014), DOI: 10.1111/1467-954X.12191
© 2014 The Author. Editorial organisation © 2014 The Editorial Board of the Sociological Review

and more fruitful to undertake' (2011: 3). But, as we shall see, it is true that many approaches rather than dealing with the issue of the articulation of levels or registers, prefer to give preference to only one, providing a unidimensional response to the problem.

Avoiding psychological or sociological deviations

A first answer to this challenge does indeed take us off course and deviates toward psychology. Violent behaviour is sometimes so disconcerting or so bound up with characteristics which appear to be highly personal that the space for an explanation in terms of sociology, politics or ethnology is extremely restricted. In this case, the analysis tends to veer toward the psychological, even medical. There is a tendency to isolate the personality of the actor, to examine his or her antecedents, trajectory and family background and in some cases to resort to psychiatry and consider the violence as a form of madness, or pathology. In extreme cases, the implication or the consequence of a perspective of this type is to absolve the perpetrator of any responsibility for the violence, since he or she was driven by impulses and was not knowingly the perpetrator.

This type of opinion is not necessarily to be rejected but it is only acceptable on condition that empirically we have ascertained that this is in fact the case. The acknowledgment of irresponsibility should only be made once there has been an in-depth examination of other hypotheses and certainly not because it is invoked by the perpetrator or, for example, by lawyers. Thus the thesis attributed to Hannah Arendt, with some exaggeration, of the irresponsibility of Adolph Eichmann in the disappearance of the Jews in Europe, has frequently been advanced. Thus the vulgate considers that for Arendt, Eichmann is said to have acted, not out of hatred for Jews, or out and out anti-Semitism but because he was placed in a situation where he was obliged to obey a legitimate authority for purely administrative reasons. The vulgate also considers that this thesis recalls the students in Stanley Milgram's (1974) well-known experiments who obeyed a professor ordering them to inflict pain on a victim (using a confederate as guinea pig) when they gave the wrong answers to the questions asked. In fact, Arendt in no way confuses Milgram's experiments, which demonstrate the principle of submission to a legitimate authority, with her reflections on Eichmann's responsibility.

The difficulty with psychological approaches is that they tend to minimize or eliminate the social, cultural, political or historical dimensions of collective violence and to reduce individual violence to the working of conscience, lack of awareness or indifference to society. These approaches take either no account of the meaning of the action, or separate the meaning from the action; they are not interested in the person or group in question.

Nevertheless, these approaches, which we refer to as tending to the psychological do also have an essential interest. They do tell us something about the acting out of desires, the particular point or the individual processes which lead to it and where the action takes place. This is an important point.

In contrast, many analyses neglect the psychology of the actors, and with it the 'micro' level, in favour of general social and cultural rationales which could explain violence: poverty, the desire to become rich, racism and its spread in society, the political crisis, the formation of a fascist movement or religion, for example. But an approach which is restricted to this 'macro' level leaves the reader yearning for more.

A purely sociological or similar explanation will, indeed, often leave to one side, the fact that only a few individuals, sometimes only one, act out their desires, whereas thousands, or hundreds of thousands, are of the same opinion, have the same ideas, share their emotions and their orientations, or yet again have known a comparable social trajectory. Sociology and similar disciplines do not really enable us to understand why an act of violence is the doing of one individual person and not others. Let us illustrate this remark.

An illustration

Let's take the case of those whom the press and similar types of literature have, since the attacks in Boston in 2013, at times referred to as 'lone wolves' – terrorists acting alone, or almost alone. For example, in Norway, on 22 July 2011, Anton Behring Breivik killed 77 young people in cold blood in the name of an extreme right, anti-Muslim, anti-immigrant ideology mingled with a few surprising references, in particular to Israel. The police succeeded in arresting him; he was imprisoned and judged. His defence in court did the utmost to have him considered responsible for his acts, and therefore as having acted in a political manner. The case is unique and exceptional but did to some extent resonate with extreme right sympathizers, including in his own country.

In France, in March 2012, Mohammed Merah killed first three soldiers, according to him the personification of an army active against Islam, then three Jewish children and a teacher in a Jewish school in Toulouse, thus expressing an anti-Semitism which knew no bounds. The man appeared to have acted alone or at least with very few accomplices. The violence was a highly personal, deliberate choice made on his own. Analytically, it is the act of an individual, however it corresponded to feelings shared by part of the Muslim youth in France and elsewhere. We find countless expressions of this on the Internet or in the social networks. But these youths do not act out their desires.

Finally, the Tsamaev brothers, who planted bombs at the finishing line of the Boston Marathon in April 2013, also apparently acted on their own, but their attacks – even if to this day their ideology or Muslim religious feelings do seem somewhat vague – may correspond to the orientations of people other than themselves who can recognize themselves in this act. There again, these isolated actors are connected via the Internet to worldwide networks.

In the three cases, the acting out of the desire is individual and highly personal, but the meanings of the act may concern a much wider population. This is why the analysis must go from one perspective to another, from the individual to the socio-political or cultural context in which he or she has acted.

The political, ideological, possibly religious meanings of the act are clear here, even obvious, and they are shared by many others. But when a lone – or practically – lone individual, acts out a desire, a purely sociological approach does not really enable us to apprehend the violence appropriately. Symmetrically, psychology or criminology, by leaving aside the meaning attributed to their acts of violence by actors like these 'lone wolves', is not wholly satisfactory. In the eyes of the law, they are criminals. This does not mean to say they are mad; moreover they are more than capable of a degree of rationality and they do wish to attribute a political, or geopolitical, meaning to the murders which they have committed.

Is it possible to reconcile an approach focusing on the meaning of the action, its social, political and historical scope, its collective dimensions and the concern of the perpetrator of violent acts to have an impact on world order on one hand, and, on the other, an approach which takes his or her personality into consideration? This is in fact possible and two major orientations merit discussion here. Their examination will show that rather than merely trying to discuss the articulation of the 'macro' and the 'micro', in classical fashion, and the respective merits of each approach, it might be interesting to consider how to approach the deciding issue of the commitment to action.

Interactions

A first approach here is interactionist and has in fact recently begun to be developed in connection with violence. To begin with, let's set this orientation in its recent history. Its point of departure is to be found in the major deconstruction which took place from the 1960s, when the social sciences wished to end with the 'grand narratives' described by Jean-François Lyotard (1979), enter postmodernity and free themselves of 'grand' theories. At that time, research moved away from structuralism and ceased to devote considerable space to Marxism in its different variations. Above all, it abandoned functionalism, in particular as personified by Talcott Parsons. In this evolution, modes of approach which were interested in the study of interactions, particularly restricted interaction, were rejuvenated – sometimes, with ethnomethodology, out of the debris of functionalism, but not necessarily. These approaches suggested that the best way to understand the social was to understand how human beings live together and for that, detailed, ethnographic observations were decisive. They demonstrate how the interactions which, in the last resort, create the social fabric, develop.

These approaches, of which the most outstanding figure is undoubtedly Erving Goffman, stand apart from politics and history. Nor, until very recently, were they very interested in violence – at least not to the point of making it a central problem. But in 2008, Randall Collins published a book in which he set out an interactionist theory of violence, which owes a lot to the perspectives opened up by Jack Katz (1999) in his sociology of the emotions, and which deserves our attention.[6]

Collins, known to date for his Weberian orientations and his reading of Max Weber, analyses violence in a perspective which is becoming micro-sociological and interactionist – an approach which he had already indicated at the beginning of the year 2000 (Collins, 2004). His approach is pragmatic in intent. The analysis moves from being sociological to being rather ethnological; in any event it is based on ethnographic studies, like those of Elijah Anderson. It also owes a lot to the work of historians such as Samuel L. A. Marshall who studied the behaviour of American soldiers in battle during the Second World War (Marshall, 1947). Collins, who has carefully examined photographic documents, and videos, and who has himself also done fieldwork observation, considers in close detail the facial expressions and body postures of the actors at the time of the violence – the noise and the sounds emitted, the rhythm of the bodies and movements in a real-life situation, the attempts to impose a rhythm on the opponent. In his opinion, violence finds its causes not in the subjectivity of its protagonists but in the dynamic of the situations in which they find themselves.

If we follow his reasoning, violence arises in real-life situations; it is the outcome of an emotional barrier of confrontational tension/fear which is circumvented or, in the last resort, resolved in violence. In this perspective, understanding violence therefore involves taking into account the material issues at stake when tension and, possibly fear, arises and when some people in these instances, if necessary, resort to violence. For Collins, the 'confrontational tension' only rarely leads to violence, and then usually only in part. He considers that when there is immediate social interaction, or when 'antagonists are face-to-face', it is difficult to implement violence and, in his words, 'violent threats most of the time abort'.

He considers that in most cases violent situations are extensions of a-violent situations, that is, situations which are not in themselves violent. Violence is not explained by motivations – being 'motivated' is not enough. Collins therefore sees violence as a 'circumventing of confrontational tension' which is sometimes based on a power struggle – the strong attack the weak, the group attacks the isolated individual – or possibly on the attitude of the public, which may encourage the move to violence, on the creation of a distance – it is preferable to fight at a distance – and therefore on the depersonalization of the victims – the face-to-face or psychological confrontation is avoided.

Collins invites us to be specific and he is right. He states, for example, that if one examines closely the documents relating to a violent episode, one makes observations which eliminate the stereotypes. He insists on the importance of the emotional domination which he considers precedes physical destruction. He is also right in saying that violence is not an easy thing and that, on the contrary, it is difficult to implement.

The Sociological Review, 62:S2, pp. 50–64 (2014), DOI: 10.1111/1467-954X.12191

Collins is well aware that a micro-sociological approach does not entirely explain violence and he refers to an intended publication which will enable us to move to a macro-sociological approach. But for the moment, we must content ourselves with his pragmatic interactionism and with the idea, which adds nothing to our understanding of violence, that the techniques used by the actors in the interactions then spread within the society considered, and beyond, becoming what might be understood as 'micro-patterns' – an idea which seems to articulate a perspective similar to Gabriel Tarde, when the author deals with the laws governing imitation, and the theme of repertoires of forms of collective action as proposed by Charles Tilly.[7]

Can we reduce violence to an 'interactional accomplishment' in situations where emotion dominates? Can we in the last resort accept the idea that it is the situation and not the actors which takes precedence?

In the first instance, we will observe that it is not difficult to find situations or historical experiences which negate Randall's statements, or in any event, which impair any claim to their general nature or theoretical validity. For example, how can we account for extreme experiences in which those who are closest to us, the neighbours, or those with whom one used to play football, are the objects of the worst outbursts of violence as in the ethnic cleansing in Rwanda or in ex-Yugoslavia? In the latter case, there were not only snipers shooting while remaining invisible – to whom Collins attaches great importance – but also murderers attacking people who saw them and who knew them.

But above all, what is striking, in the approach developed by Collins, is the reduction of meaning, or its disappearance: the actors can only be understood in real-life situations, they are determined only in and by the interaction, without which violence is groundless. Inter-subjectivity reigns here: there is no need to be interested in subjectivity, nor is this useful.

A specific example will enable us to demonstrate in what way an intellectual stance of this type is inadequate, if the aim is to propose a general theory of violence. This will give us a better understanding of what is at the centre of Collins's criticism. His point of view entirely disregards what happens to the perpetrators, individually or collectively, before they commit an act of violence. It disregards what occurs prior to the action, preparing this move – what creates the possibility, what makes it in the last resort inevitable, possibly structures it long before the subjectivities meet.

The death of Clément Méric

This example should be favourable to Collins because the death of the young man which we shall discuss is effectively the outcome of an interaction – at least in appearance. On 6 June 2013, a young extreme-left militant, Clément Méric, died in Paris after a fight with skinheads, the previous day. An explanation in terms of the economic and social crisis, unemployment or the difficulties of young people in working-class areas must immediately be dismissed: the incident took place in the centre of Paris, in a pleasant area, and, more precisely, after Clément Méric and some friends had encountered the skinheads in a private apartment where there was a sale of garments of a brand popular with both extreme left and extreme right militants. The skinheads and the extreme left youths did not expect to meet at this sale; there was no sort of appointment organized in any way between rival political gangs; their meeting was totally fortuitous. It would appear that it was the extreme left youths who began to be verbally abusive and to provoke the skinheads and who suggested that they meet outside. There, the fight began and a skinhead killed Clément Méric with one or two punches.

At the outset it is therefore totally appropriate to refer to the pragmatic interactionism proposed by Collins: a situation, furthermore totally unforeseen, generated a verbal exchange which was followed by a fight which degenerated. Death was neither expected nor intended; it was accidental.

True. But let's take a closer look at the perpetrators of the violence. Having studied a group of French skinheads[8] some 25 years ago (the leader of which, what is more, became the main leader of the extreme right organizations which gives an ideological direction to this type of actor), I can ascertain that they are more concerned with physical preparation for violence, than political or ideological preparation. Usually, they are trained in combat techniques and they eat accordingly. The research which I piloted, consisted in organizing meetings between a group of a dozen or so 'skinheads' and a series of interlocutors before inviting them to discuss my analysis of their action. I spent about fifty hours with them and with the exception of their leader, who was physically fit for violent action, they were all very concerned about their physical fitness. This did not, however, prevent them from drinking considerable amounts of beer. I presume that Clément Méric's murderer and his friends differed from the skinheads in my study only in details.

Clément Méric's death was accidental, true, but the accident would not have taken place if the skinheads had not been actors ready to exercise a considerable degree of physical violence and determined to do so should the occasion arise or if necessary. The interaction does indeed owe a lot to chance but this is not the only factor; thus, the private sale which the participants in the drama had attended did target, amongst others, a very specific, extremist public.

The French political right, and even the *Front national*, which we should really consider to be a radical or extremist right, have distinctly distanced themselves from the skinheads. As soon as the news was known, the dominant interpretation, on the left, consisted in minimizing the interaction dimensions of the drama, and in raising the spectre of the extreme right, proposing comparisons with 1934 – a period of considerable political anxiety concerning fascism. There was a demand for the banning of extreme right organizations, which, though somewhat remote, may have been a source of ideological inspiration for the murderer. This was implemented a few days later. On the contrary, what was needed, and I personally said so in several interventions in the media, was to shed light on the reality of the facts and the nature of an interaction which had degenerated – which could mean that Collins is right. But these facts would not have existed if, previous to the situation or the instant, the actors had not been amply prepared; both subjectively and physically, to act out their fantasies. Death was accidental and the consequence of the interaction; the violence has another explanation.

The interaction itself only took place because two subjectivities confronted one another and clashed, at first in verbal aggression and provocation, then violently with, at least for one party, a strong propensity towards a transposition of this type. For this reason, while recognizing the utility of an approach focusing on the situation and the interactions which it enables, it seems to me preferable, for an in-depth understanding of the violence, to envisage a second line of thought which is profoundly different in terms of theoretical grounding, namely an approach in terms of subject, subjectivity and, better still, in terms of subjectivation and desubjectivation.

The subject and violence

Consequently let us move from approaches which give preference to interaction and therefore intersubjectivity and focus on the subjectivity of those who act out violence and therefore on the meaning inherent to the violence, even if it is rather strange, and somewhat warped in comparison with more commonplace social, political or cultural meanings. This implies defining the concept more specifically and those associated with it – subject, subjectivation and desubjectivation.

We will deal with this in two stages.

The first stage in the theoretical considerations consists in adopting a perspective focusing on the concept of the subject.

This perspective was relaunched in the humanities and social sciences after a long period of purgatory dominated by different variants of structuralism pursuing the subject and advocating his or her death. In Michel Foucault's last period – in *La Volonté de Savoir* or *The Will to Knowledge* and not the Foucault of *Les Mots et les Choses* (*The Order of Things: An Archaeology of the Human Sciences*) – the subject was central to his thought. Since then, sociology, social anthropology, history and political science, in liaison with philosophy, have developed numerous researches which are most frequently based on a positive, almost romantic, conception of the 'subject'. For example, in the work of Alain Touraine or Hans Joas,[9] the subject is defined by his or her capacity to act; it evokes images of liberty, self-possession, the capacity to choose, to decide and to control one's experience. The subject is a responsible being, endowed with a sense of the community, because in order to be a subject oneself, one must admit that other human beings enjoy the same possibility. The 'subject' in the humanities and present-day social sciences is totally remote from any idea of subjection, which is synonymous with submission to domination. The subject is the assertion of liberty and of responsibility. The return of the subject took place with the idea that the subject was distancing itself from subjection, that is to say from a relation of subordination and belonging to a power which deprived it of the capacity to think and to be autonomous. The present-day subject challenges authority, resists norms and rules; it exists for and in itself – it is part of the *Souci de Soi* or 'Care of the Self' described by Foucault (1984, 2001).

Not everything is always perfectly clear in the theoretical proposals which underlie this image of the subject; we do not necessarily know whether the subject is a virtuality which pre-exists action or whether it is constituted in the action, in experience. The subject of the social sciences is sometimes a relatively abstract or indeterminate anthropological property which is, or is not, transformed in action. In contrast, it is sometimes a social, civic, cultural or religious property. For example, the subject may be a class conscious worker, or yet again an individual person belonging to a cultural or religious community; in these instances the subject is rooted in a real, material world. Whatever the case may be, the subject here is liberty, emancipation, resistance, self-construction and self-assertion.

But when the issue is one of violence, other questions deserve to be raised: can the concept of subject be used to deal with evil – barbarity, theft, rape, terrorism or crime? It can, on condition that we put forward a renewed concept of the subject which takes account, precisely, of the negative connotation of violence. This is why, as I have previously stated (Wieviorka, 2009), I propose a conceptualization which is based on several of the leading types of subject including, in particular:

- *the 'floating subject'*: this is the subject who resorts to violence because the possibility of becoming an actor is precluded by conditions which are particularly unfavourable: exclusion, racism, the impossibility of asserting social demands, for example. Thus, in the recent urban violence in the United Kingdom or in France, a rage of this type was expressed demonstrating the curbing of the actor's expression as a subject and his or her existence as such.
- *the 'hyper-subject'*, like the floating subject, cannot become an actor as a result of the social, economic, cultural or political conditions which prevent it from doing so. But the transition to violence is preceded, or accompanied by a process of search for meaning, an overload of meaning which may take an ideological or religious turn. Violence is then inseparable from an intellectual construction which results in legitimating it and conferring on it a particular strength. This is how particularly radical variants of Islam can provide meaning for an action which becomes possible in the form of extreme, destructive violence and, in the case of Islamist martyrdom, self-destructive. This was also the case in the 1970s and 1980s in the diverse variants of extreme-left terrorism, with their ballast of Marxist ideologies, in a context of decline of the working-class movement to which they purported to belong in an increasingly artificial manner.
- *the 'non-subject'* acts in a violent manner while at the same time declaring he or she is not responsible, and is not apparently involved as subject. For example, the non-subject claims to be obeying a legitimate authority, like

The Sociological Review, 62:S2, pp. 50–64 (2014), DOI: 10.1111/1467-954X.12191

Eichmann, who claimed that he would even have killed his own father if Hitler had asked him to do so. Let me add that this image of Eichmann is an over-simplification and perhaps even a distortion when compared with the reality of the person. It may thus constitute a legal argument, leading to the idea of a lack of criminal liability.

- *the anti-subject* acts violently from pleasure, they practise pure violence, violence for the sake of violence; they dehumanize their victims, acting out of cruelty or sadism, like the soldiers in the American army in the Abu Ghraib detention centre.

Thus it is possible to deconstruct the notion of violence by setting oneself in the perspective of the subjectivity of the actors and by observing that there are separate instances or approaches. Wishing to be a subject, for example, but not being able to do so, except in a 'floating' manner, is not the same thing as acting as an anti-subject and gaining pleasure from the suffering of others.

With this outline of a typology, we begin to have a slightly more sophisticated concept of the subject. From this point we can envisage the sensitive question of the emergence from violence: each type of subject in fact calls for a different answer.[10] For example, when confronted with the anti-subject only repression can be efficient, whereas the violence of the floating subject can be countered with social or cultural policies, or yet again by transforming unmet demands into discussions and institutionalized conflict.

In concrete terms, the figures of the subject become incorporated or intertwined or yet again fade into one another, which can only complicate the action of those who wish to act against violence. Above all, violence quickly becomes unstable; it is a phenomenon which is always susceptible to change, always difficult for its actors to control and to maintain at a level desired for strategic, instrumental reasons: violence quickly spirals upwards and races out of control. This is why the actors of violence in some instances present an image which is subject to profound transformations, for example between the first tentative, hesitant moments of an action which is apparently controlled and the furious, barbarous, totally inhuman outburst of a violence which knows no limits.

The subject of violence is therefore not in itself a figure which is necessarily stabilized, or controlled. The subject may, for instance, at the outset be floating and in no way murderous, simply a rioter for one night for example, and then become radical, a hyper-subject driven by uncontrollable/undying hatred, leading to extreme violence where cruelty can make its appearance. This is why the concept of subject – even if our proposals are an improvement, is inadequate. If the protagonist of violence enters into violence and then possibly confers on it a meaning and expressions which changes, then we have to focus, not on the idea of a subject defined once and for all, but on the idea of a process in which the meaning inherent to or contained in the violence, changes as does the subjectivity of the actor.

Subjectivation and desubjectivation

The move from the subject and subjectivity to the processes of subjectivation and desubjectivation therefore means adopting a different form of argument which avoids any essentialization or naturalization of the 'subject' and enables us to go beyond the questions concerning the actual status of the subject which we have seen does present problems since it can either be defined as being prior to any action or experience, or be conceived as inseparable from practice.

These processes are of two orders; they fall under two different approaches which can nevertheless be presented together. On one hand, violence can be produced during the process of subjectivation. Thus, for example, many young people living in deprived, working-class areas in France or the United Kingdom, state, after their first experience of an urban riot, that the latter had enabled them to give a meaning to their lives. Their participation played a defining role on the basis of which they re-examined their way of life, and decided to become religious, or join a musical, or sports, association. Sometimes also they entered into the spiral of delinquency or of an ever greater violence a theme developed in the social anthropology of violence by writers such as René Girard (1972).

But on the other hand, and much more broadly speaking, violence develops at the same time as the meaning of the action becomes lost, deviates, changes position to make of the actor, increasingly, an individual or a group, drawing closer to pure violence, violence for the sake of violence, retreating into the spiral of loss of meaning, or into its replacement by an ideology or a radical form of religion. The rationale, then, is one of desubjectivation.

There again, the responses to violence vary, depending on whether it is a subjectivation provisionally ensured through violence, or of a more or less advanced desubjectivation. If it is a question of a provisional rationale of subjectivation, then the action against the violence should consist in encouraging the inflexion of this subjectivation so that it is directed, after the defining instant, towards other forms of action, possibly set in institutionalized conflicts. Whereas, if it is a question – which is more frequent – of a rationale of desubjectivation, the return to meaning is only possible if this rationale is not yet too advanced; if not, only repression will prove to be efficient. In all cases, for those who wish to think about action against violence, thinking in terms of process implies a definition of the modalities enabling the process to be curbed as soon as possible.

Thus, a new paradigm of violence can take shape, originating in the exhausting of the most classical forms of approach, in the criticism of interactionist reasoning and by close consideration of a concept of the subject itself – a concept developed or taken further by the idea of the process of subjectivation and desubjectivation.

The ethnographic observation of violence and the interactions in which it erupts – or does not erupt, despite being not far off – is an invitation to reject sociological determinisms. But it says nothing about what could possibly have

The Sociological Review, 62:S2, pp. 50–64 (2014), DOI: 10.1111/1467-954X.12191

led the perpetrators of violence to be receptive to it, to be capable of resorting thereto, or of accepting or suffering from the conditions which make for its emergence here and there. Research which focuses on perpetrators of violence, on processes of subjectivation and desubjectivation and loss of meaning which may lead to violence is not necessarily less empirical than that which claims to act in the name of ethnology or interactionism. I myself have spent hundreds of hours in collective or individual interviews about terrorism, urban violence or racism and anti-Semitism[11] and I have been close to, or spent many hours, apart from the interviews properly speaking, with perpetrators of violence. If the approach which I suggest does seem to me to be distinctly more relevant than that of Collins' it is also for the very good reason that he accepts – its relevance to the practical consequences for action to alleviate violence.[12] Approaches to evil, including violence, can be evaluated in terms of their findings. If one approach sheds more light than another and offers better perspectives to those who intend to act on the ground to reduce violence or to enable a way out of violence is it not more acceptable? This is an issue which also deserves to be examined at length: modes of approach could be tested in terms of the policies which could possibly be based thereon.

Notes

1 The best representative of this orientation was the historian-sociologist Charles Tilly; cf. for example Wieviorka (1978).
2 Cf. for example Gurr (1970).
3 An important source of this way of thinking is the survey carried out by Adorno *et al.* (1950).
4 Cf. for example, McDermott *et al.* (2009).
5 Randall Collins, 'The invention and diffusion of social techniques of violence. how micro-sociology can explain historical trends' (2011a), followed by Michel Wieviorka: 'Comment on Randall Collins/1: an approach to violence' (2011); Stathis N. Kalyvas, 'Comment on Randall Collins,/2: linking the micro and the macro in the study of violence' (2011); Paolo Magaudda, 'Comment on Randall Collins/3: the circulation of violence – techniques and the role of materiality in Randall Collins's violence theory' (2011); and Randall Collins, 'Reply to Kalyvas, Wieviorka and Magaudda' (2011b).
6 I have had the opportunity of discussing with Collins how his approach differs from my own on two occasions: orally, during the Congress of the International Sociological Association in 2010, in Göteborg, and in writing in the journal *Sociologica* (2011, No. 2), in reply to his article, 'The invention and diffusion of social techniques of violence', in which he took a critical position in relation to my work.
7 Tarde (1993 [1890]); Tilly (2003). Let me add that Collins does not quote Tarde, an author he does not seem to be familiar with.
8 Wieviorka *et al.* (1992), and more specifically Chapter 10, 'Les skinheads'.
9 Cf. for example, Dubet and Wieviorka (1995) and Joas (2001 [1992], 1996).
10 I deal with this issue in Wieviorka (2012), and more specifically in Chapter 2, 'An End to Violence'.
11 Cf. for example, Wieviorka (2003).
12 Here is what he writes in his 'Reply' (2011b: 3): 'To return now to Wieviorka's suggestion for how to adjudicate between rival research programs: examine their practical consequences for action to alleviate violence. This is a good criterion, and I accept the challenge'.

References

Adorno, T., Frenkel-Brunswik, E., Levinson, D. J. and Sanford, R. N., (1950), *The Authoritarian Personality*, New York: Harper.

Collins, R., (2004), *Interaction Ritual Chains*, Princeton, NJ: Princeton University Press.

Collins, R., (2008), *Violence: A Micro-Sociological Theory*, Princeton, NJ: Princeton University Press.

Collins, R., (2011a), 'The invention and diffusion of social techniques of violence: how micro-sociology can explain historical trends', *Sociologica*, 2. doi: 10.2383/35863

Collins, R., (2011b), 'Reply to Kalyvas, Wieviorka and Magaudda', *Sociologica*, 2. doi: 10.2383/35867

Dubet, F. and Wieviorka, M. (eds), (1995), *Penser le Sujet. Autour d'Alain Touraine*, Paris: Fayard.

Foucault, M., (1984), *The Care of the Self (Le Souci de Soi)*, Paris: Gallimard.

Foucault, M., (2001), *Histoire de la Sexualité*, vol. 3, Le Souci de Soi, Paris: Gallimard.

Gadd, D. and Jefferson, T., (2007), *Psychosocial Criminology: An Introduction*. Los Angeles: Sage.

Girard, R., (1972), *La violence et le sacré*, Paris: Hachette.

Gurr, T. R., (1970), *Why Men Rebel*, Princeton, NJ: Princeton University Press.

Joas, H., (2001 [1992]), *La créativité de l'agir*, Paris: Cerf.

Joas, H., (1996), *The Creativity of Action*, Chicago: University of Chicago Press.

Kalyvas, S. N., (2011), 'Comment on Randall Collins/2. Linking the micro and the macro in the study of violence', *Sociologica*, 2. doi: 10.2383/35865

Katz, J., (1999), *How Emotions Work*, Chicago: University of Chicago Press.

Lyotard, J.-F., (1979), *La condition post-moderne*, Paris: Minuit.

Magaudda, P., (2011), 'Comment on Randall Collins/3. The circulation of violence: techniques and the role of materiality in Randall Collins's violence theory', *Sociologica*, 2. doi: 10.2383/35866

Marshall, S. L. A., (1947), *Men against Fire*, Washington: Infantry Journal.

McDermott, R., Tingley, D., Cowden, J., Frazzetto, G. and Johnson, D. D. P., (2009), 'Monoamine oxidase A gene (MAOA) predicts behavioral aggression following provocation', *Proceedings of the National Academy of Sciences*, 106 (7), 2118–2123.

Milgram, S., (1974), *Obedience to Authority: An Experimental View*, London: Tavistock.

Tarde, G., (1993 [1890]), *Les lois de l'imitation*, Paris: réédition Kimé.

Tilly, C., (2003), *The Politics of Collective Violence*, Cambridge: Cambridge University Press.

Wieviorka, M., (1978), *From Mobilization to Revolution*, Reading, MA: Addison Wesley.

Wieviorka, M., (2003), *The Making of Terrorism*, 2nd edn, Chicago: University of Chicago Press.

Wieviorka, M., (2009 [2006]), *Violence: A New Approach*, London: Sage.

Wieviorka, M., (2011), 'Comment on Randall Collins/1. An approach to violence', *Sociologica*, 2. doi: 10.2383/35864

Wieviorka, M., (2012), *Evil*, Cambridge: Polity Press.

Wieviorka, M., Bataille, P., Jacquin, D., Martuccelli, D., Peralva, A. and Zawadzki, P., (1992), *La France raciste*, Paris: Seuil.

The Sociological Review, 62:S2, pp. 50–64 (2014), DOI: 10.1111/1467-954X.12191

Is war becoming obsolete?
A sociological analysis

Siniša Malešević

Abstract: There is a degree of consensus among scholars that the character of warfare has substantially changed over the past three decades. However, there is no agreement about the direction and causes of this change. Some argue that 'the new wars' have become more brutal, more chaotic and decentralized. These wars are linked to the globalization processes emphasizing that as the unrestrained proliferation of globalized economy intensifies so will these new wars. In contrast others insist that all forms of organized violence are on the wane: there are fewer wars, they are less lethal, more localized and shorter than in previous historical periods. Moreover they argue that the very institution of warfare is gradually but definitely becoming obsolete. This paper challenges both of these perspectives and articulates an alternative interpretation. The aim is to develop a *longue durée* sociological analysis that focuses on the macro-organizational social context and explores the dynamics of the war-state-society nexus over the past centuries. I argue that warfare is not becoming obsolete and that 'new wars' are unlikely to completely replace inter-state warfare. Instead my analysis indicates that there is more organizational continuity in the contemporary warfare that either of the two dominant perspectives is willing to acknowledge.

Keywords: war, organized violence, the state, social change, historical sociology

Introduction

One of the significant recent developments in the new sociological focus on violence is the rethinking of the relationship between war and society. Although classical sociology has been preoccupied with the analysis of organized violence much of mainstream post-World War II sociology remained oblivious to the study of war (Malešević, 2010; Joas, 2003). If and when sociologists engaged with warfare the tendency was to centre on military sociology and explore the narrow relationships between 'armed forces and society' rather than analysing the long-term impact of war on social change. Over the last two decades there has been a profound shift in research interests and war has become a central analytical concern for a number of sociologists (Joas and Knobl, 2013; Wimmer, 2013; King, 2013; Centeno, 2002; Smith, 2005; Mann, 2012, 1993; Shaw, 2005,

The Sociological Review, 62:S2, pp. 65–86 (2014), DOI: 10.1111/1467-954X.12192
© 2014 The Author. Editorial organisation © 2014 The Editorial Board of the Sociological Review. Published by John Wiley & Sons Ltd, 9600 Garsington Road, Oxford OX4 2DQ, UK and 350 Main Street, Malden, MA 02148, USA

2003; Malešević, 2010). These studies have provided both theoretical and empirically specific analyses of the relationship between war and society. For example, some scholars explore the inter-dynamics of nationalism, state formation and war (Centeno, 2002; Wimmer, 2013; Mann, 1993; Malešević, 2012), some analyse the cultural framing and coding of organized violence (Smith, 2005; Alexander, 2013) while others study the patterns of group solidarity on the battlefield (King, 2013; Collins, 2008). However, there is still a major lacuna in the sociological understanding of the long-term historical processes that shape the relationship between war and society. It is not completely clear what is happening to contemporary war and what the lasting implications of these social dynamics are.

This paper aims to explore some of these wider issues. The first part critically assesses the two dominant and contrasting perspectives on the transformation of war both of which insist on there having been radical change in the character of the relationship between war and society. The second part provides an alternative interpretation that centres on the war-state-society nexus over long stretches of time. The main argument emphasizes the role organizational power plays in these historically contingent, but for the most part cumulative and coercive, processes and contends that as long as the organizational capacity of states continues to increase the likelihood of wars becoming obsolete remains minimal.

Understanding contemporary wars: the two dominant perspectives

There is no doubt that the 20th century was by far the bloodiest and most destructive period in human history. With two global wars, thousands of middle range and smaller armed conflicts, dozens of genocides, revolutions, pogroms, riots, uprisings, military coups, political assassinations, insurgencies and terrorism, the 20th-century total death toll is somewhere between 150 and 200 million human lives (Leitenberg, 2006; White, 2013). Although this century was characterized by significant peace-time mass killings such as Stalin's purges, Mao's Great Leap Forward or the Cultural Revolution most 20th-century human casualties, including those of the largest genocides, have taken place in times of war (Shaw, 2005; Mann, 2005). In this context it is the two world wars that account for the bulk of the casualties and for the unprecedented destruction. Nevertheless, this annihilating character of modern warfare was not a sudden product of new historical conditions unique to the 20th century; instead the ever-increasing destructiveness of war was a gradual development clearly noticeable over the proceeding centuries. Even though the staggering scale of destruction might have generated a degree of astonishment among contemporaries the cumulative direction of this destructiveness was not much of a surprise as the last seven centuries have witnessed a constant and dramatic increase in war fatalities. Whereas in the combined 14th and 15th centuries the total war death toll amounted to less than 1 and 4 million respectively, the tally for the 16th and

The Sociological Review, 62:S2, pp. 65–86 (2014), DOI: 10.1111/1467-954X.12192

17th centuries rose to 7 and 8 million dead. For 19th-century wars this figure jumps to 19 million and by the end of the 20th century the total number of war casualties amounts to no less than 135 million (Leitenberg, 2006; Eckhardt, 1992).

A much greater surprise is the unprecedented and rapid decline in war casualties and the number of wars fought over the last six decades. Since World War II was the most destructive violent conflict waged on this planet its end was bound to reduce the ratio of human casualties which in its aftermath had fallen from 300 (per 100,000 people per year) to close to 25 in early 1950s (Lacina *et al.*, 2006). However, what was less expected was the continuous sharp decline in war deaths over the following five decades. Hence the world-wide battle death toll fell to close to 9 in the 1970s, 5 in the mid-1980s, 2.5 in the late 1990s and to only 0.5 per 100,000 per year in 2004 (Lacina and Gleditsch, 2005). Furthermore, the existing research indicates that the same trend can be observed when looking at the number of battle deaths per conflict. In contrast to 19th- and early 20th-century warfare most contemporary wars result in substantially lower human casualties. Thus in the 1950s the total battle deaths per conflict per year were around 68,000; in the 1960s and 70s they were reduced to 52,000 and by the 1980s they had fallen under 40,000. By the 1990s, and early 2000s these figures had dropped to astounding lows – less than 9,000 battle deaths per conflict per year (Lacina and Gleditsch, 2005). In other words, whereas in the 1950s the average size war resulted in the deaths of more than 30,000 people, the typical early 21st-century war was likely to end in less than a thousand casualties (Pinker, 2011). Moreover, for much of this period inter-state warfare was gradually replaced by civil wars as the dominant form of organized violence in the contemporary world. Instead of the intensive conventional wars between sovereign states an overwhelming majority of present day armed violent conflicts are fought by different armed groups inhabiting the same polity. For example, most wars waged in the 1950s were inter-state wars while in the first decade of this century only 7 per cent of wars fought all over the world are deemed to be inter-state (Tertrais, 2012). This quite remarkable change puzzles scholars: Why have wars become rarer and less deadly? Why has intra-state warfare replaced inter-state wars? Do these changes mean that war is gradually, but surely, vanishing from this planet?

Although there is a general agreement that the institution of warfare is undergoing a substantial transformation it is less clear what the causes and the long-term implications of these changes are. For one group of scholars the virtual disappearance of inter-state wars and their displacement by civil wars is an indicator of a broader social malaise resulting in the continuous weakening of state power. Thus Bauman (2002, 2006), Munkler (2004) and Kaldor (2007, 2013) argue that contemporary armed conflicts differ significantly from their 19th- and early 20th-century counterparts: they are decentralized, less restrained, more chaotic and brutal, less focused on territory and more on the control of population and often characterized by the deliberate targeting of civilians. Furthermore, such conflicts are understood to be generated by the unrestrained proliferation of neo-liberal globalization which in its constant search for resources, cheap labour and markets helps erode the sovereignty and capacity of many states. In some contexts this ultimately contributes to the state's loss of monopoly on the legitimate use of violence leading to privatization of violence and the emergence of rootless paramilitaries who wage wars over the remnants of state structures, scarce resources and people.

In contrast to conventional warfare these 'new wars' are seen to be strictly parasitic phenomena whereby greedy warlords politicize ethnic and religious markers and utilize militias to wage genocidal wars on civilians. While the proponents of the new war thesis agree that wars between states have dramatically declined and that battle deaths have substantially decreased they dispute the findings indicating a similar decline in civilian deaths. On the contrary both Kaldor (2013) and Shaw (2003, 2005) argue that it is extremely difficult to gauge and provide reliable evidence on the civilian casualties, not least because there are different methods for calculating these figures, and many deaths remain unreported and undocumented (especially those that are indirectly caused by war operations such as disease, malnutrition, ethnic cleansing, suicides, etc.). For example, the civilian death toll of war in Iraq ranges from 100,000 to 1 million depending on the source and methodology used. Furthermore, as the new war thesis is premised on the idea that new forms of warfare blur the distinctions between public and private, legal and illegal and most of all civilian and military, there is no reliable way to distinguish combatants from civilians. Most significantly they argue that the battle death toll is not the only measure that can capture the brutality of new wars. Instead they show that other indicators such as the forced displacement of people or the proliferation of privatized purveyors of violence are just as reliable in accounting for the changing character of war. For example, UNHCR data shows that in 2010 there were 43.7 million forcibly displaced people, which was the highest figure in the last 15 years (Kaldor, 2013). When all of this is taken into account the general argument is that as long as unimpeded neo-liberal globalization proliferates so will the new forms of war.

In contrast to the new war paradigm another group of scholars argues that the decline of war is just a symptom of the broader diminishing of all forms of violence in the contemporary world. Hence Horgan (2012), Goldstein (2011), Pinker (2011), and Mueller (2009), insist that one can observe a steady trend in the gradual waning of all forms of warfare, revolutions, genocides, riots, terrorism and other types of organized violent action. Mueller (1989) was one of the first who articulated this argument with his contention that major wars among large states have become obsolete. In his view 'war is merely an idea' comparable to duelling or slavery, all of which have been 'grafted onto human existence' and have gradually become redundant as a mechanism for solving collective disputes (Mueller, 1989: 321). More recently he has radicalized this idea further, arguing that warfare as an institution 'has almost ceased to exist' (Mueller, 2009: 297). This argument was further refined and empirically documented by Goldstein (2011) and Horgan (2012) both of whom argue that in the last three decades one

The Sociological Review, 62:S2, pp. 65–86 (2014), DOI: 10.1111/1467-954X.12192

could observe fewer outbreaks and more endings of war and that existing wars tend to be more localized, smaller and shorter than those fought in the previous decades. Nevertheless the most influential book written in this vein was Pinker's *The Better Angels of our Nature* (2011). Drawing heavily on Elias's theory of civilizing processes Pinker argues that not only warfare but nearly all forms of violence have experienced a dramatic decline from prehistory to the present day. He compares the available data on homicides, torture, human sacrifice, blood feuds, capital punishment, slavery, rape, infanticide, child abuse, inter-state, colonial, post-colonial and civil wars, revolutions, pogroms and other forms of organized violence and concludes that all types of violence exhibit similar, downward, trajectories. Moreover, unlike most other scholars working within this paradigm Pinker does not see the 20th century as being the most violent period in human history but instead insists that one should use relative rather than absolute numbers to gauge the level of destructiveness for a particular historical period. Hence he rates the An Lushan revolt (8th-century China) and the Mideast Slave Trade (7th–19th century) as being far ahead in terms of human casualties than the two world wars, Mao's Great Leap Forward and Stalin's purges combined (Pinker, 2011).[1] To account for this trend he deploys the explanatory apparatus of evolutionary psychology and history of ideas. He maintains that the gradual decline of warfare and other forms of violence is rooted in the inner working of our brain which has an inherent propensity towards violence. As he puts it bluntly: 'most of us-including you, dear reader – are wired for violence' (Pinker, 2011: 483). This inborn proclivity, in Pinker's view, was gradually tamed by ideological and institutional transformations: the growth of state power, increasing literacy, the development of cosmopolitan and humanitarian worldviews, the expansion of trade and the wider civilizing processes all of which have allegedly helped control our violent impulses and have increased the empathetic qualities of modern human beings.

Although Goldstein, Mueller, Horgan and others working in this tradition do not utilize evolutionary theory to explain the apparent decline of warfare they too emphasize the impact that Enlightenment ideas and social movements and political organizations inspired by such ideals have played in reducing the proliferation of warfare. For example, Mueller (2009: 307) highlights the significance of the post-World War II norms that made state borders almost sacrosanct and territorial conquest profoundly illegitimate. Goldstein (2011) emphasizes the role that the UN, EU, NATO and other international organizations play in the pacification process. In addition he also identifies the humanitarian agencies and popular movements which focus on human rights discourses and as such have played a substantial role in delegitimizing the use of violence and war in political disputes. Horgan (2012) sees war as a matter of individual and collective choice and contends that once political leaders and citizens embrace fully the goal of a peaceful world this is likely to become a reality. Hence, despite the pronounced differences between the individual positions of scholars involved they are unanimous in the view that all forms of war are experiencing a dramatic and potentially irreversible decline.

Both of these perspectives identify some significant features of contemporary war and other forms of organized violence. However, as they provide conflicting diagnoses of social reality it is not clear what exactly is happening with the institution of warfare. While there is general agreement that intra-state wars have replaced inter-state wars, that the direct battle death tolls have been substantially reduced and that warfare has become more localized and shorter in duration there is no consensus on such questions as: Is war as such becoming obsolete? Are new wars replacing inter-state warfare for good? Is the decline of organized violence a temporary or permanent phenomenon? Are our progeny likely to live in a war-free world?

Despite some obvious merits neither the new wars thesis nor the decline of violence perspective can provide convincing answers to these questions. As I have argued elsewhere (Malešević, 2008, 2010) the new war paradigm suffers from economic reductionism which attributes too much power to the forces of neo-liberal globalization and ignores geo-politics, organizational dynamics and ideological transformations. This perspective also has a short historical memory: neither globalization nor privatization of violence are novel historical processes. In some important economic and political respects the late 19th and early 20th century was just as globalized as today's world (Conrad, 2006; Hall, 2000; Hirst *et al.*, 2009) but whereas our predecessors were waging numerous colonial and inter-state wars culminating in World War I the scale of today's warfare has been substantially reduced. Hence, if the same or similar processes were at work before why are the outcomes so different?

The decline of violence perspective exhibits a different kind of reductionism: it is deeply grounded in idealist epistemology[2] that generates very functionalist arguments. The view that the reduction of human casualties in war, or the diminishing of all types of violence, can be attributed to 'the humanitarian revolution', the gradual expansion of human rights discourses and civilizing norms is for the most part un-sociological. While ideas and beliefs play a significant role in social relations they do not determine long-term historical changes. This logic of reasoning cannot explain why the discourses of human rights, moral equality and civilizational advancement have become so influential in today's world but not before, even though they were formulated at the inception of modernity and were in some form of institutional use for the past two hundred years or so. More importantly these norm-centred explanations are prone to functionalist argumentation that regularly end up in tautological conclusions. In other words to explain the decline of war they confuse (functional) needs with causes and make explicit what is already present in the premises of this approach. Much of this reasoning is unfalsifiable and not a single author from this tradition has managed to make a direct, causal, link between the post-World War II dominant values and the decline in organized violence (Malešević, 2013b; Popper, 2005).

The key argument of this paper is that despite some illuminating and valuable insights made by the two dominant perspectives they do not provide adequate analysis of contemporary warfare. As such their forecasts for the future of war

The Sociological Review, 62:S2, pp. 65–86 (2014), DOI: 10.1111/1467-954X.12192

do not seem plausible. The most significant weakness of both of these perspectives is the fact that they analyse large-scale social transformations without devoting much or any attention to the complex macro-sociological processes involved. More specifically to fully understand the character of warfare it is crucial to utilize a *longue durée* sociological analysis that contextualizes the transformation of warfare in broader long-term social processes and especially the macro-organizational dynamics that underpin the war-state-society nexus. When contemporary wars are analysed from this long-term perspective it becomes clearer that there is more continuity than discontinuity in the institution of warfare than is recognized by either of the two dominant approaches.

The historical sociology of warfare

Although the study of war is as old as war itself, there is no universally accepted definition of this phenomenon. However, since the 1970s onwards most empirical, particularly quantitative oriented, research on war has tended to congregate around Singer and Small's (1972) proposition that defines any armed conflict which results in at least 1,000 battle deaths per year as war. This almost exclusive focus on the size of human casualties as the determining feature of warfare has proved useful for developing large-scale datasets for the comparative analyses of wars. Nevertheless, the excessive quantification was also highly detrimental for understanding the complexities and subtleties of social changes and the correspondingly diverse historical trajectories of war in time and space. While battle deaths might be a useful indicator to assess the scale and size of particular wars they are not comprehensive enough to capture the full dynamics of social change instigated by specific wars. Many historically highly significant violent conflicts did not involve a large number of casualties nor mass destruction. For example, the storming of the Bastille was a tremendously important event that substantially changed the course of human history, yet it involved only a single human casualty with a further six individuals being killed after they surrendered (Lusebrink and Reichardt, 1997). Similarly the highly significant Indian Wars of 1865–1898 and the Mexican-American War 1846–1848, events that have shaped the size and character of the future world super power, each involved quite small number of casualties with only 919 and 1,733 dead American soldiers respectively (Clodfelter, 1992). Furthermore, most warfare before the modern era was characterized by, comparatively speaking, small human casualties with many wars resembling pushing matches (as in the ancient Greek world) or the ritualistic skirmishes between nobility whereby the number of dead soldiers or civilians played a minor role in determining the outcome of war and an even lesser role in the social change that followed specific violent events (Mann, 1993; Collins, 2008; Malešević, 2010). What is important to emphasize is that the overwhelming focus on quantity of human casualties might wrongly suggest that war is a historically constant and uniform phenomenon shaped by similar, if not identical, trans-historical social processes. Nevertheless, to provide a comprehensive answer to the questions about the present and future of war one needs to rethink the relationship between war, state and society in the past.

War-state-society nexus

The key point here is that just as world societies have been in constant flux over the past 12,000 years so has the institution of warfare. When one talks about society and state today and the polities and social orders that occupied the world of 2,000 or 400 years ago one is not discussing the same forms of social organization. The early forms of polity such as chiefdoms, pristine empires or city-states were entities that were profoundly different to contemporary nation-states. In contrast to nation-states which derive their *raison d'être* from the idea of popular sovereignty, moral equality and a substantial degree of cultural uniformity, the pre-modern polities utilized very different sources of legitimacy – mythologies of non-human descent, the divine origins of monarchs, imperial civilizing missions and so on. Furthermore, unlike their pre-modern counterparts that adopted different versions of patrimonial rules of social organization, nation-states are modelled on the bureaucratic principles that emphasize efficiency, division of labour, knowledge, professionalism and the impersonality and transparency of hierarchical order (Malešević, 2013a; Meyer *et al.*, 1997; Weber, 1968). The institution of warfare has also undergone a similar social transformation – from the non-fighting simple foragers, the pushing matches of antiquity, the ritualistic tussles of the medieval world, the limited violent conflicts of mercenaries, to the brutalizing wars of revolutionaries and nationalists, the mass warfare of two total wars and eventually the contemporary civil wars waged by warlords versus the high-tech interventionist wars of the Western professionals (Howard, 1976; Malešević, 2010). The fact that one is forced to use the same term 'war' for the variety of highly distinct and historically specific forms of organized violence often leads to the misleading strategy that treats all these armed conflicts as if they are the same phenomenon. Nevertheless, to understand these fundamental changes it is necessary to briefly explore the organizational underpinnings of collective violence.

In contrast to popular perceptions, shared by socio-biologists such as Pinker (2011) and van der Dennen (1995), war is, historically speaking, a relatively novel invention. As much of the available archaeological and anthropological evidence indicates, the simple hunter gatherers and other foraging nomadic groupings tended to avoid prolonged inter-group violence and had no organizational, technological, ideological or environmental means to wage wars (Fry and Söderberg, 2013; Sponsel, 2014; Fry, 2007; Kelly, 2000). As recent extensive study of a comprehensive Ethnographic Atlas data set by Fry and Söderberg (2013) demonstrates, most simple hunter-gatherers are not engaged in organized violence. Deaths due to violence are quite rare and when they do occur they resemble homicides rather than war and other forms of

The Sociological Review, 62:S2, pp. 65–86 (2014), DOI: 10.1111/1467-954X.12192

organized violence. For example, in 20 out of 21 cases analysed by Fry and Söderberg, 85 per cent of all violent acts undertaken include interfamilial feuds, group-centred executions and interpersonal quarrels whereas the cases of inter-group violence are extremely uncommon. As foraging bands are small, non-sedentary, egalitarian and fluid there is no organizational prerequisite to wage wars.

Thus war emerges on the historical scene together with social development – the rise of stratified group structures, sedentary lifestyles, agriculture, social hierarchies, and division of labour among others. Most of all the proliferation of warfare is closely linked with the emergence of the first stable, territorially focused, polities – chiefdoms, city-states and eventually pristine empires (Mann, 1993; Malešević, 2010) all of which have taken root only in the last 12,000 years. Furthermore, from its inception war, state and society have developed and changed together. If one understands war as an instrument of social and political power then as social orders change so does the nature of warfare. It is no accident that both chiefdoms and early pristine empires relied extensively on violent conquests to maintain (and expand) the existing social order. The famous chiefdoms of yesteryear such as those ruled by Arminius or Genghis Khan were despotic and hierarchical but highly unstable polities whose very existence was premised on continuous territorial expansion and war conquests. Similarly the early empires, from Romans, Chinese, Rashiduns, Srivijayas, to Ottomans, were heavily dependent on resources, slaves, serfs and territories to maintain their internal social cohesion and prosperity (Burbank and Cooper, 2011). In contrast most city-states were more stable, less hierarchical and, with few notable exceptions such as Sparta or Venice, less conquest prone. In all of these cases polity formation, internal social dynamics and warfare have had a profound and lasting impact on each other. The nature of war has often had significant impact on internal social stratification and vice versa. Protracted, symmetrical and all-encompassing wars stimulated development of citizenship rights and democratic institutions whereas asymmetric and conquest oriented warfare that utilized armies of highly skilled warriors and expensive weaponry were more likely to foster hierarchical and highly stratified social orders (Andreski, 1968; Mann, 1993; Malešević, 2010). For example, both ancient Greece and medieval Switzerland were often hailed as the first examples of participatory citizenship and advanced democratic institutions including their representative popular assemblies such as Greek *ekklêsia* and Swiss *landsgemeinde* (Sinclair, 1988; Kobach, 1993). However, it is often forgotten that this unusual degree of social freedom and popular decision making was built on large-scale participation in wars. These were societies composed of self-armed and self-equipped communities of farmer-soldiers who were able and willing to use their arms and military skills to maintain their rights.

War has also played a decisive role in the advent of modernity. As Tilly (1985), Mann (1993), Giddens (1986) and Hirst (2001) have convincingly demonstrated the intensive preparations for war and the escalation of European warfare since the late 16th century onwards provided unprecedented stimulus for state development and social change. The ever-increasing geopolitical competition forced rulers towards greater fiscal reorganization, the expansion of administrative structures, the growth of the banking sector, and investment in the development of science, technology and the military. The direct corollary of these transformations was the extension of parliamentarism, citizenship rights and greater welfare provisions as the rulers were forced to trade political and social rights for more popular support, increased public taxation and the willingness of citizens to fight in wars. The onset of industrialization was heavily dependent on the technology pioneered in the military sphere and from the mid-19th century onwards social development in the civilian sector regularly went hand in hand with the industrialization of warfare (McNeill, 1982; Giddens, 1986). The two total wars of the 20th century were a culmination of this ever-expanding link between the state, war and society: mass production, mass politics and mass communications were all mobilized for mass destruction. What started off as a traditional military confrontation was gradually redefined as a vicious conflict to the death between entire populations. Nevertheless, the long-term consequence of these two extremely destructive conflicts was further extension of citizenship rights, greater gender equality, delegitimization of racism and the establishment of welfare states (Mann, 2013). Hence, over the past several centuries one could notice the constant increase in the destructiveness of war which was often preceded, or followed by, substantial social changes. However, this continuous increase of synergy between war, state and society cannot easily explain what happened to war over the last sixty years. Does the fact that inter-state wars have dramatically diminished and that human casualties have been substantially reduced suggest that that our age is experiencing a radically different relationship between the state, society and war, as suggested by the two dominant perspectives? The simple answer is: no.

What one can observe when looking historically at the nexus war-state-society is that their dynamics were largely shaped by similar processes over very long stretches of time and this has not substantially changed today. Since for 98 per cent of their existence on this planet humans were nomadic foragers characterized by malleable and weak social ties, it took millions of years for rudimentary social organizations to emerge. However, once the first elements of social order and statehood developed they tended to arise in tandem with warfare. Hence what is truly distinct about the last 12,000 years is how quickly and forcefully the nexus war-state-society has transformed the face of this planet. One of the key processes spawned by the interplay at this nexus was the continuous expansion of organizational power. Since Weber's early works (1968) analysts have become aware that any effective social action entails the presence of organizations. Nevertheless once in place social organizations are inclined to grow, expand, control its personnel and engage in confrontations with competing social organizations. Hence all influential social organizations have a coercive foundation (Malešević, 2010, 2013a). The prevalence of warfare

The Sociological Review, 62:S2, pp. 65–86 (2014), DOI: 10.1111/1467-954X.12192

over the past centuries has helped expand and increase the coercive capacity of polities. This process was already visible at the birth of the first empires when the expanding state power depended on the proliferation of 'social caging' with individuals being forced to trade personal liberty for state provided security (Mann, 1993). Over the years social caging was combined with 'political rack-eteering', that is populations being required to pay taxes and finance costly wars in exchange for some citizenship rights and protection from other states and domestic threats (Tilly, 1985). Nevertheless it is only in the past 200 years that this cumulative bureaucratization of coercion has significantly accelerated. The transformation of empires, composite kingdoms and city-states into sovereign nation-states was accompanied by technological, scientific and production changes all of which have had an enormous impact on the war-state-society nexus. As wars expanded and became more destructive and costly the organizational power of states and their ability to control their populations grew exponentially. Not only have modern states increased their infrastructural reach and capacity but they have also managed, for the first time in history, to legitimately monopolize the use of violence, taxation, legislation and education (Weber, 1968; Elias, 2000; Gellner, 1983). The pinnacle of this process was the two world wars. To wage such protracted and costly wars states were forced to further increase their organizational powers including their ability to mobilize millions of individuals to fight or labour for the war effort. The intensive popular mobilization had long-term effects that galvanized intensive social changes. For example, the shortage of manpower on the battlefields fostered the introduction of universal conscription which, among other things, expanded the citizenship and some welfare rights of urban poor and peasantry that could not be easily revoked after the war. In a similar vein the mass deployment of men to fronts and the expansion of war industries caused a shortage of industrial labour. This ultimately compelled state authorities to open up the factories and other industries to women workers, thus introducing policies which have pro-foundly undermined traditional patriarchal relationships. Once women gained economic independence it was extremely difficult to re-establish the gendered status quo. Furthermore, the mass war casualties and the war time ideals of national solidarity stimulated gradual delegitimization of the sharp class divides and forced the state authorities to extend welfare policies and health protection in many European and, to a lesser extent, North American states. All of these substantial social transformations had a deep impact on post-war states and societies. Despite the enormous human casualties and material destruction post-war social organizations became stronger than ever. The further expansion of science, technology and industry together with the continuous growth of the administrative sector provided impetus to multiply organizational power in a variety of domains. Hence the second half of the 20th century witnessed a dramatic acceleration in the state's ability to collect information on all of its population, to tax its citizens at source, to fully police its borders, to control public education, health sector, employment and immigration policies, to inter-fere in family and sexual life and to successfully introduce mass surveillance programmes (ie biometric passports, ID cards, birth certificates, census data, CCTV cameras, etc.) (Lyon, 2001; Dandeker, 1990; Mann, 2013). It is war that was a prime catalyst of these changes.

The fact that most of Europe, North America and the rest of the developed world have not experienced much or any warfare on their soil over the past seven decades might suggest that the war-state-society nexus has been broken or displaced by the less coercive structural mechanisms of development. This, however, is not the case. The immediate aftermath of World War II was not permanent peace but instead a protracted and highly intensive cold war occasionally enhanced by brutal and devastating proxy wars[3] (ie Korea, Vietnam, Afghanistan, Angola, Nicaragua etc.) directly supported by the two superpowers. This period (1946–1991) was characterized by the continuous preparation for war together with the political mobilization of citizenry all of which have helped stimulate further increases in the organizational powers of states. Not only the USA and Soviet Union but all members of the two military alliances utilized military advancements and the perpetual threat of war to increase their organizational power. It was the political and military competition between the two power-blocks that gave impetus to technological, scientific, industrial and state development. As in the previous historical periods most significant scientific and technological inventions were pioneered in the military sector and then gradually found their way into civilian use (Giddens, 1986). Despite the lack of human casualties in Europe and North America the proxy wars and the permanent threat of nuclear Armageddon proved to be key organizational devices for substantial social change throughout the world. The cold war was certainly the golden age of economic prosperity, political stability, welfare provisions and social mobility for large sectors of the population on both sides of the political divide (Hobsbawm, 1994; Mann, 2012). Just as in the previous three centuries social development, state enhancement and military expansion advanced together. The war-state-society nexus was not significantly dented, it just became accommodated to the different historical constellations.

Although the late 20th and early 21st centuries have witnessed some significant changes in the relationship between war, state and society, these are far from being radical transformations. In fact these changes indicate the continuous strengthening of the war-state-society nexus and further increase in the cumulative bureaucratization of coercive power (Malešević, 2010, 2013b). The popular view of globalization as undermining the strength of nation-states and dramatically transforming social relationships between the states is an overstatement lacking empirical validation (Mann, 2012, 2013; Hirst *et al.*, 2009; Hall, 2000). The argument that globalization inevitably weakens state power is often premised on the idea that before the current wave of globalization nation-states were strong and sovereign. However, historically nuanced analyses show that for most of the 19th and early 20th century full sovereignty and political independence were largely unachieved ideals, something that most rulers strived for but were unable to achieve. It is only the Great Powers that could attain and afford full state sovereignty and control of their territories whereas most other

The Sociological Review, 62:S2, pp. 65–86 (2014), DOI: 10.1111/1467-954X.12192

states have not possessed possess sufficient state capacity for, nor were they allowed to achieve, full sovereignty (Smith, 2010). Hence, the fact that some states have more political might and independence today than others is not particularly new. In fact it is only in the last few decades that most states have gained so much organizational power that even their strongest 19th-century predecessors could not imagined possible. Similarly the pre-2008 economic liberalization was not profoundly different to its late 19th- and early 20th-century predecessor and in both of these cases opening up of world markets went hand in hand with the increase in the organizational and coercive potency of the states (Mann, 1993, 2013; Conrad, 2006; Lachman, 2010). Instead of being mutually exclusive forces neo-liberal capitalism and bureaucratization often underpin one other (Lachman, 2013; Hall, 2006; Vogel, 1996). Even the appearance of new technologies has not substantially shifted this balance. On the contrary the new technological advancements and inventions – from satellites, internet, mobile phones, robotics, laser weapon systems to nanotechnologies and many others – have helped reinforce the organizational power of states which are now much more able and willing to control and police their borders, populations, tax intake, transgressions of law, immigration, education, sexuality and so many other aspects of everyday life.

The continuous expansion of state power is also followed by the extension of its coercive reach and capacity both internally (policing one's own population) and externally (using military might to shape foreign policy). This growth of organizational strength allows most powerful states to engage in periodic but quite regular military interventions all over the world. Since the end of the cold war the USA, UK, France, Russia and Israel, among others, have been involved in a number of wars and military interventions including Iraq, Afghanistan, Mali, Georgia, Lebanon, Palestine, Libya, Sierra Leon, Chad, Central African Republic, Ukraine etc. It is true that these military undertakings have generated a smaller number of casualties than similar interventions before and during the cold war. However, the key point is that analysts' focus should shift from such a crude measure (that is military or civilian casualties) in the direction of whether or not such wars make significant social and political impact. What matters sociologically is not whether a particular war caused more or less damage and human destruction but what kind of social and political change it generates. If viewed through these lenses it is possible to see that much of contemporary warfare has not engendered dramatic social transformations. Neither the so-called high-tech warfare waged by most powerful states nor the predatory civil wars fought by militias and the remnants of state armies have produced historically novel social conditions. The outbreaks of civil war tend to emerge in regions where the existing state structures are already quite weak and are challenged by competing social organizations. These often include not only the neighbouring states, the domestic competitors dissatisfied and capable of challenging the weakened state but also the world powers who pursue their own geo-political ambitions. This obviously is not a historically novel situation. As Tilly (1985) shows, European state formation went through a very similar process – it started with 1,000 polities in the 14th century, which by the 16th century were reduced to 500 and by the early 20th century protracted warfare was instrumental in reducing this number to only 25 states. As the running of modern social organizations becomes ever more expensive, state structures that cannot keep up with the demands of cumulative bureaucratization of coercion often lose their monopoly on the legitimate use of violence. In other words, the dominance of civil wars today is not a new phenomenon (Kalyvas, 2001); they are just more visible as there are no wars between powerful states. What is distinct about these conflicts is that, unlike their 15th-, 16th- or 18th-century European predecessors, most contemporary civil wars cannot be 'played out' to their logical conclusion, the outcome of which would be fewer but more powerful states (Herbst, 1990; Centeno, 2002). The main reason why such conflicts are labelled 'civil wars' and contained within the existing state borders is the coercive dominance of international regulations that explicitly prohibit any violent change of interstate borders. In previous historical periods many wars that started off as intra-state conflicts were later, if and when insurgencies won, redesigned as inter-state wars. However, the contemporary geo-political context does not allow for such a transition from civil to inter-state war to occur. In contrast to Mueller and other representatives of the decline of violence perspective who see the existing norms on the sanctity of inter-state borders as a simple reflection of the universally shared Enlightenment principles, it is much more plausible to view these rules as something initiated, imposed and policed by the winners of World War II. As such, these regulations are the ideological expression of the contemporary geo-political constellations as they firmly reinforce the geo-political status quo.[4]

Although the last twenty years have seen numerous high-tech wars and military interventions waged by powerful states most of these violent conflicts did not generate major social change. The reliance on sophisticated technology, science and industry has reduced the need for the use of mass armies and has led to the abolition of conscription in Europe and North America. Although the introduction of mass conscription gave birth to the welfare state, there is no reliable evidence that the ever-increasing professionalization of the military directly causes the shrinking of welfare provisions (Lachman, 2010). The new technological advancements in military and medicine have also been instrumental in decreasing the number of human casualties among the military personnel of the powerful states. However, these changes had very little to do with humanitarian ethics and civilizing processes and much more to do with the organizational capacity of powerful states to use sophisticated technology to minimize political and military risks. As Shaw (2005) demonstrates, much of this warfare is premised on minimizing life-risks to Western military personnel by transferring these risks to the weaker enemy. From the Falkland War of 1982, to the 1991 Gulf, 1999 Kosovo, and most recent wars in Afghanistan, Iraq, Libya and Mali the reliance on technologically sophisticated weapons has helped create the systematic transfer of risks from the elected politicians to military personnel and from Western militaries to enemy combatants and their civilians. Neverthe-

The Sociological Review, 62:S2, pp. 65–86 (2014), DOI: 10.1111/1467-954X.12192

less, the use of new technology and science did not alter the social and political context of warfare. In other words, in Korea, Vietnam and the Soviet war in Afghanistan, what was pursued by relying on the millions of recruits and mass mobilization of entire societies is now achieved through the use of high altitude bombing, long-distance missile launches, the remotely navigated combat drones, the use of demolition vehicles and other robotic devices.

The future of warfare

If the war-state-society nexus has not been significantly weakened, why have wars become rarer, and less deadly? And why has inter-state warfare been displaced by civil wars? To answer these questions one needs again to engage with the historical sociology of war and its role in the post-World War II world. When war is conceptualized not as a simple political instrument of rulers but as an outcome of complex and contingent historical processes involving competition between social organizations then its proliferation is heavily dependent on the strength and coercive reach of particular social organizations.[5] The historical record shows that the prevalence and expansion of warfare tends to be linked with the increased capacity of social organizations. Hence, scholars have identified several periods of revolutionary acceleration of warfare ranging from southern Mesopotamia in the late 4th and early 3rd millennium, eastern Mediterranean and China at the end of first millennium BCE, and the European induced warfare expansion between the 1500s and 1945 (Levy and Thompson, 2011; Gabriel, 2002; Gray, 2002). In all three of these cases one can witness the significant interplay between war, state development and social transformation. The war-state-society nexus generated unprecedented social changes in military (army sizes, weaponry production, etc.) society (greater urbanization, technological inventions, shift to mass scale production in agriculture and later in industry, etc.) and polity formation (greater political centralization, expanding infrastructural power, etc.). The direct outcome of these changes was an escalation in wars as ever-expanding states attempted to establish regional hegemonies and/or prevent other such polities becoming new political hegemons (Levy and Thompson, 2011). In this context the post-World War II period is not the end of (war) history. It is just an end of the long-term process that was initiated with the military revolution of the early 15th century.

However the relative peace established in Europe and North America in the last several decades still remains grounded in the similar historical processes that have shaped social and political life in the previous centuries – the organizational power and the ability of large-scale social organizations such as modern day nation-states to establish their political, economic, ideological and military dominance. During the cold war era the bipolar stability, mutually recognized regional hegemony and the threat of nuclear destruction prevented escalation of violence in the northern part of the globe. The further decline of inter-state warfare after the cold war is tightly linked with the unprecedented military supremacy of the USA and the combination of inability and unwillingness of other powerful social organizations (ie EU, Russia, China, Japan, etc.) to challenge the US military and political hegemony. For much of the past sixty years American military power has been so overwhelming that no other state, not even the Soviet Union at the peak of its military might, would willingly provoke a war with the USA. The military omnipotence of this state is historically unprecedented: this is the only state that has a substantial military presence, including large-scale army bases, in more than 150 countries all over the world; the US military budget is larger than the total combined military expenditure of its next ten competitors – China, Russia, UK, France, Japan, India, Saudi Arabia, Brazil, Germany and Italy (SIPRI, 2013); American airpower is so overwhelming that no other state is anywhere near its technological supremacy; and the US's military technology in laser guided missiles, aircraft carrier ships, refuelling facilities, military robotics and many other areas is far ahead of any other military in the world (Collins, 20132013; Mann, 2003). This unparalleled military hegemony remains the cornerstone of contemporary geo-political stability in the world. The US military supremacy averts any attempts to engage in inter-state warfare in the northern part of the globe and strongly discourages the potential outbreaks of inter-state war within the US's, extremely wide, interest zone. The fact that the American military shield (through NATO or other arrangements) incorporates much of Europe and Japan means that this *Pax Americana* acts as a brake on the escalation of any potential conflicts within its very wide domain. In this sense, as Burbank and Cooper (2011), Munkler (2007) and Mann (2003) remind us, US military hegemony in many important respects resembles its imperial predecessors – the military supremacy of the Roman, Mongol and British Empires were decisive in generating extensive periods of peace not so dissimilar to the period we are currently experiencing. Hence it is the geo-political configuration not the humanitarian revolution or civilizational advancement that gave birth to *Pax Romana*, *Pax Mongolica*, *Pax Britannica* just as much as to *Pax Americana*.

Nevertheless, what distinguishes the contemporary world from its predecessors is the considerable increase in the organizational capacity of most modern states and other social organizations. Whereas Roman, Mongol and other empires usually waged wars against polities with feeble organizational power most contemporary states possess high infrastructural capacity which makes any potential inter-state war extremely costly and difficult to fight. Unlike their patrimonial counterparts, which in most important respects were puny leviathans, most present-day states are built around bureaucratic principles that foster the continuous expansion of their coercive capacity and reach (Malešević, 2010, 2013). For example, while the Roman Empire could subdue relatively quickly and cheaply the chiefdoms and composite kingdoms of Sabines, Etruscans, Goths, Illyrians or Galls, the late 20th- and 21st-century inter-state wars, typified by the Iran–Iraq war (1980–1988), are extremely destructive, costly and difficult to win. Nevertheless, it is important to emphasize that the ever-increasing organizational power is not just confined to states but also to other overtly and covertly coercive social organizations (including

The Sociological Review, 62:S2, pp. 65–86 (2014), DOI: 10.1111/1467-954X.12192
© 2014 The Author. Editorial organisation © 2014 The Editorial Board of the Sociological Review

terrorist networks, private corporations, social movements etc.). This is best illustrated by the fact that despite the enormous military presence of US, UK and 47 other highly developed militaries in one of the poorest and infrastructurally least developed countries in the world, the Taliban insurgency has been able to wage successful guerrilla war for more than a decade. On the surface this looks as if the most powerful state in the world cannot easily overpower one of the weakest polities in the world. However, the point is that the US and its allies are not fighting the Afghan state which is infrastructurally and organizationally extremely weak but are engaged in a fierce struggle with the highly organized, effective, hierarchical and coercive insurgency network – the Taliban. In this sense the Taliban is similar to other insurgency movements such as Hamas ISIS, Hezbollah or FARC: all of them have substantially increased their coercive organizational powers at the expense of the nation-state they inhabit (Malešević, 2013a, 2014).

Hence, paradoxically, even though the continuous expansion of organizational power was decisive for the escalation of 20th-century total wars it is this very same process that plays a major role in containing inter-state warfare today. Simply put, inter-state wars have become rare and less deadly precisely because the organizational power of many contemporary states, and most of all the USA, has so substantially increased to the point that initiating an inter-state war is extremely difficult, hugely expensive and, with the exception of a couple of powerful states, likely to generate enormous devastation, if not complete self-destruction.

None of this is to suggest that the cumulative bureaucratization of coercion will ultimately lead towards the obsolescence of war. On the contrary, as geo-political and environmental configurations change it is likely that the long-term future will bring about more violent conflicts between social organizations with increasingly uneven power structures. Once *Pax Americana* weakens and other states and non-state associations and networks gain even more organizational capacity one is likely to see an enormous geo-political world-wide transformation. Moreover, as climate change and other environmental variations intensify including global warming, continuous population expansion and the excessive consumption of non-renewable resources, the nature of the war-state-society nexus is likely to become even more prominent. As much of the available, evidence based, forecasting demonstrates, climatic changes are bound to further increase CO_2 emissions which ultimately are likely to bring about a less hospitable planet – severe water shortages for large parts of the world, dramatically rising tides of oceans and seas with periodic tsunamis, the gradual disappearance of fossil fuels, the scarcity of minerals, the lack of arable land, and so on (Klare, 2002; Dyer, 2011; Mann, 2013). These major changes are likely not only to make the global ecosystem unsustainable but might also cause an organizational collapse and potential disintegration of state structures in some regions of the world. Once these states prove unable to feed and protect their citizens this is likely to spark large-scale migrations of people moving from the uninhabitable to the habitable parts of the globe. Such unprecedented population movement might trigger violent responses: 'Global warming will force mass migrations on a scale never seen in human history. Governments lack the organizational capacity and almost certainly the desire to accommodate those refugees; many, however, will have the military means and popular support to repel needy migrants' (Lachman, 2013: 3). Thus future geo-political and environmental transformations could bring about a very different world with some states continuing to increase their organizational powers and channelling those powers in the direction of building large militaries and police forces whereas others would struggle to survive in the remnants of failed states. In other words one is likely to see a much more dystopian world of the future. On the one side the expanded cumulative bureaucratization of coercion is likely to be used to engage in new wars of conquest for scarce resources while simultaneously creating and keeping fortress-like borders to exclude potential refugees. On the other side one might expect the appearance of quasi Hobbesian organizational wastelands populated by stateless groups and organizations fighting for the survival. Although this almost apocalyptic imagery might sound unrealistic and far-fetched its small-scale incarnation is already borne out in the social reality of several contemporary civil wars. From Somalia and DR Congo to Syria, Chad, Sudan and Yemen one can encounter large areas of destroyed and environmentally desolate areas where people struggle to endure or escape the never-ending war-induced shortage of water and energy, the periodic famines, untreated contagious disease, chronic homelessness and unemployment (Hendrix and Salehyan, 2012; Hironaka, 2005). In contrast to these zones of despondency the ever-increasing organizational capacity of most powerful states creates conditions for the real and substantial transformation of warfare in the future: the gradual displacement of human military and work force with their robotic counterparts. The mass reliance on the use of unmanned drones in Afghanistan, Syria, Iraq and Yemen navigated by 'civil servants' in Nevada is probably a reliable indicator of how some wars will be waged in the future. It is quite conceivable that human warfare might give way to armed conflicts between robotic soldiers (Coker, 2013). In this context where there is no direct human presence on the battlefields but where devastation and demolition continue to escalate it will quickly become obvious how futile it is to rely on human casualty counts as the barometer of war's destructiveness.

Conclusion

Whereas in the late 18th and early 19th century Enlightenment thinkers could only dream about perpetual peace among European states this has largely become a reality today. Over the past decades not only Europe but most parts of the world have witnessed a substantial decline in all forms of warfare. Interstate wars have become extremely rare and even civil wars tend to generate fewer casualties than before. This rather unusual historical situation has polarized scholars with some insisting that all forms of organized violence are gradually but surely disappearing from our horizon, while others argue that globalization induced 'new wars' bring about more destitution and destruction. In contrast to these two perspectives I have attempted to show that rather than indicating a radical transformation, the current decline of warfare is in fact a temporary phenomenon rooted in the same organizational logic that shaped our world over the last twelve millennia. In other words, instead of reflecting a profound and permanent shift in historical development and a significant change in human attitude to war the contemporary decrease of organized violence is a product of specific geo-political and organizational constellations. As these constellations are produced by the same long-term processes that historically have shaped and continue to shape the war-state-society nexus as long as they are in motion it seems unlikely that the institution of war will become obsolete in the future.

Notes

1 As I argue elsewhere (Malešević, 2013b) this methodological practice is highly problematic for two reasons. First, Pinker measures quite incompatible events: the long-term historical processes such as the Mideast Slave Trade which lasted 1,250 years and the direct battlefield casualties of two world wars which happened over couple of months, weeks or even days. Secondly, Pinker uses highly unreliable and in many cases essentially flawed statistics for much of his historical evidence. The most notable examples are his death estimates for pre-historical violence, the An Lushan revolt and the Mongol invasions under Genghis Khan (Ferguson, 2013; Fairbank and Goldman, 2006).

2 Pinker is only a partial exception here. He too utilizes idealist arguments to explain the decline of violence on the macro level but he also adopts cognitive evolutionary psychology and the Eliasian analytical framework to explain human propensity for violence. However, this is an even more problematic approach as it operates with a rigid, essentialist and primordialist epistemology. For extensive criticism of this perspective see Malešević (2010, 2013a, 2013b) and Malešević and Ryan (2013).

3 As Mann (2013) indicates, these proxy wars resulted in a loss of at least 20 million human lives.

4 The most memorable attempt to violate this norm was Saddam Hussein's invasion of Kuwait which instantly triggered the US and European armed punishment: the Gulf War of 1991.

5 Although the nation-state remains the most powerful political actor in the contemporary world there are other non-state organizations which have also increased their coercive-bureaucratic power. These include private corporations (such as Shell, McDonalds, Toyota, Microsoft etc.), religious institutions (the Catholic Church, Scientology, Russian Orthodox Church etc.), terrorist networks (Al Qaida, Hezbollah, Continuity IRA, ISIS etc.), and the established social movements (Zapatistas, Animal Liberation Front, Earth Liberation Army etc.). I explore this more extensively in Malešević (2014).

References

Alexander, J., (2013), *The Dark Side of Modernity*, Cambridge: Polity Press.
Andreski, S., (1968), *Military Organization and Society*, London: Routledge & Kegan Paul.
Bauman, Z., (2002), *Society under Siege*, Cambridge: Polity Press.
Bauman, Z., (2006), *Liquid Fear*, Cambridge: Polity Press.

Burbank, J. and Cooper, F., (2011), *Empires in World History*, Princeton, NJ: Princeton University Press.

Centeno, M. A., (2002), *Blood and Debt: War and the Nation-State in Latin America*, University Park, PA: Penn State University Press.

Clodfelter, M., (1992), *Warfare and Armed Conflicts: A Statistical Reference*, Vol. I, Jefferson, NC: McFarland and Company.

Coker, C., (2013), *Warrior Geeks*, London: Hurst.

Collins, R., (2008), *Violence: A Micro-Sociological Theory*, Princeton, NJ: Princeton University Press.

Collins, R., (2013), 'Does nationalist sentiment increase fighting efficacy? A skeptical view from the sociology of violence', in J. A. Hall and S. Malesevic (eds), *Nationalism and War*, Cambridge: Cambridge University Press.

Conrad, S., (2006), *Globalisation and Nation in Imperial Germany*, Cambridge: Cambridge University Press.

Dandeker, C., (1990), *Surveillance, Power and Modernity: Bureaucracy and Discipline from 1700 to the Present Day*, New York: St Martin's Press.

Dyer, G., (2011), *Climate Wars: The Fight for Survival as the World Overheats*, New York: One World.

Eckhardt, W., (1992), *Civilizations, Empires and Wars: A Quantitative History of War*, Jefferson, NC: McFarland.

Elias, N., (2000 [1939]), *The Civilizing Process: Sociogenetic and Psychogenetic Investigations*, London: Blackwell.

Fairbank, J. and Goldman, M., (2006), *China: A New History*, New York: Belknap Press.

Ferguson, R. B., (2013), 'Pinker's list: exaggerating prehistoric war mortality', in D. Fry (ed.), *War, Peace and Human Nature*, Oxford: Oxford University Press.

Fry, D. S., (2007), *Beyond War*, Oxford: Oxford University Press.

Fry, D. S. and Söderberg, P., (2013), 'Lethal aggression in mobile forager bands and implications for the origins of war', *Science*, 341 (6143): 270–273.

Gabriel, R., (2002), *The Great Armies of Antiquity*, Westport, CT: Praeger.

Gellner, E., (1983), *Nations and Nationalism*, Oxford: Blackwell.

Giddens, A., (1986), *The Nation-State and Violence*, Cambridge: Polity Press.

Goldstein, J. S., (2011), *Winning the War on War: The Decline of Armed Conflict Worldwide*, New York: Dutton.

Gray, C., (2002), *Strategy for Chaos: Revolutions in Military Affairs and the Evidence of History*, London: Frank Cass.

Hall, J. A., (2000), 'Globalisation and nationalism', *Thesis Eleven*, 63: 63–79.

Hall, J. A., (2006), 'Plaidoyer pour L'Europe des Patries', in R. Rogowski and C. Turner (eds), *The Shape of the New Europe*, Cambridge: Cambridge University Press.

Hendrix, C. S. and Salehyan, I., (2012), 'Climate change, rainfall, and social conflict in Africa', *Journal of Peace Research*, 49 (1): 35–50.

Herbst, J., (1990), 'War and the State in Africa', *International Security*, 14 (4): 117–139.

Hironaka, A., (2005), *Neverending Wars*, Cambridge, MA: Harvard University Press.

Hirst, P., (2001), *War and Power in the 21st Century*, Cambridge: Polity Press.

Hirst, P., Thompson, G. and Bromley, S., (2009), *Globalisation in Question*, Cambridge: Polity Press.

Hobsbawm, E., (1994), *The Age of Extremes*, New York: Vintage.

Horgan, J., (2012), *The End of War*, New York: McSweeney.

Howard, M., (1976), *War in European History*, Oxford: Oxford University Press.

Joas, H., (2003), *War and Modernity*, Cambridge: Polity Press.

Joas, H. and Knobl, W., (2013), *War in Social Theory*, Princeton, NJ: Princeton University Press.

Kaldor, M., (2007), *New and Old Wars: Organised Violence in a Global Era*, Cambridge: Polity Press.

Kaldor, M., (2013), 'In defence of new wars', *Stability* 2 (1): 4.

The Sociological Review, 62:S2, pp. 65–86 (2014), DOI: 10.1111/1467-954X.12192

Kalyvas, S., (2001), ' "New" and "old" civil wars: a valid distinction?' *World Politics*, 54: 99–118.

Kelly, R., (2000), *Warless Societies and the Origins of War*, Ann Arbor, MI: University of Michigan Press.

King, A., (2013), *The Combat Soldier*, Oxford: Oxford University Press.

Klare, M., (2002), *Resource Wars: The New Landscape of Global Conflict*, New York: Owl Books.

Kobach, K., (1993), *The Referendum: Direct Democracy in Switzerland*, Aldershot: Dartmouth Publishing.

Lachman, R., (2010), *States and Power*, Cambridge: Polity Press.

Lachman, R., (2013), *What is Historical Sociology?* Cambridge: Polity Press.

Lacina, B. and Gleditsch, N. P., (2005), 'Monitoring trends in global combat: a new dataset of battle deaths', *European Journal of Population*, 21 (2–3): 145–166.

Lacina, B., Gleditsch, N. P. and Russett, B., (2006), 'The declining risk of death in battle', *International Studies Quarterly*, 50 (3): 673–680.

Leitenberg, M., (2006), 'Deaths in war and conflicts in the 20th century', Cornell University Peace Studies Program Occasional Paper 29.

Levy, J. and Thompson, W., (2011), *The Arc of War*, Chicago: University of Chicago Press.

Lusebrink, H. and Reichardt, R. (1997), *The Bastille: A History of a Symbol of Despotism and Freedom*, Durham, NC: Duke University Press.

Lyon, D., (2001), *Surveillance Society: Monitoring Everyday Life*, London: Oxford University Press.

Malešević, S., (2008), 'The sociology of new wars? Assessing the causes and objectives of contemporary violent conflicts', *International Political Sociology*, 2 (2): 97–112.

Malešević, S., (2010), *The Sociology of War and Violence*, Cambridge: Cambridge University Press.

Malešević, S., (2012), 'Wars that make states and wars that make nations: organised violence, nationalism and state formation in the Balkans', *European Journal of Sociology*, 53 (1): 31–63.

Malešević, S., (2013a), *Nation-States and Nationalisms*, Cambridge: Polity Press.

Malešević, S., (2013b), 'Forms of brutality: towards a historical sociology of violence', *European Journal of Social Theory*, 16 (3): 273–291.

Malešević, S., (2014), 'Nationalism and military power in the 20th century and beyond', in R. Schroeder (ed.), *The Global Powers*, Cambridge: Cambridge University Press (in press).

Malešević, S. and Ryan, K., (2013), 'The disfigured ontology of figurational sociology: Norbert Elias and the question of violence', *Critical Sociology*, 39 (2): 165–181.

Mann, M., (1993), *The Sources of Social Power II*, Cambridge: Cambridge University Press.

Mann, M., (2003), *Incoherent Empire*, London: Verso.

Mann, M., (2005), *The Dark Side of Democracy*, Cambridge: Cambridge University Press.

Mann, M., (2012), *The Sources of Social Power III*, Cambridge: Cambridge University Press.

Mann, M., (2013), *The Sources of Social Power IV*, Cambridge: Cambridge University Press.

McNeill, W., (1982), *The Pursuit of Power*, Chicago: University of Chicago Press.

Meyer, J., Boli, J., Thomas, G. and Ramirez, F., (1997), 'World society and the nation-state', *American Journal of Sociology*, 103 (1): 144–181.

Mueller, J., (1989), *Retreat from Doomsday: The Obsolescence of Major War*, New York: Basic Books.

Mueller, J., (2009), 'War has almost ceased to exist: an assessment', *Political Science Quarterly*, 124 (2): 297–321.

Munkler, H., (2004), *The New Wars*, Cambridge: Polity Press.

Munkler, H., (2007), *Empire*, Cambridge: Polity Press.

Pinker, S., (2011), *The Better Angels of our Nature*, New York: Allan Lane.

Popper, K., (2005), *The Logic of Scientific Discovery*, London: Routledge.

Shaw, M., (2003), *War and Genocide: Organized Killing in Modern Society*, Cambridge: Polity Press.

Shaw, M., (2005), *The New Western Way of War: Risk-Transfer War and its Crisis in Iraq*, Cambridge: Polity Press.

Sinclair, R. K., (1988), *Democracy and Participation in Athens*, Cambridge: Cambridge University Press.

Singer, J. D. and Small, M., (1972), *The Wages of War 1816–1965*, New York: Wiley.

SIPRI Military Expenditure Database, (2013), http://www.pgpf.org/Chart-Archive/0053_defense-comparison#sthash.cgDq2KLF.dpuf

Smith, A., (2010), *Nationalism*, Cambridge: Polity Press.

Smith, P., (2005), *Why War? The Cultural Logic of Iraq, the Gulf War, and Suez*, Chicago: Chicago University Press.

Sponsel, L., (2014), 'Peace and nonviolence, anthropological aspects', in J. Wright (ed.), *International Encyclopedia of the Social and Behavioral Sciences*, Amsterdam: Elsevier Press (in press).

Tertrais, B., (2012), 'The demise of Ares: the end of war as we know it?' *Washington Quarterly*, 35 (3): 7–22.

Tilly, C., (1985), 'War making and state making as organized crime', in P. Evans, D. Rueschemeyer and T. Skocpol (eds), *Bringing the State Back In*, Cambridge: Cambridge University Press.

Van der Dennen, J., (1995), *The Origin of War*, Groningen: Origin Press.

Vogel, S., (1996), *Freer Markets, More Rules: Regulatory Reform in Advanced Industrial Countries*, Ithaca, NY: Cornell University Press

Weber, M., (1968), *Economy and Society*, New York: Bedminster Press.

White, M., (2013), *Atrocities*, New York: W. W. Norton.

Wimmer, A., (2013), *Waves of War*, Cambridge: Cambridge University Press.

The Sociological Review, 62:S2, pp. 65–86 (2014), DOI: 10.1111/1467-954X.12192

Family honour and social time

Mark Cooney

Abstract: Violence is a dynamic event, not a static state. The cause of violence, therefore, cannot lie in static variables such as individual propensities (eg self-control) or aggregate properties (eg inequality). But what changes cause violence? A new theory developed by Donald Black traces violent acts to movements of social time. Social time moves when actors' statuses rise or fall (vertical time), when relationships increase or decrease in intimacy (relational time), and when cultural diversity expands or contracts (cultural time). The present paper applies the new theory to one particular type of violence – that committed in the name of family honour. Typically perpetrated by men against their female relatives, family honour violence is triggered by several movements of social time, but particularly vertical time, in the form of challenges from below by women seeking to make independent lifestyle decisions.

Keywords: family honour, honour killing, violence against women, pure sociology, social time

Introduction

The central question in the study of violence seems clear: what causes violence? Unfortunately, the answer to the question is not clear. Theories locate the causes of violence variously, in the body (biology), the mind (psychology), or the society (sociology). Other theories favour combinational causes, such as the body and mind (evolutionary psychology), the body and society (biosocial explanations) or, very commonly, the mind and the society (social psychology). Together, these theories help to explain a considerable amount of variation in violent behaviour across individuals, groups and societies. Yet they suffer from a simple but critical logical problem: their causes are static while violence is dynamic (conduct changes from non-violence to violence). A static variable cannot cause a dynamic event such as a beating, lynching, rape, or war (Black, 2011, 2015). Genes, personalities or structural variables (eg inequality) may be important background conditions, but they do not and cannot explain why a given act of violence occurs. For violence to take place, something must change.

Consider, for example, family honour violence (hereafter simply 'honour violence'). Found in communities from North Africa through the Middle East

The Sociological Review, 62:S2, pp. 87–106 (2014), DOI: 10.1111/1467-954X.12193
© 2014 The Author. Editorial organisation © 2014 The Editorial Board of the Sociological Review. Published by John Wiley & Sons Ltd, 9600 Garsington Road, Oxford OX4 2DQ, UK and 350 Main Street, Malden, MA 02148, USA

to south-east Asia, honour violence is typically committed against women by their male relatives (fathers, brothers, cousins, uncles) for bringing the family's good name into disrepute usually, though not exclusively, through sex before or outside marriage.[1] For instance:

> Güldünya Tören, 22, an unmarried woman from a large family in southeastern Turkey, became pregnant by a married man who refused to marry her. On learning of her condition, Güldünya's family locked her in a room before deciding to send her away to her uncle in Istanbul. An older brother followed her to the city, and attempted to strangle her. Güldünya took refuge with an imam and his family. After her son was born she gave him up for adoption. Her brother then returned and took her away, ostensibly to visit their aunt. Once they had left the house, a second brother appeared and shot Güldünya. As she lay in hospital recovering from her wounds Güldünya was shot by the second brother, again. She was pronounced brain dead. Two days, later her family cut off life support. (Pope, 2012: 189–191)

A UN estimate puts the number of women killed annually for reasons of honour at 5,000 (UNFPA, 2000). Regardless of the accuracy of that estimate, it is clear that a large number of women (and some men) are beaten and killed every year both in traditional honour communities and among their emigrants in Western countries.

The most commonly cited cause of honour violence is patriarchy (Kulczycki and Windle, 2011). Settings in which honour violence occurs have starkly unequal gender arrangements, and the violence is typically seen as a mechanism for the perpetuation of male dominance: beat or kill one woman and ten others will be cowed into submissiveness (see Sev'er and Yurdakul, 2001). But while patriarchy is clearly central to honour violence, helping to account, for instance, for the distribution of honour violence across countries, it cannot explain the cause of particular instances of such violence. Patriarchy is a constant; violence is dynamic. Something must change in order to trigger the attack. Honour violence thus recapitulates the larger problem of violence causation.

A bold new theory of conflict developed by Donald Black (2011) offers a way forward. Black's theory proposes that all conflict has a single fundamental cause: the movement of social time. Black's theory has important implications for the understanding of violence in general. Here I illustrate and apply his theory to violence by concentrating on the causes and severity of its honour-related form. To do so, I draw on the considerable though incomplete body of empirical findings developed in a variety of settings by anthropologists, sociologists, journalists, human rights workers and others.

Social time

Social time is the dynamic aspect of social space (Black, 2011). Just as physical time is the fluctuation of physical space (eg the revolution of the earth), so social time is any fluctuation of social space (Black, 1976). Social time moves when people or groups form or sever relationships, when their fortunes soar or plunge, when they challenge or resist challenge to authority, when they acquire reputations for deviance or for virtue, or when they embrace or reject new people, ideas, religions, art forms, or morals.

Conflict

Conflict – the clash of right and wrong – is an inescapable part of the human experience. Yet although conflict is universal it is not ubiquitous. The episodic nature of conflict logically implies that it cannot be triggered by static conditions; something must change (Black, 2011). Change occurs in time, indeed change *is* time: social time. Movements of social time are the fundamental cause of conflict, including violence (Black, 2011). Conflict forges and severs relationships and creates winners and losers: it moves social time and hence causes more conflict. Conflict is a particular type of social time, moral time.

Although highly diverse, movements of social time can be grouped into three main types: vertical, relational, and cultural. *Vertical time* moves when inequality increases or decreases. Increases in inequality occur because some actors rise ahead of others or fall below others in hierarchies of wealth, organizational power, social integration, or moral standing. Decreases in inequality occur because inferiors rise or superiors fall. *Relational time* moves when actors become more or less intimate with one another. *Cultural time* moves when cultural diversity increases or decreases (through rejection). The greater and faster the movement of social time, the greater the conflict it causes. Sudden and sharp changes in people's social circumstances produce the most severe clashes of right and wrong.

Movements of social time depend on what people do, and to whom they do it. Homicide, for instance, drastically reduces a victim's ability to earn and accumulate wealth and, as such, is a large movement of vertical time (Black, 2011). But the killing of a wealthy person is a greater fall in status than the killing of a poor person, and hence tends to attract more severe sanctions, legal and popular, all else equal (Black, 1976; Cooney, 2009a).

Theories of violence

The theory of moral time is extremely general, seeking to provide a testable explanation not just of violence but of the many ways people pursue conflicts (including running away, negotiating, mobilizing a mediator, calling police, suing etc.). To accomplish that ambitious goal the theory necessarily deviates from conventional theories of violence. Such theories typically employ one of three principal units of analysis: actors, aggregates or events.

Actor theories explain differences among individuals (and groups) in their propensity to commit violence. They emphasize core characteristics, such as individuals' levels of social learning, social control, or self-control. Such characteristics are relatively invariant. Self-control, for example, is a constant, set for life, according to the theory, at about age 8–10 (Hirschi and Gottfredson, 2001). Yet violence is extremely episodic. Even the most violent individuals are violent only rarely (Collins, 2008). Self-control (and other characteristics of individuals) helps to explain which actors are likely to be more or less violent at some point (see Agnew, 2005). But such characteristics cannot explain when actors will be violent, in what way they will be violent, or against whom they will be violent (Black, 2004a). Nor can they explain the critical transition from non-violence to violence – what triggers the violence. When it comes to explaining acts of violence, actor theories lack both precision and dynamism.

Aggregate theories address violence committed by individual actors but combined up to the level of a social grouping such as a city, province or country (see Blau and Blau, 1982; Nisbett and Cohen, 1996). Nominating a variety of cultural, economic and demographic variables in the ambient social environment, aggregate theories are valid in that they successfully distinguish settings with high and low rates of violence (see McCall *et al.*, 2010). But resource deprivation, percentage divorced, violent values or other aggregated variables cannot explain acts of violence themselves – who will commit violence, against whom, when (Black, 2004a). Moreover, those variables are static and hence cannot account for the movement into violence (Black, 2011). The percentage of divorced men in a city, for example, does not change nearly quickly enough to account for the many acts of episodic violence that occur within the urban area. Like actor theories, aggregate theories are insufficiently precise and dynamic.

Event theories go to the very heart of violence – the incidents out of which it arises. Because they zero in on incidents rather than people, groups or aggregates, event theories can overcome the inherent imprecision of actor and aggregate theories – provided they are testable. Full testability requires, however, that the theories eschew reliance on subjective features of violent incidents – how they are experienced or evaluated by the situational actor.[2] To date, only one theory does that.

The geometry of violence

Black's (1976, 1993) earlier work on conflict management provides the first general, testable theory of violent events. The theory is derived from Black's wider perspective known as pure sociology (Black, 1995). Founded on the premise that social life is a realm of reality independent of biology or psychology, pure sociology explains behaviour with its location and direction in social space, or its social geometry. To discover the geometry of a form of behaviour, isolate the events from which the behaviour arises. Since most violence is a response to wrongful conduct by the other party or his or her group, the relevant event is typically a conflict (Black, 1983). The crucial difference between violent and non-violent conflicts lies in their social geometry (see Phillips, 2003). The geometry is known objectively – by the relative position of the parties in multiple dimensions of social space (Black, 1995). Are the parties equals or unequals?

The Sociological Review, 62:S2, pp. 87–106 (2014), DOI: 10.1111/1467-954X.12193

Intimates or strangers? Integrated or marginal? Culturally close or culturally distant? Respectable or deviant in reputation? Each form of violence, moreover, has its own peculiar social geometry. Terrorism, for instance, occurs when lower-status groups have long-standing grievances against wealthier and more powerful groups that are relationally, culturally, and functionally distant yet physically close (Black, 2004b). Lynching travels downwardly and distantly, toward those with few or no partisan supporters who have offended higher status people supported by close and solidary groups of partisans (Senechal de la Roche, 2004).

Black's theory is a major advance. It is precise – capable, in principle, of explaining who commits what type of violence against whom, under what circumstance. It is testable, eschewing all subjective variables that cannot be measured. And it is valid: scholars have successfully applied geometrical reasoning to several forms of violence (apart from terrorism and lynching) including genocide (Campbell, 2009, 2011), vigilantism and rioting (Senechal de la Roche, 1996), feuding (Black, 2004a), criminal homicide (Cooney, 1998; Phillips 2003), suicide (Manning, 2012), intimate partner violence (Baumgartner, 1993), and family honour violence (Cooney, 2014).

But for all its merits, the theory is incomplete. For one thing, it does not address the underlying conflict. Holding constant the conduct causing the conflict, the theory posits that the conflict will attract violence under particular geometrical configurations. But why an insult, unpaid debt, act of infidelity or other conduct triggers conflict in the first place is not explained. Second, while most violence arises out of conflict, not all does. Black's earlier theory therefore does not cover the full range of violent behaviour, in particular, that committed in the course of other events, such as exploitation (eg robbery). Third, and perhaps most crucially of all, the theory does not yield a causal explanation. It does not explain when a non-violent event will transition to a violent event. Isolating the causes of violence requires more than just a focus on events; it requires, in addition, a focus on change in events. Static states, even geometrical ones, cannot explain the eruption of violence.

The cause of violence

The new theory of moral time fills these theoretical gaps, in particular adding the elusive dynamic element: the event acquires a history (Black, 2011). The theory begins by reconceptualizing violence itself. The concrete act of violence fades away (Black, 2011, 2015). Violence becomes a movement of social time. Violence is primarily a movement of vertical time in that it sharply reduces people's ability to survive and prosper, thereby undermining the most basic status of all – health. Violence simultaneously invades the physical boundaries of another and, as such, is a movement of relational time.

Violence is not just a movement of social time, however; it is caused by a prior movement of social time. As social time moves, conflicts emerge. The conflict may not be with the one who moves social time. Some violence is triggered by an event that has little connection to the target of violence or even the group to which he or she belongs but is rooted instead in the circumstances of the aggressor's life (eg a robbery prompted by an addict running out of cash). Whatever its source, violence, especially lethal violence, represents a high degree of conflict – a large movement of social time – and is more likely itself to be caused by substantial movements of social time. Thus, violence is more likely to be triggered by an assault than an insult (more vertical time), by an extra-marital sexual relationship than an extra-marital friendship (more relational time), and by the meeting of radically different than slightly different traditions (more cultural time) – especially when these changes are sudden rather than gradual, and continuing rather than occasional.

In sum, like the theory of social geometry, the theory of moral time is general, testable, parsimonious and precise. But it also offers a radically new conception of human conduct that purports to explain the critical transition to violence. If the theory is valid, it should be able to specify the triggers of violence regardless of the form it assumes – brawling, duelling, feuding, mass shootings and so forth. Here I invoke the theory in a bid to explain many of the known facts of one particular type of violence – that committed in the name of family honour. For while a good deal of empirical information about family honour has accumulated from different communities and countries, no theory yet specifies the causes of particular instances of violence perpetrated in its name.

Honour violence

Many, perhaps most, incidents of family honour violence never come to the attention of the police or researchers. But since murders are harder to conceal, more data are available about lethal honour violence. Drawing on reports published worldwide in English-language publications of 172 incidents and 230 victims, Chesler (2010) provides the most comprehensive look to date at homicide committed in the name of family honour. Ninety three per cent of the victims were female. One hundred were killed in Western countries (33 in North America; 67 in Europe), the remaining 130 in predominately Muslim countries (eg Pakistan, Iran, Saudi Arabia, Egypt). She estimated that 91 per cent of the perpetrators were Muslim, 42 per cent killed in collaboration with someone else, and 66 per cent were members of the woman's family of origin, with fathers participating in 37 per cent of the killings. The female victims fell into two categories: young women with an average age of 17, and older women with an average age of 36. Younger women were typically killed by their family of origin, whereas a majority of older women were killed by husbands or boyfriends, though multiple perpetrators were involved in 30 per cent of their cases.

Valuable though these data are they do not explain what causes the violence in the first place. Chesler (2010) reports that 56 per cent of the cases were motivated by the woman being 'too Western' while the remaining 44 per cent

The Sociological Review, 62:S2, pp. 87–106 (2014), DOI: 10.1111/1467-954X.12193

arose out of sexual impropriety. But why is either type of conduct deviant at all? A second limitation is that not all honour violations are punished with violence, let alone lethal violence. Ethnographic research reveals that families employ a variety of tactics in the face of dishonourable conduct, real or merely alleged (see Ginat, 1997; van Eck, 2003; Kardam, 2005). These include tolerating, scolding, threatening, arranging an abortion, sending away to relatives, arranging a marriage, or agreeing to a divorce. Honour violence is just the visible tip of a much larger mass of honour conflicts.

What triggers honour conflicts? And why do some result in killing? To these two critical questions existing theories provide no answers (but see Cooney, 2014). The most prominent theories address variation in rates of honour violence across groupings such as societies and ethnicities. The theories invoke a range of variables including cultural beliefs and values, corporate family sovereignty, and, especially, male supremacy (see Delaney, 1991; King, 2008; Gill *et al.*, 2012).

Culture, family structure, patriarchy and other such variables possess considerable explanatory power. But because they invoke static variables they cannot explain the cause of the conflict. And because they are pitched at the aggregate level they cannot, logically, explain the violent event: why one honour violation, real or alleged, leads to violence while another does not.[3] Even so, they provide the social background against which individual acts of honour violence take place. Within the broad parameters these factors establish, social space fluctuates, social time changes. Particular movements of social time trigger particular acts of honour violence. Consider, first, vertical time.

Vertical time

Recall that vertical time is any movement up or down a system of stratification – a change in social status as measured, for example, by wealth, power or authority. Vertical time moves when inequality increases (overstratification) or decreases (understratification). One type of understratification – underinferiority – is the central cause of honour violence.

Underinferiority

Underinferiority – the rise of an inferior – is a reliable trigger of conflict in all societies, particularly when sudden and extreme. A common source of underinferiority conflict is a challenge from below, any actions that reduce or eliminate the superiority of higher status actors.[4] Upward challenges are highly risky. Revolutions, actual or attempted, invariably meet with strong, even savage, resistance from the state, particularly in autocratic regimes. Uprisings by slaves, peasants, workers, and prisoners and other disturbances of hierarchy similarly generate swift and severe sanctions. More recently, many societies have experienced major upheavals in the wake of movements for racial, gender and sexual equality. Entrenched systems of privilege do not give up without a fight.

Rebellion occurs at the micro level as well – when somebody questions, undermines or overthrows the authority of another. Micro-rebellions from below meet comparably strong resistance from above. To disobey a commanding officer is to risk court-martial. To defy a judge is to face jail for contempt of court. To disrespect a police officer is to invite an arrest or beating. To disobey a teacher is to earn a trip to the Principal's office.

An honour offence is a micro-rebellion; honour violence is its quashing (Black, 2011). The woman's offence is to make autonomous decisions about how she will live her life. In so doing, she usurps the right of her family to make those decisions for her. Her rebellion may take many forms: rejecting the spouse chosen by her parents, becoming pregnant before marriage, refusing to clean up after the men of the house, living like a Westerner, or otherwise disobeying her family. These actions, particularly when done repeatedly, challenge three entrenched forms of stratification: patriarchy (male rule), corporateness (group rule), and gerontocracy (elderly rule). Consider each briefly.

Gender stratification is perhaps the most salient sociological feature of honour conflicts. Wherever such conflicts occur, women invariably occupy a lower place in the domestic and social hierarchy over the course of their lives. The very birth of girls is less celebrated than that of boys (see Pope, 2012). As youngsters, they often receive less food, schooling and parental affection than their brothers. They are granted less freedom, especially after puberty, when they become subject to sartorial and behavioural restrictions. Girls, but not boys, have to veil and conceal their bodily form. While boys are trained to become heads of households by keeping a close eye on their female siblings, girls are socialized to provide domestic labour, to marry when told, and to produce children – especially boys. As adults, women are subject to a sexual double standard. They are not free to roam in public places. They may not be able to testify in court or, if they do, their word counts for less (Pope, 2012). The most prestigious jobs are rarely open to them. And they must be careful not to interact with unrelated men.

But men are not without restrictions either. Men and women alike 'owe allegiance to the family, the community, or the tribe first and foremost, and the collective interests of the group take precedence over their personal wishes' (Pope, 2012). Of the groups owed loyalty, the family is the most central. Honour-sensitive families are typically corporate entities – large, extended, and centralized.[5] They tend to hold land and other resources (eg animals) in common, are hierarchically organized, and make important decisions collectively – including the decision to eliminate one of their own (see, eg, Payton, 2011). Importantly, they choose the marriage partners of their members. They act as a unit toward outsiders and outsiders treat their members as parts of a whole. An offence against one member is therefore an offence against all (see İnce *et al.*, 2009). And an offence by one member impugns the reputation of the entire group (see, eg, Abu-Lughod, 1999).

The Sociological Review, 62:S2, pp. 87–106 (2014), DOI: 10.1111/1467-954X.12193

In honour settings, age is equated with wisdom and power is correspondingly placed in the hands of older people. The young are subject to the authority of their elders. Young men must submit to their fathers and uncles. 'Children have no right to speak' a Turkish patriarch told a journalist who notes that he was 'making it quite clear that he ruled over the fate of his adult sons as well as his daughters' (Pope, 2012: 98). A boy is subject to the day-to-day authority of his father. A girl must primarily obey her mother, a young wife her mother-in-law. As a woman ages, some of the restrictions of her gender may ease (see Pope, 2012).

A young woman, then, is trebly subordinated. The authority of each form of stratification is vested in her father and, later, her husband. They are her masters to whom she must submit.[6] She must restrict her movements and carefully monitor her interactions. She must not stand out or assert herself. She must freely contribute her labour to the family economy, carrying out whatever domestic chores are requested of her. She must accept her family's choice of marriage partner, whether he is 18 or 80 years old. And she must confine her sexuality strictly to the marital bed – even a rape may not be excused.

The greater the inequality between the woman and her family the greater the challenge to family authority any given act of autonomous disobedience represents and the more severe the response it elicits. The same act of independence will cause more conflict in a highly patriarchal family than in a mildly patriarchal family. In a male-dominant family, merely talking to an unrelated man might get a woman killed; an out-of-wedlock pregnancy might be ignored in a more gender-egalitarian family.

The amount of conflict further depends on the nature of her rebellious conduct. Refusing to cook or clean, for example, is an act of disobedience that disturbs the normal functioning of a household. Somebody else must perform the neglected tasks or they will remain undone. Either way, the refusal is a nuisance. It does not, however, undermine the family's ability to negotiate its very future. In particular, her refusal does not usurp family authority. Loss of virginity, on the other hand, does. Marriage decisions are family decisions. A woman who sheds her virginity undercuts her family's ability to determine whom she will marry and with what family it will be allied – she weakens family sovereignty (King, 2008). Her family consequently has fewer and less desirable options when forging future relationships. She has no more right to do that than a junior diplomat has to sign an international treaty on behalf of his country.

To act autonomously, then, is to challenge family authority, especially when done frequently (see Pope, 2012). If others learn of it, the woman's conduct becomes even more deviant. The one invariant power a woman has is the power to stigmatize her family. She cannot add to family honour, but she can subtract from it (see Hasan, 2002). However, her deviant conduct only reduces the family's status if outsiders come to know of it (see Abu-Rabia, 2011). Should the family manage to conceal the offending conduct, the woman is likely to be spared. The family's first response to a breach therefore is often to hush the matter up or, if questioned, to dissemble (see Kardam, 2005). Still, mere rumours of dishonour are harmful (see King, 2008). Hence, the woman's offence may be merely alleged rather than actual (Husseini, 2009). Either way, gossip about the woman constitutes an additional movement of social time: overstratification, in particular, overinferiority.

Overinferiority

Overinferiority occurs when one actor falls below another in status (Black, 2011: 60). Overinferiority is important in honour conflicts because just as the woman's independent conduct raises her status relative to that of her family, especially its male members, so its public dissemination simultaneously reduces their status relative to that of other families (Black, 2011). Her gain is their loss.[7]

Gossip plays a central role in honour violence (see Glazer and Abu Ras, 1994; Faqir, 2001; Gill *et al.*, 2012). Communities are close. People are naturally interested in the lives of their neighbours and routinely share news, exchange opinions, and pass judgement on one another. The consequences can be socially toxic, severely stigmatizing the family concerned. Eliminating the subject of the gossip is one of the few ways the family can reclaim its lost status. An uncle whose teenage niece was lured back from Sweden and killed in Iraq stated:

'We couldn't accept Pela's behaviour, because it gave the family a bad reputation. Despite many family meetings, which aimed at dealing with the problem, we weren't successful because the victim insisted on carrying on with her bad behaviour.

I am a brother of Pela's father and I believe in my heart and because of the badness I saw and the awful things I heard about her in the foreign country, that she deserved worse than death. This I say because she was ruining the reputation of an old, honourable family, highly respected among the Kurds'. (quoted in Wikan, 2008: 43)

The loss of honour is palpable, often resulting in shunning. A Turkish farmer who killed his daughter said,

'I would not have want [*sic*] to harm my own child, but I had no choice. Nobody would buy my produce. I had to make a living for my other children'. (quoted in Sev'er and Yurdakul, 2001: 990)[8]

The dishonour is particularly acute for the male members of the family who have failed to monitor their own. A man who emigrated from Pakistan to Norway stated in an interview:

'When a Pakistani woman is raped, she is shamed. This is how a man feels if a woman in his family has an improper relationship with a man. You feel raped somehow'. (quoted in Wikan, 2008: 205)

Virginity cases are especially serious because the family loses not just moral but economic status as well. Virginity is property. It commands a price in the marriage market in the form of bridewealth paid by the groom and his family.

The Sociological Review, 62:S2, pp. 87–106 (2014), DOI: 10.1111/1467-954X.12193

The family, not the bride, receives the bridewealth. Hence, the woman is merely the custodian of that sexual property; the family is the owner. By losing her virginity, the woman deprives her family of a valuable economic asset. Consequently, her family becomes downwardly mobile compared to other families who still have their sexual property or who have exchanged it for material goods in the marriage market place.

By paying bridewealth the groom acquires ownership of his wife's sexuality. She has no right to share his property with another. An affair with another man is thus another form of theft, depriving the man of the exclusive access to his wife that he purchased. Hence, she may be punished or even killed.

The family's loss of status is compounded when the man with whom the woman has an unauthorized relationship is himself of low status. A downward relationship (with a lower status man) is more damaging than an upward relationship (with a higher status man). Thus, her family is more likely to define a liaison with a man from a poorer, less influential family as dishonourable than one with a man from a wealthy or powerful family (Chakravarti, 2005; Kardam, 2005; Kressel, 1981).[9] A downward relationship is particularly dishonourable if the woman thereby rejects a high status fiancée chosen by her family (Tintori, 2007). In contrast, the consequences of a higher-status liaison are less serious for her (Onal, 2008). However, not many wealthy families are likely to welcome a dishonoured woman from an impoverished family.

Relational and cultural time

Honour offences primarily attract punishment because they move vertical time. But sometimes they move relational and cultural time as well. When they do, the conduct is more dishonourable and triggers more severe – more lethal – punishment.

Overinvolvement and underinvolvement

Relational time is a change in relational distance or intimacy – participation in the life of another (Black, 1976).[10] An increase in intimacy is overintimacy; a decrease in intimacy is underintimacy (Black, 2011). One type of overintimacy is overinvolvement, an increase in contact with another.

Overinvolvement is a common source of trouble. An extreme example is rape – a large and rapid increase in unwanted physical contact, particularly when committed by a stranger (Black, 2011). Trespassing invades a person's private space as well, and is invariably resented. Overstaying one's welcome at a social occasion is a minor breach of the same underlying offence – imposing oneself on others.

Honour conflicts often include some overinvolvement, typically a relationship with another person (usually a man). The more overinvolved the relationship, the graver the violation of honour. It is more serious for a woman to talk to than merely look at an unrelated man; more serious for her to touch than to talk; more serious to touch him repeatedly than just once; more serious to have sexual intercourse – particularly if she is a virgin – than to embrace, and more serious to have sexual intercourse serially than singly. To become pregnant is more serious again, and giving birth to an illegitimate child is still more serious.

Overinvolvement varies with the prior involvement of the parties. The same amount of contact travels greater social distance when the parties are strangers. A woman who takes up with an outsider is therefore at greater risk than one who takes up with a man from the same village or town (see Blum and Blum, 1965; Onal, 2008). And a woman who chooses a man from outside her own clan may be in greater danger as well (see Scott, 2008). By contrast, being linked with a relationally close man is less likely to be treated as a dishonourable offence requiring execution (see Ginat, 1997).

Black (2011) argues that intimacy is a zero-sum phenomenon: if A becomes intimate with C, she draws away from her former intimate, B. Reductions of involvement – underinvolvement – are a frequent source of human conflict. Leaving a romantic partner for another person is one of the most common occasions for homicide everywhere. So too is initiating a sexual affair with someone not one's spouse (see Daly and Wilson, 1988). Parents who abandon their children attract hostility from others. Politicians who switch party evoke particular ire. And traitors who forsake their country are reviled.

A woman who has an unauthorized relationship with a man does not just commit overinvolvement but underinvolvement. Her relationship with him decreases her intimacy with her own family. That relationship has typically been very intense. In Iraqi Kurdistan, for example:

> A typical female lives with family members, never alone. Nor does she travel anywhere alone, and she is never left home alone. The household members ensure that if she goes to school or college, she is transported with kin or in an approved manner such as on a school bus. She does not have a job outside the home or one inside the home that would require her to receive non-kin visitors. Her social life revolves around the household, immediate neighbours, and kin. (King, 2008: 320).

The more intimate a woman's relationship with a man, the greater the reduction in intimacy with her family. From the family's point of view, her relationship is a form of desertion. By taking up with him, she is less available to them. Should the relationship result in her giving birth, her time and attention will be absorbed even more and her underinvolvement be all the greater.

A woman may also commit the offence of underinvolvement more directly – by separating from or divorcing her husband (see Black, 2011). Among the Pakistani Muslim Mirpuri community in the UK, for instance, 'it is not uncommon for women who leave marital relationships, even when the cause is violence, to be branded by their community as dishonourable . . . In extreme circumstances women will face the possibility of "life on the run" from the perpetrator, or death if they are found' (Latif, 2011: 30).

The Sociological Review, 62:S2, pp. 87–106 (2014), DOI: 10.1111/1467-954X.12193

Overtraditionalism and undertraditionalism

Cultural time moves when actors become more or less culturally distant from one another.[11] More cultural distance is overdiversity; less cultural distance is underdiversity. One type of overdiversity is overtraditionalism – an increase in contact between cultures.

Overtraditionalism commonly incites conflict among people and groups (Black, 2011; Campbell, 2013). Sudden contact with Europeans had calamitous consequences for the indigenous peoples of Africa, America and Australia. Clashes between racial and ethnic groups continue to trigger occasional rioting in many countries today (Horowitz, 1993). And cultural outsiders often bear the brunt of individual acts of discrimination – particularly in settings unaccustomed to diversity (see Cooney, 2009c).

Intimate relationships that span greater cultural distances appear to have more conflict than those that span smaller cultural distances. In America, for instance, marriages between parties of different religions or different levels of education have a higher risk of divorce (Cherlin, 2009). Mixed-culture couples in Muslim societies may have more conflict than same-culture couples, though no data appear to be available on the point.

Culturally diverse relationships can cause another type of conflict as well – between one or both of the parties and the members of their own culture. The source of the trouble is rejection or abandonment of traditional culture, or undertraditionalism (Black, 2011). The rejection does not have to be explicit – simply by gravitating toward another culture people distance themselves from their own culture. A woman who moves away from her native culture offends those she leaves behind. The more deeply her family are immersed in traditional culture, the greater the undertraditionalism and the more serious her offence.

Abandonment of culture is a recurring theme in honour violence, particularly in Western countries where the opportunities to adopt a non-traditional lifestyle are pervasive and plentiful. Recall that Chesler's (2010) cross-national review of some 230 honour killings reported in English-language media outlets found that a majority were apparently motivated by the woman becoming 'too Western'. The women's offences included wearing Western clothing or cosmetics, wanting an education or career, and forming friendships across ethnic lines. For example:

> 'In one . . . case in Berlin, a young Turkish woman's brothers shot and killed her for abandoning Turkish customs and becoming too German: She had been dressing in a Western style (without a headscarf), learning to be an electrician at a technical school, and socializing with German men. A Turkish boy later described why she was killed: "She deserved what she got. The whore lived like a German" '. (Black, 2011: 127)

As in the Berlin case, undertraditionalism is especially fraught when combined with overinvolvement.[12] Unauthorized romantic relationships are apt to cause particular trouble when the partners are culturally diverse (see Ginat,

1997; Chakravarti, 2005). Van Eck (2003) reports that among ethnic Turks in Holland it is more dishonourable for an unmarried woman to have an unauthorized relationship with a Dutch man than with a Turkish man. If she is a Muslim, and especially if her family is devout, it is more dishonourable for her to form an attachment to a non-Muslim than to a Muslim (van Eck, 2003). In Turkey, a Kurdish woman who takes a Turkish lover increases her risk of being killed (Kardam, 2005). In Iraq, a Yazidi woman enters a relationship with a Muslim at her peril (Pope, 2012). Within communities that practise honour violence, the more a woman's unauthorized relationship crosses religious, linguistic or other cultural boundaries the greater her risk of being executed by her family (see Husseini, 2009). In such cases, honour violence represents a defence of tradition, an attack on those who would abandon the proud ways of the ancestors by taking up with foreign aliens.

Importantly, though, the movement of cultural time and relational time is typically subordinate to the movement of vertical time. Having a relationship with a foreign stranger is only dishonourable when the family forbids it. And a man's relationships with a foreign woman is much less dishonourable than a woman's with a foreign man (see Pope, 2012). Moreover, among the forms of vertical time, patriarchy is the most critical: honour killing is extremely unlikely to occur in corporate families ruled by elderly women but is sometimes found in small, non-corporate families ruled by men (see Onal, 2008). The immediate cause of the violence, then, is her rebellion against familial, cultural and, especially, male authority inherent in her autonomous lifestyle behaviour.

Conclusion

Our age is increasingly intolerant of violence. Social time explains why (see Campbell, 2013). More particularly, the nature and intensity of conflict, including the degree to which violence is deviant, is a product of the geometry of social time (Black, 2011). Recall that violence is a movement of vertical time, in particular a type of overstratification. Where people are relatively equal, the greatest movements of vertical time are increases in inequality, and overstratification conflict is more frequent and severe. Conversely, where people are highly unequal, the greatest movements of vertical time are reductions in inequality and understratification conflict occurs more often and more intensely. Thus, when inequality was rigid and extreme, as in agrarian societies, violence was unremarkable, part and parcel of everyday life (Elias, 2000 [1939]). But as inequality has weakened (though by no means disappeared), violence has become more deviant. Violence in a downward direction is particularly denounced today precisely because it would reinforce inequality. On the other hand, violence directed upwardly reduces inequality and hence is greeted with more ambivalence. Rebellions by oppressed peoples, wars of liberation and other forms of upward violence do not attract the same revulsion as their downward counterparts. The well-worn phrase, 'One person's terrorist is another's freedom fighter' encapsulates some of the greater acceptability of violence from below.

Violence is, in addition, the physical invasion of another person – an increase in intimacy, or overintimacy.[13] Across large expanses of relational distance the greatest movements of social time are increases in intimacy. Overintimacy conflicts are therefore more frequent and severe when people are more distant. Among those who are close, however, reductions of intimacy constitute larger movements of relational time and incite more conflict. Today, because we generally live around more strangers and enjoy more privacy than in the past, violence is a greater movement of relational time – a more significant invasion of our lives – than it once was. Similar long-term shifts in intimate relationships also explain why violence between intimates has evolved into a more serious crime. With more people residing alone, marrying later, having fewer children, uncoupling more often, and living around fewer relatives, intimate relationships are also less entangled – less intimate – than in previous eras.[14] Consequently, intimate violence has come to attract greater severity from police, judges and juries. When violence is not just intimate but downward as well (eg committed against those physically weaker, such as women or children), it is even more closely scrutinized, studied and sanctioned (Black, 2015).

Honour violence repeats the general pattern. Because of the pronounced inequality and the extreme intimacy of the family in most of the communities in which honour violence is found, such violence tends to be condoned there. Legal officials may turn a blind eye while neighbours shower praise on the perpetrators (see Cooney, 2009a). But in the more modern and urban parts of the same countries and especially in the more egalitarian and individualized settings of the West, honour violence attracts much more condemnation. 'There is no honour in honour killing' is a theme increasingly heard around the world.

Because honour violence is morally repugnant to many its sociological reality remains at least partially hidden. For honour violence is not just the repression of subordinate people. It is also the suppression of deviance, or punishment. What triggers the violence is an accusation against the woman that she did something quite wrong, thereby undermining her family's precious moral reputation, its very honour.

The notion of honour, however, is extremely elastic. No code of honour lays down in black and white what a woman may or may not do. Anthropologists tend to emphasize breaches of chastity as the source of dishonour, whereas journalists and activists are apt to stress the arbitrary, and often imaginary, nature of honour offences. The theory of moral time proffers a more abstract and general explanation: the more a woman's autonomous conduct moves social time, the more dishonourable it is. And the greater the dishonour the greater the probability of an honour killing. Movements of social time may be vertical, relational or cultural. Vertical movements (in particular, underinferiority and overinferiority) are the fundamental cause being present in virtually every instance of honour violence. Relational (underinvolvement and overinvolvement) and cultural (undertraditionalism and overtraditionalism) movements are common as well and, when present, aggravate the gravity of the offending conduct.

The theory of moral time represents a significant deviation from existing theories of violence. Many such theories address variation across social actors. Invoking stable, core characteristics, they can explain which individuals or groups are more likely to be violent. But they cannot explain when the actor will be violent, or against whom. Other theories address variation across social aggregates. They explain which neighbourhoods, cities, states, or countries are likely to be more violent (their rate). But they do not and cannot explain who commits the violence, against whom, when. Actor and aggregate theories are both supported by evidence, and therefore accomplish much of what they are designed to accomplish. But they do not seek to accomplish the most central task: isolating the social characteristics of violent events.

The theory of moral time is more precise, addressing variation across cases, now conceptualized as movements through social space. The theory can explain which event is likely to be more violent. Moreover, only the theory of moral time is also a causal theory that can explain the change from non-violence to violence.

Black's large claim that movements of social time underlie all forms of violence clearly requires considerable specification, elaboration and testing. Still, the theory has already received some support. Manning (2014) shows that suicide is typically prompted by overinferiority (falling below others in status) and by underinvolvement (losing close relationships). Looking at the other end of the spectrum, Campbell (2013) finds that genocide (mass ethnic killing) is most often triggered by overtraditionalism (clashing of cultures) and collective undersuperiority (ethnic groups losing pre-eminence). These findings are just a beginning, however: much work remains to be done identifying which movements of social time cause which type of violence.

Future work will continue to draw on Black's earlier theory of social geometry. Just as some movements of social time cause more violence than others, so some geometrical locations attract more violence than others. The effects of social time vary with their position and direction in social space – their geometry (Manning, 2014). When the geometry is strongly attractive to violence, even a small movement of social time might trigger an act of violence. When the geometry is only weakly attractive to violence, a large movement of social time may be required to ignite a physical attack. The most complete explanations of violence will come to reference not just movements in social space but their location and direction as well.

Acknowledgements

I thank Bonnie Berry, Donald Black, Bradley Campbell, Matthew Greife, Mary Kelly, and Jason Manning for their helpful comments.

Notes

1 Most violence in the name of honour involves men fighting other men (see Black, 2011). Family honour violence is a subspecies of honour violence that is primarily committed by men against women. Some family honour violence, however, is committed by men against men and some by women against women (see Amnesty International, 1999; Pope, 2012). This paper addresses violence against women only.

2 This excludes two theoretical approaches: rational choice theory and Collins's (2008) micro-sociological theory. Rational choice theory proposes that violence occurs when the net benefits of violence outweigh the net benefits of all other courses of conduct for the offender (see Cornish and Clarke, 1986). Costs and benefits of violence include such subjective factors as the value the individual places on obtaining momentary satisfaction, getting even, looking tough, experiencing pangs of conscience, enduring the disapproval of family and friends, limiting future upward mobility and other unmeasurable preference variables. Collins (2008) argues that violence erupts when people overcome the confrontational tension they experience in contemplating violence, but he does not provide a testable explanation of when the critical transition occurs (Cooney, 2009b). Neither theory, then, is fully testable at the level that matters most: distinguishing violent from non-violent events.

3 Most honour offences do not result in violence because the cases occur at a particular location in social space, where hierarchy intersects with relational closeness (Cooney, 2014).

4 A second type of understratification is undersuperiority – the fall of a superior. This too may sometimes be involved in honour violence as, for instance, when among immigrants to the West, children often fit in better than the parents, who may be unemployed, isolated and unable to speak the local language, thus causing a shift in the power dynamics of the household (Pope, 2012).

5 The strength of the family can be seen in the strong pull it exerts on its members. Some women who have sought to flee accusations of dishonour by running away have found they cannot live without their family and return home. One such Swedish Kurd teenager was then killed by her family (Wikan, 2008).

6 In some places, she can even be given to or seized by another family to compensate an offence committed by one of her male relatives (Rubin, 2012).

7 A second form of overstratification is oversuperiority – an actor rising above others (Black, 2011). Oversuperiority may sometimes be a factor in honour conflicts. For instance, a Turkish woman who did not have to work in the fields because her husband received a government salary was subject to an untrue charge of dishonour: 'envy may have played a part in the campaign against her' (Pope, 2012).

8 Because of the real loss of status attendant on known honour violations it is sociologically misleading to describe such cases as 'so-called honour killings'.

9 A liaison with a disreputable man – one who conceals his married state, for example – is more dishonourable as well, though that may make him, rather than her, the target of an honour killing (see, eg, van Eck, 2003).

10 Relational changes can be divided into fluctuations in involvement with others or exposure to others (Black, 2011).

11 Cultural time moves either when separate traditions have contact with one another (tradition-alism) or when a new item of culture comes into being (innovation) (Black, 2011).

12 As well as overinvolvement in the life of another, overintimacy includes overexposure of one's self to others, which can also feature in honour violence. For example, the final straw that led a Pakistani man living in Norway to kill his rapidly Westernizing Pakistani wife was when she 'agreed to undress in front of a male doctor during a consultation' (Wikan, 2008).

13 It may also be a rejection of diversity, a form of undertraditionalism, as in genocide (Campbell, 2013).

14 Although involvement has declined among intimates in modern society, the second dimension of intimacy – exposure – has increased. Consistent with the theory of moral time, among intimates,

overinvolvement (eg violence) has become more serious while overexposure (eg revealing oneself) has become less deviant, indeed more praiseworthy.

References

Abu-Lughod, L., (1999), *Veiled Sentiments: Honour and Poetry in a Bedouin Society*, Berkeley, CA: University of California Press.

Abu-Rabia, A., (2011), 'Family honour killings: between custom and state law', *The Open Psychology Journal*, 4 (Suppl 1-M4): 34–44.

Agnew, R., (2005), *Why Do Criminals Offend? A General Theory of Crime and Delinquency*, New York: Oxford University Press.

Amnesty International, (1999), *Violence against Women in the Name of Honour*, Amnesty International Index Number ASA 33/017/1999.

Baumgartner, M. P., (1993), 'Violent networks: the origins and management of domestic conflict', in R. Felson and J. Tedeschi (eds), *Violence and Aggression: The Social Interactionist Perspective*, 209–231, Washington, DC: American Psychological Association.

Black, D., (1976), *The Behaviour of Law*, New York: Academic Press.

Black, D., (1983), 'Crime as social control', *American Sociological Review*, 48: 34–45.

Black, D., (1993), *The Social Structure of Right and Wrong*, San Diego, CA: Academic Press.

Black, D., (1995), 'The epistemology of pure sociology', *Law and Social Inquiry*, 20: 829–879.

Black, D., (2004a), 'Violent structures', in M. Zahn, H. Brownstein and S. Jackson (eds), *Violence: From Theory to Research*, 145–158, Newark, NJ: Lexis-Nexis/Anderson Publishing.

Black, D., (2004b), 'The geometry of terrorism', *Sociological Theory*, 22: 14–25.

Black, D., (2011), *Moral Time*, New York: Oxford University Press.

Black, D., (2015), 'The beginning of social time: an interview with myself', in J. Tucker (eds), *The Pure Sociology of Right and Wrong*, Special Issue of the *International Journal of Law, Crime and Justice*, forthcoming.

Blau, J. and Blau, P., (1982), 'The cost of inequality: metropolitan structure and violent crime', *American Sociological Review*, 47: 114–129.

Blum, R., and Blum, E., (1965), *Health and Healing in Rural Greece: A Study of Three Communities*, Stanford, CA: Stanford University Press.

Campbell, B., (2009), 'Genocide as social control', *Sociological Theory*, 27 (2): 150–172.

Campbell, B., (2011), 'Genocide as a matter of degree', *British Journal of Sociology*, 62 (4): 586–612.

Campbell, B., (2013), 'Genocide and social time', *Dilemas: Revista de Estudos de Conflito e Controle Social,* 6: 465–488.

Chakravarti, U., (2005), 'From fathers to husbands: of love, death and marriage in North India', in L. Welchman and S. Hossain (eds), *Honour: Crimes, Paradigms and Violence against Women*, 308–331, London: Zed Books.

Cherlin, A., (2009), *The Marriage Go-Round: The State of Marriage and the Family in America Today*, New York: Alfred A. Knopf.

Chesler, P., (2010), 'Worldwide trends in honour killing', *Middle East Quarterly* (Spring): 3–11.

Collins, R., (2008), *Violence: A Micro-sociological Theory*, Princeton, NJ: Princeton University Press.

Cooney, M., (1998), *Warriors and Peacemakers: How Third Parties Shape Violence*, New York: New York University Press.

Cooney, M., (2009a), *Is Killing Wrong? A Study in Pure Sociology*, Charlottesville, VA: University of Virginia Press.

Cooney, M., (2009b), 'The scientific significance of Collins's Violence', *British Journal of Sociology*, 60: 586–594.

Cooney, M., (2009c), 'Ethnic conflict without ethnic groups: a study in pure sociology', *British Journal of Sociology*, 60: 463–492.

Cooney, M., (2014), 'Death by family: honor violence as punishment', *Punishment and Society*, 16 (4): 406–427.

The Sociological Review, 62:S2, pp. 87–106 (2014), DOI: 10.1111/1467-954X.12193

Cornish, D. and Clarke, R. (eds), (1986), *The Reasoning Criminal: Rational Choice Perspectives on Offending*, New York: Springer-Verlag.

Daly, M. and Wilson, M., (1988), *Homicide*, New York: Aldine De Gruyter.

Delaney, C., (1991), *The Seed and the Soil: Gender and Cosmology in Turkish Village Society*, Berkeley, CA: University of California Press.

Elias, N., (2000 [1939]), *The Civilizing Process: Sociogenetic and Psychogenetic Investigations*, Oxford: Blackwell.

Faqir, F., (2001), 'Intrafamily femicide in defence of honour: the case of Jordan', *Third World Quarterly*, 22 (1): 65–82.

Gill, A., Nazand, B. and Hague, G., (2012), 'Honour-based violence in Kurdish communities', *Women's Studies International Forum*, 35: 75–85.

Ginat, J., (1997), *Blood Revenge: Family Honour, Mediation and Outcasting*, 2nd edn, Brighton: Sussex Academic Press.

Glazer, I. and Abu Ras, W., (1994), 'On aggression, human rights, and hegemonic discourse: the case of a murder for family honour in Israel', *Sex Roles*, 30 (3/4): 269–288.

Hasan, M., (2002), 'The politics of honour: patriarchy, the state and the murder of women in the name of family honour', *Journal of Israeli History*, 21: 1–37.

Hirschi, T. and Gottfredson, M., (2001), 'Self-control theory', in R. Paternoster and R. Bachman (eds), *Explaining Crime and Criminals: Essays in Contemporary Criminological Theory*, 81–96, Los Angeles, CA: Roxbury.

Horowitz, D., (1993), *The Deadly Ethnic Riot*, Berkeley, CA: University of California Press.

Husseini, R., (2009), *Murder in the Name of Honour: The True Story of One Woman's Heroic Fight against an Unbelievable Crime*, Oxford: Oneworld Publications.

İnce, O., Aysun, Y. and Doğancan, Ö., (2009), 'Customary killings in Turkey and Turkish modernization', *Middle Eastern Studies*, 45: 537–551.

Kardam, F., (contributions from Zeynep A., İlknur, Y., & Ergül, E.), (2005), *The Dynamics of Honour Killings in Turkey: Prospects for Action*, Ankara: Population Association.

King, D., (2008), 'The personal is patrilineal: *Namus* as sovereignty', *Identities: Global Studies in Culture and Power*, 15: 317–342.

Kressel, G., (1981), 'Sororicide/filicide: homicide for family honour', *Current Anthropology*, 22: 141–152.

Kulczycki, A. and Windle, S., (2011), 'Honour killings in the Middle East and North Africa: a systematic review of the literature', *Violence against Women*, 17 (11): 1442–1464.

Latif, Z., (2011), 'The silencing of women from the Pakistani Muslim Mirpuri community in violent relationships', in M. Mohammad and A. Tahir (eds), *Honour, Violence, Women and Islam*, 29–41, Abingdon: Routledge.

Manning, J., (2012), 'Suicide as social control', *Sociological Forum*, 27 (1): 207–227.

Manning, J., (2014), 'Suicide and social time', *Dilemas: Revista de Estudos de Conflito e Controle Social*, forthcoming.

McCall, P., Land, K. and Parker, K., (2010), 'An empirical assessment of what we know about structural covariates of homicide rates: a return to a classic 20 years later', *Homicide Studies*, 14 (3): 219–243.

Nisbett, R. E. and Cohen, D., (1996), *Culture of Honor: The Psychology of Violence in the South*, Boulder, CO: Westview Press.

Onal, A., (2008), *Honour Killing: Stories of Men Who Killed*, London: SAQI.

Payton, J., (2011), 'Collective crime, collective victims', in M. Mohammad and A. Tahir (eds), *Honour, Violence, Women and Islam*, 67–79, Abingdon: Routledge.

Phillips, S., (2003), 'The social structure of vengeance: a test of Black's model', *Criminology*, 41 (3): 673–708.

Pope, N., (2012), *Honour Killing in the Twenty-First Century*, New York: Palgrave Macmillan.

Rubin, A., (2012), 'For punishment of elders' misdeeds, Afghan girl pays the price', *New York Times*. 16 February. Available from: http://www.nytimes.com/2012/02/17/world/asia/in-baad-afghan-girls-are-penalized-for-elders-crimes.html?pagewanted=all&_r=0.

Scott, J., (2008), 'Introduction', in A. Onal (ed.), *Honour Killing: Stories of Men Who Killed*, 9–17, London: SAQI.

Senechal de la Roche, R., (1996), 'Collective violence as social control', *Sociological Forum*, 11: 97–128.

Senechal de la Roche, R., (2004), 'Modern lynchings', in M. Zahn, H. Brownstein and S. Jackson (eds), *Violence: From Theory to Research*, 213–225, Newark, NJ: Lexis-Nexis/Anderson Publishing.

Sev'er, A. and Yurdakul, G., (2001), 'Culture of honour, culture of change: a feminist analysis of honour killings in rural Turkey', *Violence against Women*, 7: 964–998.

Tintori, K., (2007), *Unto the Daughters: The Legacy of an Honour Killing in a Sicilian-American Family*, New York: St Martin's Press.

United Nations Population Fund (UNPFA), (2000), *State of World Population*, available from: http://www.unfpa.org/swp/2000/english/index.html.

Van Eck, C., (2003), *Purified by Blood: Honour Killings amongst Turks in the Netherlands*, Amsterdam: Amsterdam University Press.

Wikan, U., (2008), *In Honour of Fadime: Murder and Shame*, Chicago: University of Chicago Press.

The Sociological Review, 62:S2, pp. 87–106 (2014), DOI: 10.1111/1467-954X.12193

Towards an embodied sociology of war

Kevin McSorley

Abstract: While sociology has historically not been a good interlocutor of war, this paper argues that the body has always known war, and that it is to the corporeal that we can turn in an attempt to develop a language to better speak of its myriad violences and its socially generative force. It argues that war is a crucible of social change that is prosecuted, lived and reproduced via the occupation and transformation of myriad bodies in numerous ways from exhilaration to mutilation. War and militarism need to be traced and analysed in terms of their fundamental, diverse and often brutal modes of embodied experience and apprehension. This paper thus invites sociology to extend its imaginative horizon to rethink the crucial and enduring social institution of war as a broad array of fundamentally embodied experiences, practices and regimes.

Keywords: war, violence, injury, body, experience, sensation

Introduction

War has been a crucial factor in the shaping of modernity and modern social life and it shows few signs of declining in importance or intensity in the 21st century. Despite its importance, war has historically not been a core concern for sociology. This paper attempts to rethink the significance of war and its socially generative force by paying particular attention to its fundamentally embodied nature, an analytic orientation that has received limited emphasis within sociological discourse to date.

The paper initially engages with the work of Elaine Scarry (1985) who explores the fundamental centrality of bodily injuring to war, a fact that is commonly disavowed in many prominent military and strategic traditions of thought and media and political discourses of war. For Scarry, war is 'the most radically embodying event in which human beings ever collectively participate' (1985: 71) and war's force is a fundamentally bodily making and unmaking of the world. The paper subsequently explores how, despite its undeniable and continuing significance in shaping the modern world, war has been under-analysed by a sociology whose gaze has historically been directed inwards upon an assumed pacific state. War thus remains under-examined within sociological discourse in general, and the embodied dimensions of war remain under-theorized in particular.

The Sociological Review, 62:S2, pp. 107–128 (2014), DOI: 10.1111/1467-954X.12194

The remainder of the paper explores a range of contemporary scholarship, in diverse analytic traditions from feminist international relations to medical anthropology, which has attempted to place the fundamentally embodied dimensions of war more explicitly at the forefront of its analysis. Such work has explored war as a realm of diverse embodied experiences, embodied practices and regimes of sensation and, as such, it offers sensitizing concepts and the beginnings of an analytic toolkit for the task of further fleshing out a comparative and embodied sociology of war. The paper concludes by arguing that embodiment cannot be understood as an insignificant or epiphenomenal dimension of war, and that the sociological analysis of war would thus benefit from a sustained engagement with the corporeal. War is an enduring crucible of social change that needs to be traced and analysed in terms of its fundamental, diverse and often brutal forms of embodied experience and apprehension.

War as bodily injuring

For Elaine Scarry (1985), bodily injuring is manifestly at the heart of war. While the founding figure of strategic thought Carl von Clausewitz famously argued that war is a contest to define political reality, 'the continuation of policy by other means' (1976: 87), Scarry crucially notes that this contest over differing political constructions of the world is not conducted by any available 'other means'. It is not decided, for example, by sporting prowess or by musical ability. Rather, it is always conducted by a very specific 'other means' – bodily injuring. Politics is written in war through the very specific idiom of violently injuring human bodies. For Scarry, this is because it is bodily injuring alone, as opposed to any of those other potential surrogate idioms of resolving conflicts, which uniquely carries the power of its own enforcement. The out-injured parties in war are no longer able to make the same sense of the world and as such are less able to resist the imposition of a new political reality.

Drawing particularly upon the work of Merleau-Ponty, this centrality of the body to making sense of the world, and its disruption through violence, is explicitly theorized by Mensch (2009). He argues that our ability to make sense of our surrounding environment, and of ourselves in the world, presupposes a set of bodily actions – turning the head, moving, reaching, picking up, tasting and so on – through which the perception of objects in the external world and the perception of one's own body are necessarily intertwined. Our primary sense of the world is thus one of bodily enactment, we are in the world through our doings and our projects, ultimately through what Mensch calls the co-constitution of a bodily 'I can' and the correlative world in which this 'I can' appears.

Mensch argues that what defines all *violent* phenomena is that they attack this fundamentally embodied ability to make sense of the world and one's own place in it. Violence is specifically destructive of the ability of the body to engage in sense-making and meaning-making, it 'undoes our deployment of the bodily "I

The Sociological Review, 62:S2, pp. 107–128 (2014), DOI: 10.1111/1467-954X.12194

can" in making sense of the surrounding world' (Mensch, 2009: 72–73). In a discussion of the colonial transformation of traditional aboriginal lands into divided, enclosed spaces for farming, Mensch argues that this process not only deprives the original inhabitants of their means of supporting themselves, but it also fundamentally disrupts their contexts of sense-making about the world and their place in it. Through such structural violence, aboriginal men began to lose their sense of embodiment, and hence their ability to understand themselves, as hunters or pastoralists. In a further discussion of a more direct physical assault on bodily integrity, the severing of a young woman's limbs during the conflict in Sierra Leone, Mensch relatedly argues of this violation of the body that 'What is mutilated is not just her body, but also her body-dependent projects. The mutilation extends to her pragmatic understanding of the world and her being in it' (2009: 77). For Mensch then, there is an intimate relationship between violence, embodiment, injury and the ability to make sense of the world.[1]

This noted, let us return to Scarry's argument that bodily injuring is the distinctive idiom for the political contestation of war. Importantly, she argues that this is not only down to the opponent becoming out-injured to the point where they can no longer put up any more resistance – indeed, such a scenario is historically very rare in war. Rather, Scarry argues that the additional significance of this idiom is that the very production of brutally wounded bodies provides a radical material base that can be enlisted into ending the reality contest and the 'crisis of substantiation' (1985: 150) which war entails. For Scarry, it is in those liminal and protean situations such as war, fundamentally concerned with 'the making and unmaking of the world', that bodily injury accrues a 'frightening power of substantiation' (1985: 126) and has historically been the reality-confirming force. The fact that war is fundamentally embodied is thus not only central to its prosecution but also to its eventual ending. Injuring is the basis of the contest *and* the initial source of substantiation of the winning reality:

> War is the suspension of the reality of constructs . . . and simultaneously, the mining of the ultimate source of substantiation . . . the making available of the precious ore of confirmation, the interior content of human bodies, lungs, arteries, blood, brains, the motherlode that will eventually be reconnected to the winning issue, to which it will lend its radical substance, its compelling, heartsickening reality, until more benign forms of substantiation come into being. (1985: 137)

Despite it being the manifest heartsickening reality of war, many of the ways in which war is thought and talked about frequently fail to hold steady to this central fact of bodily injuring. For Norris, the dead and injured regularly fail to become figures of phenomenology in the mediascape of contemporary war, signalling 'the human body's derealisation by technological media under military control at the end of the twentieth century' (2000: 231). Butler (2009) relatedly argues that the differential structuring of affective responses through such 'frames of war' has meant that it is only certain bodies that matter during wartime, that count and are counted, whereas others are not recognized as fully human, becoming unintelligible and 'ungrievable'. Scarry argues that 'the fact of injuring tends to be absent from strategic and political descriptions of war' (1985: 12), which are often marked instead by a profound disavowal or transference of its bodily mutilation, in the process becoming 'emptied of human content . . . a rarefied choreography of disembodied events' (1985: 70). As she notes, a level of abstraction may seem appropriate for an instrumental mode of strategic thinking. Nonetheless, fundamental ethical concerns are ruled out of court by such abstraction (Cohn, 1987; Zehfuss, 2011). And for Scarry, the crucial ethical imperative behind attempting to recognize the fundamentally embodied nature of war is that 'the more accurately the nature of war is described, the more likely the chances that it will one day be displaced by a structural surrogate' (1985: 143).

The neglected sociology of war

If bodily injuring has disappeared from many of the ways that we think and talk about war, war in general has largely been notable by its absence from sociological discourse, despite its undeniable and continuing significance in shaping the history of the modern world. As Brighton (2011: 101) notes, 'little in modern social and political life goes untouched by war' and history is replete with examples of its socially generative, complex and at times contradictory powers: from its crucial relationship to the bestowal and proving of masculinities to its empowerment of countless women mobilized into working for the war effort in 20th century Europe; from its striations and brutal entrenchments of masses of class-based lives and deaths to its significance for the history and emergence of universal welfarism; from its often ruthless racial classifications of the 'enemy' without and within to its crucial role as a site for the inclusion and recognition of otherwise marginalized and migrant others into the narratives and performances of national service and citizenship (Ware, 2012).

War, then, has never simply been about the deployal of a distant instrument of political violence at the periphery. Rather, it has also been a crucible of historical social change that has continuously mutated social relations at the core of those societies that have continuously made it (Barkawi, 2011). And yet war has not been a topic that has regularly captivated the sociological imagination, such that the sociology of war does not exist as a significant discursive sub-field with its own recognizable set of questions, debates and theories. Bousquet (2012: 180) argues that 'sociology in the main inherited one of the most prevalent assumptions of social theorists in the nineteenth century, namely that of the archaic character, and thus increasing irrelevance, of war' and that as such it assumed that 'the emerging global order of bourgeois societies, bound by trade and commerce and guided by rational economic self-interest . . . was inherently pacifistic'.[2] Even when 20th-century history proved that belief to be drastically mistaken, war has nonetheless often been thought of as the exception to normal social and political life (Shaw, 1988), or as a discrete event bounded

The Sociological Review, 62:S2, pp. 107–128 (2014), DOI: 10.1111/1467-954X.12194

in space and time (Cuomo, 1996) whose centre of gravity and primary presence has been considered to be 'elsewhere' rather than 'here' (Shapiro, 2011).

As such, and as Malešević (2010b) notes, particularly in the post-1945 period when sociology largely constituted itself as a discipline, the emphasis of sociological theorizing also 'moved on' to embrace the optimism of the times (Joas, 2003). Its focus shifted decisively towards topics such as welfare, social stratification, culture, education and health but away from any sustained analysis of organized violence, which was now regarded as a sign of failure or the absence of the social rather than its product (McDonald, 2013). It moved away also from consideration of the significance of the embodied legacies of war and of enduring preparations for war-making upon the structuring and reproduction of social life.

It has principally been within Weberian comparative historical sociology that the most distinctively sociological tradition of theorizing war has been developed. The work of Tilly (1975, 1992), Giddens (1987), Mann (1986, 1993) and Collins (1975, 1986) in particular argued that the emergence of modern bureaucratic, territorialized and centralized nation-states – marked by the monopolization of the means of violence, the extension of processes of surveillance and taxation, and the emergence of new forms of belonging and rights – was in large part the result of protracted wars and highly expensive military campaigns, a process of co-evolution whereby 'war made the state and the state made war' (Tilly, 1975: 42). Such work attempted to analyse the complex imbrications of organized violence, state formation and capitalism that were central to the emergence of modernity, whilst crucially asserting a relative autonomy of military power from simple capitalist logics. The total mobilizations of society, polity and economy for the prosecution of the 20th-century world wars were testament to war's all-consuming ability to exceed the logics of brute economic determinism (Shaw, 2005).

Whatever the strengths and weaknesses of this tradition of historical sociological scholarship, or its utility for illuminating the transformations of war in late modernity, associated in many cases with the disintegration of the state's monopoly of violence and structural integrity (Kaldor, 2012), it is crucial to note here that the embodied dimensions of war – the centrality of bodily violence, killing and injury – are given little analytic attention in such accounts. As McDonald (2013) notes, Giddens' Weberian account of the modernization of war stresses the increasing discipline, bureaucratization, and professionalization of the modern military, a process by which the soldier is turned into 'a specialist purveyor of the means of violence' (1987: 230). For McDonald (2013), this language is significant, implying that injuring and killing are potentially analytically equivalent to anything that requires a degree of refined training, such as becoming a purveyor of fine foods. He argues that, particularly as war spills out of its modern structures and across the global flows of late modernity, analysis primarily in terms of bureaucratic models of rational action fundamentally elides the increased significance of the embodied and experiential dimensions of contemporary paradigms of violence.[3]

The historical sociology of war nonetheless makes clear the generative force of war, that, as MacLeish (2013: 10–11) succinctly puts it, 'war makes the social, the rules, the nations, and the people, rather than simply corrupting, undermining or destroying those things'. War certainly involves the direct slaughter of thousands of bodies (Tirman, 2011), affective assaults upon the morale of entire populations (Anderson, 2010), the 'slow violence' of environmental and infrastructural degradations (Nixon, 2011), and the structural violence of massive investment in war-fighting capacity over domestic capacity building in alternative areas such as healthcare or jobs creation (Garrett-Peltier, 2011). But war has also been the midwife of countless transformations in domains from education to medicine, from scientific innovation to urban planning, from logistics to computation (Barkawi, 2011; Bousquet, 2012). It is at times deeply destructive, isolating and individuating, but it also produces new forms of social solidarity and binding. Reflecting upon the radical transformation of the lifeworld at the end of the First World War, Benjamin (1969: 84) thus notes that:

> Wasn't it noticeable at the end of the war that men who had returned from the battlefield had grown silent . . . a generation that had gone to school on horse-drawn streetcars now stood under the open sky in a landscape where nothing remained unchanged but the clouds, and beneath these clouds, in a field of force of destructive torrents and explosions, was the tiny, fragile human body.

This potent rendering of the body through the force field of war that Benjamin describes has however been a topic of minimal elaboration within sociological thinking. While a renewed concern with the embodiment of human life and social action has been an extremely productive feature of the social sciences over the past three decades (Shilling, 2007), with bodily issues becoming more mainstream to sociological theorizing and bodily studies proliferating in numerous empirical directions, the topics of war and militarism have largely been notable by their absence from such developments.[4] The body that has become a greater focus of Western social scientific attention has to a large extent been a pacific body, one that had already optimistically moved beyond the force field of war. While it has been regarded as producing and consuming in countless ways, it has rarely been thought of as fundamentally shaped or moved by war, preparation for war, or the legacies of war.[5] The intertwining of war and the body has thus remained an object of limited and sporadic analytic attention for the social sciences, leading to a relative paucity of theoretical resources on how to formulate and think about such linkages.[6]

Feminist international relations

Within other domains across the academic division of labour, such as security studies, military history and international relations, the topic of war has principally been approached in terms of abstract causes, strategies and aims.

The Sociological Review, 62:S2, pp. 107–128 (2014), DOI: 10.1111/1467-954X.12194

Barkawi argues that war is decentred and fragmented as an object of inquiry across such domains and further that 'neither security studies nor IR inquire into, much less theorise, war as a set of social relations and processes . . . in a world made in no small measure by ongoing histories of organised violence, we lack a social science of war' (2011: 704). Such analysis has certainly tended to elide detailed consideration of embodiment and of the bodily violations and injuries at the dark heart of war. Jabri writes of international relations that bodies 'are not deemed to constitute the subject-matter of a mature discipline that concerns itself with the abstractions of the international system' (2006: 825). However, drawing particularly on scholarship from feminist international relations, Christine Sylvester has mapped out in a series of recent publications (Sylvester, 2011, 2012, 2013) an approach to the study of war that is more distinctly sociological than the traditional international relations approach to the topic. She asks: 'What if International Relations (IR) were to turn its usual view of war around and start not with states, fundamentalist organisations, strategies . . . and not with the aim of establishing the causes of war, as has so often been the case? What if we think of war as experience, as something ordinary people observe and suffer physically and emotionally depending on their locations?' (2012: 483). For Sylvester, ordinary people are crucial agents of, and experiential participants in, global geopolitics although they are overwhelmingly absent from mainstream accounts of international relations, politics and conflict.

The key focus of Sylvester's work, then, is to try and move beyond the abstractionism of IR to understand 'war as a realm of experience rather than a set of cause and correlates and abstract actors' (2013: 13). She argues that, as with heterosexuality, marriage or the family, war can be considered as an enduring social institution with multiple sites of authority and agency, an institution in which everyday people are involved in a myriad of ways – 'as combatants, yes, but also as mourners, protestors, enthusiasts, computer specialists, medical personnel, weapons designers, artists, novelists, journalists, refugees, portents, clergy, child soldiers, and school children' (2013: 4). Indeed, given the global nature of contemporary economic, migratory and media flows, Sylvester argues that few in today's interconnected world remain isolated from war's touch, that 'everyone has war experiences' (2013: 5) even if all these actors will 'experience the collective violence differently depending on their location, level and mode of involvement, gender, moral code, memories, and access to technologies' (2011: 125). War is far from exceptional in her understanding then and she argues that analysis needs to engage with this 'vast expanse of war's ordinary' (2013: 3), with the 'in-betweenness' of war rather than the predominant concern of IR with the reasons why war is declared or peace accords are signed.

Sylvester takes it as axiomatic that 'war is experienced through the body, a unit that has the agency to target and injure others in war and is also a target of war's capabilities' (2013: 5) and she argues that the body experiences war in terms of two key vectors – 'the physical and emotional connections with war that people live' (2013: 5). This provides the key organizing heuristic for her analytic overview of war as bodily experience. As well as the physical and emotional intimacies of war that occur when people are mutilated, raped, beaten and killed, she notes how people may be physically distant from the epicentres of violence but still intimately engaged with war in active, material and emotional ways, for example in rehabilitating the war-injured or in protesting, as well as how people may be distanced from war both physically and emotionally in their mundane lifeworld, only indirectly touched when they see war on television or learn about war as part of national curriculums (2012: 496). It is important to note that those physically located at the epicentres of war's violences also often force themselves, or are forced, to retain emotional control and distance (Ben-Ari, 1998; Hinton, 1998). MacLeish (2013: 132) relatedly describes the broad military labour of *not feeling* as 'the self-conscious mastery of affect, emotion, and physical pain by soldiers and spouses, and the institutionally imposed haze of medication, emotional and bodily discipline, and compelled endurance'.

Sylvester also takes as axiomatic several key insights from feminist studies of war and militarization.[7] First, that a consideration of women's lives has often troubled commonplace understandings of war such that, for example, it may be more accurate experientially to speak of a 'continuum of violence', and of gender relations underpinned by violence, rather than any clear demarcation between times of war and peace (Cockburn, 2009). But secondly, that women's experiences of war occur in a variety of complex ways – certainly as the actual victims of injury, killing and sexualized violence (Olujic, 1998; Leatherman, 2011), and through the discursive invocation of their bodies as being a primary target that militarized masculinity seeks to protect (Zarkov, 2007); but also as workers centrally involved in war efforts via the armaments industry or medical rehabilitation as well as being the often underacknowledged providers of the emotional and sexual labour that underpins military life (Enloe, 2000); or indeed as female fighters in the paramilitaries and armed opposition groups of 'new wars' (Coulter, 2009; MacKenzie, 2012), and increasingly in Western state militaries (Mathers, 2013). Women's bodily experiences then, though rarely credited with historical importance in the study of war, are certainly not ontologically outside the 'war matrix' (Jabri, 2010). Moreover, it is the detailed examination of the myriad war experiences of both men and women that is central to Sylvester's project to 'pull the bodies and experiences of war out of entombments created by theories operating at higher levels of analysis and into the open as crucial elements of war' (2012: 503).[8]

A particularly prominent motif of many of the ethnographic and literary accounts of war experience that Sylvester draws upon is the complex and shifting trajectories and fluidity of experiences in wartime. She notes how, particularly at the everyday level of the personal politics of survival and coping, wars are often experienced through a complex and unruly range of interrupted identifications and tactical adjustments of allegiance, embodied 'masquerades' and sophisticated concealments of ambiguous identity, and the fluid negotiation of whatever circumscribed agentic possibilities emerge fleetingly and unexpectedly

The Sociological Review, 62:S2, pp. 107–128 (2014), DOI: 10.1111/1467-954X.12194

from within the chaos of war.[9] For Sylvester, then, at the heart of war there is often a radical mismatch that we are only beginning to understand between, on the one hand, people's actual embodied experiences of conflict and, on the other, institutional myths of identity, masculinity and glory in war as well as the sophisticated arguments Western theorists have often constructed about war's prosecution. She argues that a crucial task is to investigate in much more detail the myriad and often contradictory ways in which people in multiple positions experience and narrate the interruptions and changes to their lives before, during and after experiencing war. It is through analytic attention to such embodied lives that we may better come 'to know war as a comprehensive whole that has a teeming life alongside and sometimes in defiance of what statesmen, militaries, strategists and IR specialists say about it' (Sylvester, 2012: 503).

Embodied practices of war

Alongside such work within feminist International Relations, a related analytic agenda has been developed in recent sociologically informed scholarship by McSorley (2012, 2013) as well as in ethnographic work on warfighting by Hockey (2009, 2013) and Higate (2013) and medical anthropology concerned in particular with the veterans of recent US wars (MacLeish, 2013; Wool, 2013). It is the elements of this scholarship that can contribute towards developing an embodied sociology of war that will be considered in the following section.

Shaw (2005: 40–41) has argued that 'the defect of most social theory of war and militarism is . . . that it has not considered war as practice, i.e. what people actually do in war'. For McSorley (2012), one key way to attempt to address this omission is via a more explicit analytic focus upon the *embodied* practices through which war and militarism take place. Although, as Sylvester notes, the structures of feeling and lived experiences that constitute war as a social institution are multiple and diverse, the development of soldiers' bodies and warfighting ability within militaries, and the wider resonances of these martial body projects across the social field, is clearly one highly significant dimension of the making and doing of war. As MacLeish (2013: 11) notes, 'The body's unruly matter is war's most necessary and necessarily expendable raw material . . . the wars in Iraq and Afghanistan could not carry on without the physical presence of tens of thousands of such bodies'. Relatedly, Basham (2013: 140) argues that considering how 'soldiers perform and experience war and war preparedness may go some way towards helping us to think through how the geopolitics of war materialises'.

The embodied practices of war thus include the systems of basic training and further discipline through which the soldier's skills, capacities, reflexes and habits are inculcated, developed and indeed resisted (Newlands, 2013). Such an analytic focus upon the production of martial bodies has a certain, if modest, analytic history.[10] McNeill (1997), for example, has examined how the practices of drill and marching together in time foster 'muscular bonding' and have been central to the creation of military 'esprit de corps' across history. Foucault (1977) has famously explored the military as a foundational laboratory of disciplinary power where the docile bodies of recruits are subject to, and ultimately subject themselves to, various practices of corporeal transformation through which specific martial dispositions and competencies become inculcated. As Higate (2013: 140) notes, the ultimate aim of this embodied military training 'is to reconfigure body-selves towards the functional imperatives of military objectives'.

Drawing on ethnographic data, Hockey (2013) has explored the ensemble of corporeal competencies and sensory practices that infantry troops develop and deploy as they go about their work. He details the skilful coordinated choreography of patrol, its acute sense of communal time and secure collective movement; the endless weapons drills that establish a pre-reflective relationship with the rifle, so ingrained that it is ultimately thought and felt an extension of the body; and the haptic adaptations to nature that foster a capacity to 'soldier on' as adversity, cold and fatigue seize bodies. In particular, he points to how the senses become militarized, attuned particularly to the discernment of enmity and threat. The development of suspicious sensory practices occurs across the sensorium and includes heightened olfactory awareness of lingering smells that might signal enemy presence, auditory alertness to unusual changes in the mundane soundscape such as uncanny silence, and a cynical way of seeing that is constantly monitoring and parsing terrain in terms of potential protection and peril.

Hockey thus argues that infantry display a specific kind of corporeal engagement with the world and come to inhabit a very particular 'somatic mode of attention' (Csordas, 1993) that is encapsulated, and sometimes specifically summonsed, by the occupational exclamation 'switch on'. For Hockey, 'this single utterance invokes the embodied world particular to infantry' (2013: 102). This vigilant sensory apprehension of the world becomes such an ingrained part of the soldierly habitus that militarized reflexes to potential threat are capable of being unthinkingly elicited in pressurized situations, as well as being incredibly durable over time. Higate (2013) notes how the work of privatized security contractors relies upon the persistence of this mode of situational awareness and the embodied skill-set developed in prior military training. The increasingly important global institution of private military contracting thus fundamentally depends upon the tenacity of this sensory practice, as well as upon cravings for the intensity and exhilaration of professional warfighting that are often the emotional sediment underpinning the desire to continue a particular form of corporeal career beyond military life.

Relatedly, Wool (2013), in an ethnographic analysis of the transformations of the lives of US soldiers following their intense experiences of the wars in Iraq and Afghanistan, notes the inability to 'switch off' upon return from combat and associated severe difficulties in reorientation to the rhythms of regular life. Developing an analysis that stresses in particular the importance of movement in wartime as a fundamental part of making sense of the world, she argues that the experience of being and moving in a warzone can affect deep ontological transformations that irrevocably alter the experience of being and moving anywhere: 'These [experiences] endure, becoming part of the sensibility of all spaces soldiers see and move through . . . this sensibility is not strictly experienced just as a transformation of their own bodies, senses, and movements; it is also a transformation of space itself . . . into lines of sight, routes of escape, pockets of potential danger' (2013: 17). As such, post-combat the mundane material world can become a newly tentative place as 'a new experiential knowledge of the vulnerability of solid objects, like bodies, cars, and buildings, has transformed the experience of seeing, feeling, and moving in the world' (2013: 19). As an alternative to the currently dominant medical frameworks for understanding post-combat struggles in terms of psychic discontinuity and post-traumatic stress disorder, Wool draws attention to the texture and continuity of embodied experience, stressing that it is sensing bodies in motion that encounter the demands of post-combat reorientation and reworlding. She argues that such an 'analytics of movement offers a sense of the vertiginous new worlds soldiers inhabit, which suggests ontology, rather than pathology, as the ground for understanding the matter of US soldiers' being after combat' (2013: 1).

These bodily practices of discipline, sensing and moving that produce persistent soldierly being also crucially co-exist alongside military systems of bodily maintenance and care, as well as within a wider constellation of social relations and networks of care-giving and intimacy in which the soldier is embedded. In MacLeish's ethnography of everyday life in the military community of Foot Hood, Texas, he thus argues that 'soldiers' bodies are not end points for power but rather places in which it abides and transforms, 'relays' in which it moves on to other bodies and still others' (2013: 13). MacLeish understands the soldier's body not as the bounded focus for an analysis of war but as a crucial 'stepping-off point for understanding the affective currents and exchanges in which soldiers are enmeshed: *the lived affects of war*' (2013: 13). The soldier's bodily reality is ultimately of being invested with the power to destroy other bodies, and of concomitant exposure to forces that can extinguish their own life at a moment's notice. MacLeish argues that there is no really meaningful narrative into which the constant confrontation with these unceremonious facts of death and destruction can be easily contained, save the brute stoicism of soldiering on. As such, the resonances of these embodied realities of constant exposure to harm and stoical perseverance begin to bleed into, to reshape and define, the wider bonds of intimacy and care within which the soldier is enmeshed.

Drawing in particular upon Butler's (2009) analysis of the always precarious, susceptible and fundamentally interdependent nature of human embodiment,[11] MacLeish argues that vulnerability 'spreads outwards from the soldier to the persons and institutions linked to him . . . as a sort of productive contamination that is less a strain on or disruption of attachment than it is the stuff of attachment itself' (2013: 16–17). Moreover, the stresses and vulnerabilities that families and communities absorb during the physical separations that tours of duty entail do not end when such tours finish, and they are not easily reversible.

For MacLeish then, the soldier's embodied experiences resonate powerfully through, and reshape, wider structures of feeling in which love 'both domesticates and relays outwards the shock and awe of war' (2013: 178). In his account, war moves 'by lateral and incidental routes – not just through an IED or an insurgent's bullet, but in a nightmare, a cold sweat, a doctor's suspicion, a lover's incomprehension, or a bureaucrat's obstinacy – to take shape in affects: in leaps, increments, sedimented layers, and sudden upheavals nestled among other concerns, stresses and relations' (2013: 13).

The wider resonances of soldiers' embodied worlds are also the focus of attention in my analysis of the importance of footage recorded from helmet-mounted camcorders in recent public mediations of the Afghanistan conflict (McSorley, 2012). In stark contrast to the abstraction and radical disembodiment of the mediascape of hi-tech 'virtual war' (Ignatieff, 2001), soldiers' helmetcam footage provides the viewer with a lo-fi boots-on-the-ground immersion into the rhythmic kinaesthetics of patrol, the domestic routines and intimate touch of mundane life on base, and the visceral dramas and bodily risks of 'contact'. As such it offers the viewer an invitation to 'switch on' to a specific somatic mode of attention and a seductive cultural enrolment into particular militarized forms of sensory conduct. I argue that the helmet-cammed Western soldier has thus become a key assemblage in the emergence of a particular contemporary regime of 'somatic war', and further that this has become a dominant 'regime of sensation' through which the Afghanistan war is currently being experienced by wider Western audiences. Soldiers' bodily rhythms and sensory practices have become a key idiom through which wider public apprehensions of the war are being entrained, and understandings of the aims and rectitude of military conduct are being shaped and negotiated.

This is not to say that a particular politics can be straightforwardly read from this regime of 'somatic war' – its resonances are complex, numerous and at times contradictory. Certainly when bodies are not seen or felt to be put on the line, warfare may be exposed to accusations of inauthenticity and moral hypocrisy (Ignatieff, 2001; Shaw, 2005), and this may be particularly important in a case such as Afghanistan where the war is protracted and the war aims are confused and contested. 'Somatic war' may thus primarily be an idiom through which such a conflict becomes re-enchanted – 'given a moral or expressive meaning beyond the merely instrumental' (Behnke, 2006: 938; Coker, 2004).[12] The emphasis here upon the thrill, daring and vulnerability of soldiering may predominantly act as a legitimation for the continuation of the war. However, the increased salience of bodily risks and injuries in this regime of sensation may also be felt in certain constituencies as an underlying symptom of the wider degeneracy and futility of the continuing war. Far from a legitimation, then, it may be laying down the emotional sediments of eventual withdrawal from a protracted campaign. However it is felt, I argue that it is predominantly in the various resonances and intensities of this regime of 'somatic war' that the meaning of the conflict in Afghanistan has recently been made most perceptible and palpable.[13]

Relatedly, I have argued that the analysis of militarism needs to be attentive to its embodied, sensory and affective dimensions (McSorley, 2013). Classic discussions of militarism often exhibit a cognitivist bias in terms of their emphasis upon specific militaristic attitudes, beliefs or ideologies.[14] However, as Lutz (2009) notes, despite the largely uncritical acceptance in the US of what she terms the 'military normal', people rarely articulate militarist beliefs in any great detail or as a clearly thought through set of rational principles concerning the necessity of war readiness and the legitimacy of the state having vast military force. Rather it is often through mundane embodied practices and idioms that a broad and subtle form of militarism assumes an implicitness and becomes something not explicitly thought but simply felt to be habitually right, often from an early age.[15] In an analysis of how the recent military-supported 'Too Fat to Fight' campaign lobbied for changes in US schoolchildren's diets, Burridge and McSorley (2013) argue that there is a pervasive militarization of the body that operates across multiple constituencies and domains in everyday life, from fashion and diet to leisure and fitness, and that often resonates with wider pacific, neo-liberal discourses of self-actualization, thrill and body image. It is through such everyday practices that broad recruitment into a particular 'embodied community' (Basham, 2013) involved in supporting the global activities of war and war preparedness may take place. In contrast to a simple post-military society thesis (Shaw, 1991) that emphasizes the contemporary reduction in directly conscripted bodies then, many Western states have been marked by a profound remilitarization in the last decade, a widespread mobilization that has often been fundamentally embodied and affective (see, eg, Massumi, 2005; Ó Tuathail, 2003).

The body of work outlined above thus develops an analysis of war and militarism as prosecuted, lived and reproduced through a panoply of embodied practices, movements, resonances and regimes of sensation. Taken together with Sylvester's emphasis upon war as a wide-ranging realm of experience, it also begins to constitute a conceptual tool kit, offering sensitizing concepts for the task of further fleshing out a more embodied sociology of war. Such an analytic undertaking may seek to further develop the understanding of different conflicts via the comparative analysis of their distinctive methods of injury and 'woundscapes' (Terry, 2009), modes of somatic engagement and flow, affective resonances, body pedagogics and the inculcation of militarist structures of feeling. For example, recent forms of predatory conflict that Kaldor (2012) has categorized as 'new wars'[16] have often been characterized by, and constituted through, specific embodied experiences such as the massive displacement of peoples, confinement to camps, child soldiering and visceral assaults on bodily integrity. Mbembe (2003) notes that recent conflicts in Africa, where many postcolonial states' monopolies of violence have been fundamentally eroded, have been characterized by 'technologies of destruction that have become more tactile, more anatomical and sensorial' (2003: 34), including publically visible and admonitory assaults such as the severing of limbs and the production of abject bodies through campaigns of sexualized violence (Diken and Laustsen, 2005; see also, eg, Baaz and Stern, 2009; Leatherman, 2011).

Indeed, anthropological literature on collective violence in Burundi and Rwanda (eg Malkki, 1995; Taylor, 1999) has relatedly emphasized how acts of atrocity have often been perpetrated and narrated in very particular ways, involving the brutalization of specific body parts, that are not merely instrumental but expressive and productive of a dehumanizing discourse that connects putative physical with moral difference. Appadurai (2006) thus argues that, particularly in an uncertain and globalized world, much collective violence against minorities should not be understood simply as a response to pre-existing differences in identity, but rather as a specifically embodied and intimate idiom through which opposing, antagonistic identities are produced and ambivalent and uncertain identities are rendered invalid and dangerous to hold. Furthermore, he argues that the excessive violation of the body of the victim that often characterizes such violence can be understood as an explicit classificatory attempt to establish or 'unmask' the underlying 'reality' of ethnic status: 'Large-scale bodily violence becomes a forensic means for establishing sharp lines between normally mixed identities. Bodily violence in the name of ethnicity becomes the vivisectionist tool to establish the reality behind the mask. And of course, such violence inevitably confirms its conjecture, for the dead, disabled, or deconstructed body of the suspect always confirms the suspicion of its treachery' (2006: 89). For Appadurai then, close analysis of embodiment is absolutely critical to illuminate an understanding of particular regimes of contemporary war and collective violence.

As a further and very distinct example of contemporary conflict, practices such as the increased use by the US of unmanned drones in locations including the Yemen, Somalia and the Federally Administered Tribal Areas of Pakistan represent a significant transformation of war characterized by the asymmetric instantiation of myriad mobile zones of violent exception attached to individual bodies (Gregory, 2011; Chamayou, 2013). While much debate around such practices has focused upon interrogating the techno-cultural apparatus and the particular legal armature through which specific bodies can come to be identified as 'legitimate' targets for killing in particular spaces, it is also crucial to note that the reality on the ground in the areas where such operations take place is an experience of embodied terror that is far from delimited. Rather the production of drone-fearing bodies is manifest and widespread in such areas (International Human Rights and Conflict Resolution Clinic, 2012; Amnesty International, 2013). In addition, the embodied experience of drone operators themselves is not simply marked by the detachment of physical distance, but is rather punctuated by disruptive new mediated intimacies (Gregory, 2011) and by the schizoid experience of daily de/compression between modes of war and peace (Asaro, 2013; Brant, 2013; Williams, 2011).

Clearly then different wars are fundamentally characterized by distinct modes of bodily injury, somatic engagement and rhythm, regimes of sensation, embodied militarisms and so on. Moreover, embodied experiences are distinctive for,

The Sociological Review, 62:S2, pp. 107–128 (2014), DOI: 10.1111/1467-954X.12194

and productive of, many different social groups within particular conflicts.[17] A key direction for future elaboration in the analysis of war and its various instantiations, transformations and reproductions will thus be paying further analytic attention to this centrality of embodiment and to the diverse embodied experiences of multiple constituencies in wartime.

Conclusion

War has been a hugely significant factor in the shaping of modernity and modern social life and it shows few signs of declining in importance or intensity in the 21st century. It is violently destructive, productive and protean, 'a field of contingent unmaking and remaking in which familiar or taken-for-granted objects of knowledge and structures of meaning are overwhelmed and trans-formed' (Brighton, 2011: 102). As such, Holmqvist (2013) asks how are we to study its excessive force? The necessarily incomplete answer that this paper has advanced has been to suggest a plural and corporeal turn in war studies. For, as Scarry (1985) notes, war is never simply politics by any other means. It is politics incarnate, politics written on and experienced through the thinking, feeling bodies of countless men and women. Indeed, for Scarry, war is 'the most radically embodying event in which human beings ever collectively participate' (1985: 71). Understood as such, war's force is a fundamentally bodily making and unmaking of the world. It is via the occupation and transformation of myriad bodies in numerous ways from exhilaration to mutilation that war itself is made.

The embodied dimensions of war have been subject to a series of significant erasures within sociological, academic and wider discourse. Indeed, in an attempt to continue the legitimation of war as a viable instrument of policy despite its inevitable degeneracy, various bodies at war have historically been subject to a series of disavowals within prominent military and strategic tradi-tions of thought and allied media and political discourses. This paper argues that embodiment cannot be understood as an insignificant or epiphenomenal dimension of war. War is an enduring crucible of social change, whose lived affects are felt and modulated widely, and it needs to be traced and analysed in terms of its fundamental, diverse and often brutal forms of embodied experience and apprehension.

Sylvester argues that it is through the embodied trajectories of multiple lives and deaths that the constantly shape-shifting but enduringly injurious 'transhistorical and transcultural social institution of war' (2013: 5) lives and breeds. An important theme for future elaboration is understanding not just how war is multiply written upon the body, but how war is continually reiterated through a range of embodied continuities and resonances, such as the corporeal career and cravings of the private military contractor (Higate, 2013), as well as tracing how transformations and differences between wars may further be understood in terms of their distinctive modes of embodied experience and apprehension. Furthermore, a focus on embodiment and lived experience brings to the fore that war is fundamentally not apart from the rest of social life. The work discussed here has highlighted embodied and sensory practices and regimes that bleed across, resonate through, and fundamentally blur the spatial, temporal and ontological distinctions between war and peace.

If war was ever really distant from liberal Western societies, the events that September 2001 inaugurated have made such a position appear increasingly untenable. As McDonald (2013: 1) notes, the violence that once appeared to be contained by key dimensions of modern society is now significantly more fluid, fundamentally integrated into the global and technological connectivities and flows of late modernity. For Hardt and Negri (2004: 14) the current situation can be defined as one where 'the limits of war are rendered indeterminate – both spatially and temporally', leading to the emergence of 'the everywhere war' (Gregory, 2011) and 'the forever war' (Filkins, 2009). Although war has histori-cally not been a core concern for a sociological imagination whose gaze has been directed upon an assumed already pacific state, sociology can no longer avoid a reckoning with this most pressing of concerns if it is to retain a claim to provide relevant critical analysis of the key forces shaping the 21st century.

While sociology has not been a good interlocutor of war, I have argued in this paper that the body has always known war, and that it is to the corporeal that we should turn in an attempt to develop a language to speak of its myriad violences and its socially generative force. None of this is straightforward. The difficulties of talking, and theorizing, about violence are well documented (Das, 2006; Scarry, 1985). For example, work on the intergenerational transmission of war-related trauma (Cho, 2008; Kidron, 2009), and on veteran experience has consistently pointed not only to the significant and persistent nature of the corporeal aftermaths and emotional inheritances of war, but also of a funda-mental struggle to be able to adequately comprehend, and articulate, these effects and affects of war. Bodies carry war in ways that are at once intensely felt and intractable, and yet seemingly unstable and unknowable. Developing a language supple enough to track this ontology of warfare is not simply an analytic challenge, but is also often an existential struggle. Despite its historical aversion to considering issues of war, sociology is nonetheless potentially well placed to contribute to such an undertaking given its significant recent record of thinking through the significance of embodiment in a way that attempts to combine a concern with questions of cultural and institutional reproduction, lived experience, and political power. This article invites sociology to extend its imaginative horizon to rethink the crucial and enduring social institution of war as a broad array of fundamentally embodied practices, regimes and experiences.

Notes

1 Butler relatedly argues that embodiment is both the very condition of possibility of our inter-dependent human flourishing and simultaneously of our vulnerability to violence and to war:

'the skin and the flesh expose us to the gaze of others, but also to touch, and to violence, and bodies put us at risk of becoming the agency and instrument of all these as well' (2004: 26).

2 Malešević (2010a) argues that an alternative 'bellicose tradition in classical sociology' fell out of favour as the 20th century progressed.

3 McDonald (2013) notes the significance of somatic apprehension for various contemporary transformations in violence and war. For example, he argues that Jihadi testimony often refers to the revelation of hidden meanings through embodied encounters with the 'extraordinary', and points to the somatic apprehension of intensely repetitive and decontextualized violence as a principal medium for apprehending this 'reality' of the world in terms of holy war. He points to the integration of the Abu Ghraib victims into the violent pornographic imaginary of their torturers, and the wider mediated and affective flows of this process, as a further example of the complex ways in which various zones of private experience and war increasingly bleed into each other. For McDonald, the embodied apprehension of distant violence and the types of publics and imaginaries constructed around it are thus increasingly important encounters in a world where the old borders established to contain war no longer hold.

4 For example, within canonical texts on the body such as Turner (1984) *The Body and Society*, O'Neill (1985) *Five Bodies*, Featherstone, Hepworth and Turner (eds) (1991) *The Body: Social Process and Cultural Theory*, Shilling (1993) *The Body and Social Theory*, the topic of war is given minimal attention. Recent anthologies such as Fraser and Greco (eds) (2004) *The Body: A Reader* and The Aberdeen Body Group's (2004) edited five-volume set *The Body: Critical Concepts* continue this trend, excerpts from Scarry's (1985) *The Body in Pain* being the only work that addresses war in both collections.

5 The significant role for body studies of Elias's (1978) work on the civilizing process in Europe was one significant influence in establishing this baseline image of a contemporary pacific, civilized body.

6 Indeed, it is not from the social sciences but from autobiography and fiction that the embodied experiences of war have emerged most clearly as a salient and important theme of public discussion. The elegiac reconstruction of the horrors of past wars in war literature and written testimonies haunted the 20th century and continues to do so into the 21st. While the reasons underpinning such war writing are complex and plural – catharsis, 'truth-telling', a duty that those who can write do so for those who cannot, an attempt to impose some verbal order on that which may otherwise seem incomprehensible (McLoughlin, 2009) – such writing has generally been much more attuned to exploring the precarious phenomenological status of all bodily life in wartime rather than attempting to understand war in terms of its causes, strategies or within the telos of future policy. A significant motif of much war writing is that it regularly foregrounds its own inadequacy, the impossibility of adequate sense-making in the disorientating fog of war, the futility of representation faced with the war's overwhelming reality. As such, the search for some meaningful grounding has often led such war writing to focus upon 'the physical ordeal and the indignities war imposes on the body' (Rau, 2010: 3).

7 See, for example, Cockburn (2007); Cohn (2013); Enloe (2000); Kronsell and Svedberg (2012); Parpart and Zalewski (2008); Sjoberg (2013); Sjoberg and Via (2010).

8 It is important to note that, although there is a principled rejection of much of the theoretical abstraction with which war has historically been understood in Sylvester's work, she in no way adheres to a naïve empiricism that views certain experiences as the ultimate location of the true meaning of war, or asserts the unproblematic existence of simple translations between war experience and war knowledge. Rather the category and lens of experience is understood as an analytic and methodological reorientation, one that invites the narrow focus of war research to be widened to attend to war's multiple centres of agency, everyday lives and social relations, as part of a 'process of opening doors for the ordinary to enter into standards of knowledge and comprehension' (2013: 99).

9 These include, for example, the regular switching of sides of combatants in many conflicts, the false claiming of injured or victim status to access humanitarian resources (Utas, 2005), negotiating the 'choiceless decision' to become a female fighter rather than embracing passive

victimhood (Coulter, 2009), and tenacious emotional and physical refusals to accept the imposed terms of 'bare life' (Courtemanche, 2003; Shilling, 2008). See also McSorley (2015) on the precarious negotiations necessitated by a condition of permanent disruption, uncertainty and anxiety in the everyday interaction order in wartime Chechnya.

10 See, for example, Woodward (1998), Lande (2007). As Hockey (2013) notes, the fact that there are relatively few studies that attempt to grapple with directly embodied material in researching soldiers' lives is largely due to the positivist nature of most military sociology.

11 For Butler, 'the body is a social phenomenon: it is exposed to others, vulnerable by definition' (2009: 33).

12 Many war films narrate tales of re-enchantment, where the purpose of war becomes redefined in increasingly existential or self-referential terms, such as a fight to save one's own soldiers by rescuing the left behind, supporting the besieged, or salvaging honour for the fallen (Wetta and Novelli, 2003).

13 Of course, it is also crucial to remember that this regime of 'somatic war' is not a rendering of conflict as a wide-ranging medium of embodied experience. It is decisively linked to the embodied experiences and vulnerabilities of Western soldiers, rather than to those of other combatants, civilians, victims or others touched by the war.

14 For example, Mills (1956: 222) writes of a 'military metaphysics' among the power elite – 'the cast of mind that defines international reality as basically military'. Mann (1987: 35) defines militarism as 'a set of attitudes and social practices which regards war and the preparation for war as a normal and desirable social activity'.

15 As Scarry (1985: 109) notes, once ingrained 'the body's loyalty to these political realms is likely to be . . . more permanently there, less easily shed, than those disembodied forms of patriotism that exist in verbal habits or in thoughts about one's national identity. The political identity of the body is usually learned unconsciously, effortlessly and very early'.

16 For Kaldor (2012), new wars are degenerate and predatory social formations where a range of forces – decaying state armies, paramilitaries, mercenaries, criminal gangs – sustain themselves politically and economically particularly through the spread of violence against 'enemy' civilian groups and accumulation by dispossession. Her analysis has been extremely influential, if contentious both in terms of its normative underpinnings and its analysis of how such wars are experienced and understood by its participants (see, eg, Drake, 2007; Malešević 2010b; Chan, 2011). Gregory (2010: 169) cautions that the entire representational and analytic opposition between uncivilized 'new wars' and hi-tech Western wars may sustain a rhetorical privileging of the latter as more rational, modern, surgical and ultimately more legitimate, thus foreshortening critical examination of the bodily mutilation and lethality that is necessarily at the heart of all wars including hi-tech Western wars.

17 Notably of course, war will consist of very different embodied experiences for those positioned on different 'sides' of the conflict or those caught in the middle, such that their understandings may even be of radically different wars – of insurgency and counterinsurgency for example.

References

Aberdeen Body Group (eds), (2004), *The Body: Critical Concepts in Sociology*, London: Routledge.

Amnesty International, (2013), *Will I Be Next? US Drone Strikes in Pakistan*, London: Amnesty International Publications.

Anderson, B., (2010), 'Morale and the affective geographies of the "war on terror" ' *Cultural Geographies*, 17 (2): 219–236.

Appadurai, A., (2006), *Fear of Small Numbers*, Durham, NC: Duke University Press.

Asaro, P., (2013), 'The labor of surveillance and bureaucratized killing: new subjectivities of military drone operators', *Social Semiotics*, 23 (2): 196–224.

Baaz, M. E. and Stern, M., (2009), 'Why do soldiers rape?' *International Studies Quarterly*, 53: 495–518.

The Sociological Review, 62:S2, pp. 107–128 (2014), DOI: 10.1111/1467-954X.12194

Barkawi, T., (2011), 'From war to security: security studies, the wider agenda and the fate of the study of war', *Millennium*, 39 (3): 701–716.

Basham, V., (2013), *War, Identity and the Liberal State*, London: Routledge.

Behnke, A., (2006), 'The re-enchantment of war in popular culture', *Millennium*, 34: 937–949.

Ben-Ari, E., (1998), *Mastering Soldiers: Conflict, Emotions and the Enemy in an Israeli Military Unit*, New York: Berghahn Books.

Benjamin, W., (1969), *Illuminations*, edited by H. Arendt, New York: Schocken Books.

Bousquet, A., (2012), 'War', in E. Amenta, K. Nash and A. Scott (eds), *The Wiley-Blackwell Companion to Political Sociology*, 180–189, Oxford: Wiley-Blackwell.

Brant, G., (2013), *Grounded*, London: Oberon Books.

Brighton, S., (2011), 'Three propositions on the phenomenology of war', *International Political Sociology*, 5 (1): 101–105.

Burridge, J. and McSorley, K., (2013), 'Too fat to fight? Obesity, bio-politics and the militarisation of children's bodies', in K. McSorley (ed.), *War and the Body: Militarisation, Practice and Experience*, 62–77. London: Routledge.

Butler, J., (2004), *Precarious Life: The Powers of Mourning and Violence*, London: Verso.

Butler, J., (2009), *Frames of War*, London: Verso.

Chamayou, G., (2013), *Théorie du drone*, Paris: La Fabrique.

Chan, S., (2011), 'On the uselessness of new wars theory', in C. Sylvester (ed.), *Experiencing War*, London: Routledge.

Cho, G., (2008), *Haunting the Korean Diaspora*, Minnesota: University of Minnesota Press.

Clausewitz, C. von, (1976), *On War*, Princeton, NJ: Princeton University Press.

Cockburn, C., (2007), *From Where We Stand: War, Women's Activism and Feminist Analysis*, London: Zed.

Cockburn, C., (2009), 'The continuum of violence', in U. Linke and D. Smith (eds), *Cultures of Fear*, 158–173, London: Pluto Press.

Cohn, C., (1987), 'Sex and death in the rational world of defence intellectuals', *Signs*, 12 (4): 687–718.

Cohn, C. (ed.), (2013), *Women and Wars*, Cambridge: Polity Press.

Coker, C., (2004), *The Future of War: The Re-enchantment of War in the Twenty-first Century*, Oxford: Blackwell.

Collins, R., (1975), *Conflict Sociology*, New York: Academic Press.

Collins, R., (1986), *Weberian Sociological Theory*, Cambridge: Cambridge University Press.

Coulter, C., (2009), *Bush Wives and Girl Soldiers: Women's Lives through War and Peace in Sierra Leone*, Ithaca, NY: Cornell University Press.

Courtemanche, G., (2003), *A Sunday at the Pool in Kigali*, London: Canongate.

Csordas, T., (1993), 'Somatic modes of attention', *Cultural Anthropology*, 8 (2): 135–156.

Cuomo, C., (1996), 'War is not just an event: reflections on the significance of everyday violence', *Hypatia* 11 (4): 30–45.

Das, V., (2006), *Life and Words: Violence and the Descent into the Ordinary*, Berkeley, CA: University of California Press.

Diken, B. and Laustsen, C., (2005), 'Becoming abject: rape as a weapon of war', *Body and Society*, 11 (1): 111–128.

Drake, M., (2007), 'Sociology and new wars in the era of globalisation', *Sociology Compass*, 1/2: 637–650.

Elias, N., (1978), *The Civilising Process*, Oxford: Blackwell.

Enloe, C., (2000), *Bananas, Beaches and Bases*, Berkeley, CA: University of California Press.

Featherstone, M., Hepworth, M. and Turner, B. (eds), (1991), *The Body: Social Process and Cultural Theory*, London: Sage.

Filkins, D., (2009), *The Forever War*, London: Vintage.

Foucault, M., (1977), *Discipline and Punish*, London: Penguin.

Fraser, M. and Greco, M. (eds), (2004), *The Body: A Reader*, London: Routledge.

Garrett-Peltier, H., (2011), *The Job Opportunity Cost of War*, available at: http://costsofwar.org/sites/default/files/Garrett-PeltierJobs.pdf (accessed November 2013).

Giddens, A., (1987), *The Nation-State and Violence*, Cambridge: Polity Press.

Gregory, D., (2010), 'War and peace', *Transactions of the Institute of British Geographers*, NS 35: 154–186.

Gregory, D., (2011), 'From a view to a kill: drones and late modern war', *Theory, Culture and Society*, 28 (7–8), 188–215.

Hardt, M. and Negri, A., (2004), *Multitude: War and Democracy in the Age of Empire*, New York: Penguin.

Higate, P., (2013), ' "Switching on" for cash: the private militarised security contractor', in K. McSorley (ed.), *War and the Body: Militarization, Practice and Experience*, 106–127, London: Routledge.

Hinton, A., (1998), 'Why did you kill? The Cambodian genocide and the dark side of face and honour', *The Journal of Asian Studies*, 57 (1): 93–122.

Hockey, J., (2009), ' "Switch on": sensory work in the infantry', *Work, Employment and Society*, 23 (3): 477–493.

Hockey, J. (2013), 'On patrol: the embodied phenomenology of infantry', in K. McSorley (ed.), *War and the Body: Militarization, Practice and Experience*, 93–105, London: Routledge.

Holmqvist, C., (2013), 'Undoing war: war ontologies and the materiality of drone warfare', *Millennium*, 41 (3): 535–552.

Ignatieff, M., (2001), *Virtual War*, London: Vintage.

International Human Rights and Conflict Resolution Clinic, (2012), *Living under drones*, available at http://www.livingunderdrones.org (accessed November 2013).

Jabri, V., (2006), 'Shock and awe: power and the resistance of art', *Millennium*, 34 (3): 819–839.

Jabri, V., (2010), *War and the Transformation of Global Politics*, 2nd edn, London: Palgrave.

Joas, H., (2003), *War and Modernity*, Cambridge: Polity Press.

Kaldor, M., (2012), *New and Old Wars*, 3rd edn, Cambridge: Polity Press.

Kidron, C., (2009), 'Silent legacies of trauma', in N. Argenti and C. Schramm (eds), *Remembering Violence: Anthropological Perspectives on Intergenerational Transmission*, 185–220, New York: Berghahn Books.

Kronsell, A. and Svedberg, E., (2012), *Making Gender, Making War*, London: Routledge.

Lande, B., (2007), 'Breathing like a soldier: culture incarnate', *The Sociological Review*, 55 (s1): 95–108.

Leatherman, J., (2011), *Sexual Violence and Armed Conflict*, Cambridge: Polity Press.

Lutz, C., (2009), 'The military normal', in Network of Concerned Anthropologists (eds), *The Counter-Counterinsurgency Manual*, 23–38, Chicago: Prickly Paradigm Press.

MacKenzie, M., (2012), *Female Soldiers in Sierra Leone*, New York: New York University Press.

MacLeish, K., (2013), *Making War at Fort Hood*, Princeton, NJ: Princeton University Press.

Malešević, S., (2010a), 'How pacifist were the founding fathers? War and violence in classical sociology', *European Journal of Social Theory*, 13 (2): 193–212.

Malešević, S., (2010b), *The Sociology of War and Violence*, Cambridge: Cambridge University Press.

Malkki, L., (1995), *Purity and Exile: Violence, Memory, and National Cosmology among Hutu Refugees in Tanzania*, Chicago: University of Chicago Press.

Mann, M., (1986), *The Sources of Social Power I*, Cambridge: Cambridge University Press.

Mann, M., (1987), 'The roots and contradictions of modern militarism', *New Left Review*, 162 (March–April): 35–50.

Mann, M., (1993), *The Sources of Social Power II*, Cambridge: Cambridge University Press.

Massumi, B., (2005), 'Fear (the spectrum said)', *Positions*, 13 (1): 31–48.

Mathers, J., (2013), 'Women in state military forces', in C. Cohn (ed.), *Women and Wars*, 124–145, Cambridge: Polity Press.

Mbembe, A., (2003), 'Necropolitics', *Public Culture*, 47 (1): 11–40.

McDonald, K., (2013), *Our Violent World*, London: Palgrave.

The Sociological Review, 62:S2, pp. 107–128 (2014), DOI: 10.1111/1467-954X.12194

McLoughlin, K., (2009), 'War and words', in K. McLoughlin (ed.), *The Cambridge Companion to War Writing*, 15–24, Cambridge: Cambridge University Press.

McNeill, W., (1997), *Keeping Together in Time: Dance and Drill in Human History*, Cambridge, MA: Harvard University Press.

McSorley, K., (2012), 'Helmetcams, militarized sensation and "somatic war" ', *Journal of War and Culture Studies*, 5 (1): 46–62.

McSorley, K., (2013), 'War and the body', in K. McSorley (ed.), *War and the Body: Militarisation, Practice and Experience*, 1–32, London: Routledge.

McSorley, K., (2015), 'The fangs behind the mask: everyday life in wartime Chechnya', in C. Sylvester (ed.), *Masquerades of War*, London: Routledge.

Mensch, J., (2009), *Embodiments: From the Body to the Body Politic*, Evanston, IL: Northwestern University Press.

Mills, C. W., (1956), *The Power Elite*, Oxford: Oxford University Press.

Newlands, E., (2013), 'Preparing and resisting the war body', in K. McSorley (ed.), *War and the Body: Militarization, Practice and Experience*, 35–50, London: Routledge.

Nixon, R., (2011), *Slow Violence and the Environmentalism of the Poor*, Cambridge, MA: Harvard University Press.

Norris, M., (2000), *Writing War in the Twentieth Century*, Charlottesville: University of Virginia Press.

Olujic, M., (1998), 'Embodiment of terror: gendered violence in peacetime and wartime in Croatia and Bosnia-Herzegovina', *Medical Anthropology Quarterly*, 12 (1): 31–50.

O'Neill, J., (1985), *Five Bodies*, Ithaca, NY: Cornell University Press.

Ó Tuathail, G., (2003), ' "Just out looking for a fight": American affect and the invasion of Iraq', *Antipode*, 35 (5): 856–870.

Parpart, J. and Zalewski, M. (eds), (2008), *Rethinking the 'Man' Question in International Relations*, London: Zed Books.

Rau, P., (2010), *Conflict, Nationhood and Corporeality in Modern Literature: Bodies-at-War*, Basingstoke: Palgrave.

Scarry, E., (1985), *The Body in Pain: The Making and Unmaking of the World*, Oxford: Oxford University Press.

Shapiro, M., (2011), 'The presence of war: "here and elsewhere" ', *International Political Sociology*, 5 (2): 109–125.

Shaw, M., (1988), *Dialectics of War*, London: Pluto.

Shaw, M., (1991), *Post-Military Society*, Cambridge: Polity Press.

Shaw, M., (2005), *The New Western Way of War*, Cambridge: Polity Press.

Shilling, C., (1993), *The Body and Social Theory*, London: Sage.

Shilling, C., (2007), 'Sociology and the body: classical traditions and new agendas', *The Sociological Review*, 55 (s1): 1–18.

Shilling, C., (2008), *Changing Bodies: Habit, Crisis and Creativity*, London: Sage.

Sjoberg, L., (2013), *Gendering Global Conflict*, New York: Columbia University Press.

Sjoberg, L. and Via, S. (eds), (2010) *Gender, War, and Militarism: Feminist Perspectives*, Santa Barbara: Praeger Publishers.

Sylvester, C., (2011), 'Pathways to experiencing war', in C. Sylvester (ed.), *Experiencing War*, London: Routledge.

Sylvester, C., (2012), 'War experiences/war practices/war theory', *Millennium*, 40 (3): 483–503.

Sylvester, C., (2013), *War as Experience*, London: Routledge.

Taylor, C., (1999), *Sacrifice as Terror: The Rwandan Genocide of 1994*, Oxford: Berg.

Terry, J., (2009), 'Significant injury: war, medicine, and empire in Claudia's case', *Women's Studies Quarterly*, 37 (1–2): 200–225.

Tilly, C., (1975), *The Formation of National States in Western Europe*, Princeton, NJ: Princeton University Press.

Tilly, C., (1992), *Coercion, Capital and European States*, Oxford: Blackwell.

Tirman, J., (2011), *The Deaths of Others*, Oxford: Oxford University Press.

Turner, B., (1984), *The Body and Society*, London: Sage.

Utas, M., (2005), 'Victimcy, girlfriending, soldiering, tactic agency in a young woman's social navigation of the Liberian war zone', *Anthropological Quarterly*, 78 (2): 403–430.

Ware, V., (2012), *Military Migrants*, London: Palgrave.

Wetta, F. J., and Novelli, M., (2003), ' "Now a major motion picture": war films and Hollywood's new patriotism', *The Journal of Military History*, 67 (3): 861–882.

Williams, A., (2011), 'Enabling persistent presence? Performing the embodied geopolitics of the Unmanned Aerial Vehicle assemblage', *Political Geography*, 30 (7): 381–390.

Woodward, R., (1998), 'It's a man's life! Soldiers, masculinity and the countryside', *Gender, Place and Culture*, 5 (3): 277–300.

Wool, Z., (2013), 'On movement: the matter of US soldiers' being after combat', *Ethnos: Journal of Anthropology*, doi:10.1080/00141844.2012.658428

Zarkov, D., (2007), *The Body of War: Media, Ethnicity and Gender in the Break-up of Yugoslavia*, Durham, NC: Duke University Press.

Zehfuss, M., (2011), 'Targeting: precision and the production of ethics', *European Journal of International Relations*, 17: 543–566.

On violent democracy

Karl von Holdt

Abstract: Violence and democracy are generally treated as antithetical. However, this article argues for the concept of *violent democracy* using the South African case to explore the ways in which violence and democracy may be mutually constitutive in countries of the global South, with their particular histories of violence, power, inequality and contestation. The article draws on research into intra-elite conflict and violence, as well as subaltern collective violence, to demonstrate the ways in which democratic institutions generate and shape violent practices, while violence in turn limits the access and rights promised by democracy. The article explores violence and elections, violence within organizations, political assassination, and the subversion of the state institutions of the rule of law to show how democratic institutions generate and shape violence, and violence in turn restricts and undermines the workings of democracy – which at the same time provides mechanisms for constraining and challenging violence. It argues that this kind of violent democracy emerges within a glaringly unequal socio-economic order, and that violence provides alternative sources of power through which this order may be preserved or contested. The analysis of violent democracy may reinvigorate our understanding of democracy not only in the global South, but also in the countries of the global North.

Keywords: violent democracy, election violence, social order, South African democracy, failed democracy, southern theory, violent pluralism

Introduction

Many democracies in the contemporary world are violent. This is particularly so in the postcolonial, 'developing' global South, where some of the oldest democracies – Colombia, Mexico, India – are characterized by extreme levels of social and political violence. This reality poses analytical challenges for sociology and political science, since democracy is generally considered to constitute a political system in which multiple institutions allocate and protect rights, provide voice for different interests, and allow for the peaceful resolution of social and political conflict.

How, then, do we think about societies where democracy exists alongside pervasive and ongoing violence? Should we regard such a democracy as a failed democracy, a partial democracy with 'low intensity citizenship' (O'Donnell,

The Sociological Review, 62:S2, pp. 129–151 (2014), DOI: 10.1111/1467-954X.12196

1993), a 'disjunctive democracy' (Holston, 2008), or a moment in the process of democratization? Is violence merely an anomaly, a remnant from an earlier order, something external to the functioning of democracy as such? Or is violence intrinsic to the working of such democracies, generated by contradictions that 'are internal and not incidental or extraneous to democracy's theory' (Holston, 2008: 273–274)? Should we speak of 'violent democracy' as a generic political form, or should we keep the terms separate? Is 'violent democracy' an oxymoron for something that should instead be regarded as a failed democracy – and if so, is our model of successful democracy the actually existing democracies of the developed West (Arias and Goldstein, 2010b)? More concretely, what is the specific relationship between violent practices and democratic processes and institutions, and what do they tell us about both democracy and violence?

The problem is clearly a theoretical one. How do we understand democracy, politics, the state, social order? How do we understand violence? And since the difference between non-violent democracies and those that have high levels of social and political violence strikes us as the difference between the 'advanced' democracies of the West and those of the post-colonial world, this raises the question of social theory forged in the West and its adequacy for the analysis of social reality elsewhere. In brief, Western social theory assumes that overt violence declines with the formation of the modern state and democracy through a combination of the consolidation of the modern state and its monopoly of legitimate coercion identified by Weber, the political technologies of Foucault's governmentality, and Bourdieu's gentle violence of symbolic power, with the result that the study of violence is reduced to studies of deviance, criminality or war (Walby, 2013). Little attention is paid to the other face of modernity – colonial expansion and its savage systems of conquest and dispossession – histories which clearly have much to do with the persistence of violence in post-colonial democracies (Burawoy and von Holdt, 2012; von Holdt, 2013a).

In this article I discuss some of these questions through a consideration of democracy and violence in South Africa, but regarding it as a particular case of a much broader set of experiences in the post-colonial world. There is of course tremendous variation across the latter, and consideration of these variations is essential, but the task here is to shed light on general problems through a specific case where they gain a particular force, as the exuberant promise of the new democratic post-apartheid order has been tarnished by episodes of extreme violence by citizens – such as the xenophobic pogroms of 2008 – as well as by state violence against citizens – the Marikana massacre of 34 striking mine workers in 2012 being the most shocking. In this article I draw on material from the set of case studies colleagues and I undertook in order to understand the dynamics of collective violence by subalterns (von Holdt *et al.*, 2011),[1] as well as on further research I have undertaken on intra-elite violence, analysed in Von Holdt (2013b).

I begin, however, by considering some recent key texts on violence and democracy in order to orientate the concrete analysis.

Democracy and violence

Guillermo O'Donnell's 1993 paper on democratization can be seen as a seminal moment for thinking about the relation between violence and democracy in the post-colonial world. In it, he argued that processes of democratization emerging from the breakdown of authoritarianism in Latin America were producing democracies that were qualitatively different to the 'institutionalized' or 'consolidated' democracies of the West: they were states in which 'the authoritarian dimension intermixes complexly and powerfully with the democratic one', producing a 'democracy of low-intensity citizenship' characterized by 'brown zones' where the authority of the state and law 'evaporates' in the face of systems of local power 'which tend to reach extremes of violent, personalistic rule . . . open to all sorts of violent and arbitrary practices' (O'Donnell, 1993: 1358). This situation demands 'reconceptualisation' of the state and democracy (O'Donnell, 1993: 1361).

This challenge has been taken up by others. Like O'Donnell, Holston (2008) argues that the concurrence of democratization with systematic violence and injustice requires that 'democratic theory must be rethought', arguing that these contradictions are *internal* and not incidental to democracy at a theoretical level, conceiving of democratization as 'disjunctive', contested, destabilizing old powers, generating resistance, and at the same time empowering the newly enfranchised to expand its scope. This means that democracy should be thought about as incomplete, contradictory and productive, 'always unfinished', rather than as a 'totalising project' (Holston, 2008: 272–274, 311).

Arias (2006) and Auyero (2007, 2010) show that the metaphor of 'brown areas' may be misleading, and that clientilist relations bring together democratic institutions, politicians, civic leaders, police and criminal gangs in networks of violence that implicate both formal state institutions and agencies as well as informal local powers in what Auyero calls pervasive 'grey zones'. Building on this, Arias and Goldstein (2010b) argue that the analytical focus should be elsewhere – not on democratization, citizenship and the state, which inevitably leads to conclusions that such democracies are deficient and citizenship limited in relation to some or other (Western) norm, but rather on the multiplicity of violent actors both within and beyond the state, including in civil society, and the conflicts, alliances and collusions between them. Violence is then 'integral to the configuration of those institutions, as a necessary component of their maintenance, and as an instrument for popular challenges to their legitimacy' (2010b: 4). In contrast with O'Donnell's notion of a state intermixing democratic and authoritarian elements, Arias and Goldstein claim that such regimes may 'represent another type of political formation at variance from both democracy and authoritarianism' – namely, *violent pluralism* (Arias and Goldstein, 2010b: 19), with the implication that the specific workings of democracy are less important to their analysis. Violent pluralism may produce 'unique forms of political practice, order, and subjectivity that need to be studied on their own terms' rather than in the terms presented by democratic theory. Democratic institutions have no necessary transformative or developmental trajectory toward some sort of democratic norm, as posited by democratization theory; violent pluralism may constitute a social order with its own kind of stability characterized by endemic violence, or cycles of violence (Arias and Goldstein, 2010b: 9–13, 26–27).

North *et al.* (2009, 2013a) argue that institutions developed in Western democracies and transplanted into societies in the developing world may have very different meanings and outcomes, including perverse ones, in the latter, and this applies no less to democratic institutions such as elections. In their analysis, elite factions in developing societies deploy violence in order to enhance their access to rents, and elite coalitions seek to reduce violence by incorporating all factions with violent capabilities and negotiating the distribution of rents in a stable and predictable fashion. Elite coalitions become unstable and more violent when the balance of power between factions shifts within them, or new factions with violent capabilities emerge outside of them. Elections may precipitate periods of instability and violence when they produce results that are unacceptable to the existing elite coalition (North *et al.*, 2013b: 343) – or, they might have added, when they don't reflect the power of an emerging faction outside the dominant coalition. On the other hand, 'elections can be useful stabilising rituals' even if they aren't free or fair (North *et al.*, 2013b: 341–343). As a concrete example, they argue that the Arab Spring uprisings and subsequent elections cannot produce open access democracy, but rather precipitate a reorganization of the dominant coalition (North *et al.*, 2013b: 348–349) – and the kind of violence this can precipitate has become all too tragically clear in the case of Egypt.

The puzzle of violence and democracy has generated a rich and increasingly sophisticated literature, with conflicting views about the concrete relation between violence and democracy. Some, such as O'Donnell, Arias and Goldstein and North *et al.* tend to view violence (though with ambivalence) as a set of practices generated by violent actors outside of, but impacting on, shaping and attenuating, democratic institutions. In contrast, Holston argues that violence is integral to democratization. Only Arias and Goldstein use the term *violent democracy*, and they use it descriptively rather than conceptually, preferring *violent pluralism* as an analytic category.

In this article I focus on the intersection between *specifically democratic institutions* and violent pluralism in order to explore whether *violent democracy* might make sense as an analytical category rather than only a descriptive one. My aim is to consider very concretely how the interaction shapes both the forms of violence and the workings of democracy, producing what I think can be called *violent democracy*. This means that I discuss only those kinds of violence that are entwined in this way with the institutions of democracy – there are many other forms of political and collective violence, including xenophobic attacks and vigilantism, as well as wide ranges of interpersonal violence including gender violence, violence against children and violent robbery. Each of these bears

The Sociological Review, 62:S2, pp. 129–151 (2014), DOI: 10.1111/1467-954X.12196

some relation to the institutions of democracy, however tangential, and these need to be explored to provide a fuller picture of the dynamics of violent democracy; constraints of space, however, mean they cannot be addressed here.

Drawing on this concrete analysis, I argue both that democracy shapes violence in particular ways that differ from how violence might be organized in authoritarian regimes, and also that even the limited democracy that is afforded by such societies empowers citizens and subalterns in new ways. In my argument I give more weight to the significance of democratic institutions than either Arias and Goldstein or North *et al.* (2013b) do. Given this focus of attention, the analysis is unavoidably centred on state institutions, and is therefore unable to fully explore the dynamic of violent actors and social order beyond the state in the manner suggested by Arias and Goldstein.

Before moving to the concrete analysis of democracy and violence, it is important to provide some information on poverty and inequality in South Africa, as well as the link between patronage and politics. These are crucial to understanding the place of violence in South African democracy.

Poverty, inequality and democracy

Democracy was established in South Africa in 1994, as the outcome of pro-tracted negotiations between the apartheid government and the democratic movement led by the African National Congress (ANC), in the context of a transition from the colonial and apartheid structuring of socio-economic inequality along racial lines. Current socio-economic reality continues to be profoundly shaped by this legacy.

At 7, South Africa's Gini coefficient is amongst the highest in the world. The poorest 20 per cent earns about 2.3 per cent of national income, and the poorest 40 per cent earns about 6 per cent, while the richest 20 per cent earns about 70 per cent of national income. Unemployment ranges between 35 and 40 per cent, on the expanded definition, and 25 per cent on the narrow definition (those actively seeking work). On the latter measurement, 50 per cent of those between the ages of 15 and 24 are unemployed, and 30 per cent of those between the ages of 25 and 34. Forty-eight per cent of the population lives in deep poverty defined as less than $2 per day, indicating that a large proportion of those who have jobs nonetheless live in poverty. Two decades into democracy poverty remains deeply racialized – thus the median per capita expenditure in 2008 for whites was R5,668 per month, compared with R454 per month for Africans. While the proportion of Africans in the top 20 per cent of income earners had increased to 48 per cent, the white racial group had on average increased its income more than any other racial group in the democratic era (NDP, 2012: 34; NPC, 2011).

These figures give some sense of the depth of poverty and inequality, and its racial nature. The same period saw a dramatic increase in the size of the black middle class and the emergence of a black political elite and business class.

However, the opportunities for upward mobility and accumulation outside of the state remain limited, and as a result the state constitutes the main resource for wealth redistribution, upward mobility, class formation and accumulation. Access to jobs, business opportunities and rents through procurement, tenders and revenue streams are routed through the state, and the politics of 'corruption' and patronage have become increasingly important, both at local levels and nationally (Langa and Von Holdt, 2012; Ndletyana *et al.*, 2013; Plaut and Holden, 2012; Von Holdt *et al.*, 2011). The politics of patronage is not only driven by the patrons, but also by the poor in the struggle for access to opportunities, however marginal (Langa and Von Holdt, 2012; Ndletyana *et al.*, 2013). The prevalence of patronage politics and its manifestation in intense intra-elite competition is not unusual in societies where opportunities for elite accumulation are limited and levels of poverty and marginalization are high – indeed they are generally regarded as the norm (Khan, 2005; North *et al.*, 2013a, 2013b).

Transitions to democracy do not end this; rather, democratic institutions accommodate and are shaped by the politics of patronage, and political contestation in developing countries tends to be 'organized through the mobilizations of patron-client factions, rather than through the mobilization of class or economic interest groups' (Khan, 2005). In South Africa, patronage politics tends to be organized within the ANC as the massively dominant political party among black voters. It is not possible to understand the role of violence in South African politics without understanding the dynamics of patronage.

Democracy, elections and violence

Representation and elections are foundational to any theory of democracy, so any investigation of the relationship between democracy and violence needs to explore these processes. In South Africa over the past decade a growing number of community protests, often accompanied by violence both by police and protesters, have focused community grievances on the figures of elected municipal councillors. Both Booysen (2009) and Alexander (2012) explore the relation between this trend and electoral behaviour, with the former arguing that community residents employ protest and voting as a dual strategy for engaging the ANC, while Alexander argues that many protesters, especially youthful ones, join the large proportion of potential voters who refrain from voting, and focuses attention on the emergence of localized alternative electoral parties, albeit small, organized by disillusioned protesters. Both focus on the question of electoral allegiance, and neither address the relationship between violence and democracy.

In all four of our case studies of community protests, our research revealed complex dynamics surrounding councillors, representation and violence. In two of them, the protests resulted in councillors resigning, and we were able to

The Sociological Review, 62:S2, pp. 129–151 (2014), DOI: 10.1111/1467-954X.12196
© 2014 The Author. Editorial organisation © 2014 The Editorial Board of the Sociological Review

observe the resulting by-elections which were marked by contrasting voting strategies by community members, which suggests the divergent symbolic meanings election can hold.

In all cases the ANC was the majority party in control of the town council, and there were divisions within the local ANC that were linked to the protests. In each case, a faction of the local ANC and its allied organizations – the ANC Youth League and the SA Communist Party – was involved, alongside others, in the leadership of the protests, and we concluded that the protests had a dual character reflecting the concerns and interests of a faction of the local elite as well as the grievances and anger of a broad range of community members. For the elite faction, the aim was to mobilize the protests in order to reconfigure power within the local ANC, and in particular to depose the councillors and mayors who had been elected in the previous elections, in order to open up the opportunity for the protesting faction to replace them with their own candidates. The stakes were high, because councillors have opportunities to influence the allocation of jobs and lucrative tenders to their networks of supporters. For the protesting crowds the aim was to remove councillors who were alleged to be corrupt or unresponsive to their problems, and replace them with councillors who would focus on improving their lives, in the process making use of elite dissidents to gain voice within the ANC and the council. These dual motivations merged in the process of mobilizing the protests.

Again, in all of our studies, communities had a history of protesting peacefully over periods of between two and four years prior to protests becoming violent, with little significant impact. The turn to violence – burning street barricades, attacking cars, running street battles between crowds of youths and the police, and the firebombing of councillor homes and public buildings – was fuelled both by violent policing (see below) and by the anger of community members at the sense that those in power refused to listen to them. Protesters made explicit reference to the disjunction between democracy and the practices of government and the police when explaining their actions:

The Freedom Charter says people shall govern, now we are not governing, we are being governed.

The Constitution says we have rights. Freedom of speech, freedom of religion . . . we have many freedoms . . . but we get shot at for walking around at night.

You see, Casspirs remind us of apartheid, that we are not free in this democracy . . . We need police that respect human rights.

They want us to be in bed before midnight. It's taking us to the old days of curfews against Blacks. (Von Holdt *et al.*, 2011: 23–24)

Although some of the elite leaders involved in the protests attempted to distance themselves from aspects of this collective violence after the fact, it is quite clear that substantial groupings from both elite and crowds regarded violence as legitimate in their struggles. Thus a group of protesters explained, 'We thought, let's barricade the road that passes the township, burn down trains and burn everything. Maybe they will take us seriously' (Von Holdt *et al.*, 2011: 9). Violence was justified as a response to an unresponsive government:

> Violence is the only language that our government understands. Look, we have been submitting memos, but nothing was done. We became violent and problems were immediately resolved. It is clear that violence is a solution to all problems. (Von Holdt *et al.*, 2011: 49)

Political representatives are expected to take the demands of various constituencies seriously: 'Leaders must toe the line, but if they don't we will remove them like the mayor and her council' (Von Holdt *et al.*, 2011: 49). According to these protesters, violence is an *element* in a democratic system. Democracy promises a government that represents citizens and is responsive to them; if this fails, violence provides a language that communicates anger and urgency to the authorities, and it may be necessary to use force or violence to remove unresponsive representatives. Such legitimacy is articulated through symbolic references to the militant anti-apartheid struggles of the past in the kinds of chants and songs adopted by protesters, and continuities between the past and present were stressed in the rationales for burning down inadequate public facilities.

In two of our case studies by-elections for new councillors took place soon after the protests. In the first town the by-elections were an immediate consequence of the protests, as the ANC national leadership instructed the mayoral committee of six councillors to resign, and by-elections had to be held to replace them. In the second town the ANC national leadership adopted a different stance, supporting the local leadership and providing additional resources in an attempt to enhance their performance, but during a second episode of violent confrontation one of the ANC councillors resigned, forcing a by-election. In the first case, the by-elections were regarded as a victory by the protest movement, in the second they were regarded as illegitimate and boycotted, dramatizing the contrasting symbolic meanings that elections may have in different local contexts, even in the same democracy – the two towns are not more than 50 km apart.

In both cases the resignation of councillors opened up fierce contestations over the nomination of candidates within the ward branches of the ANC where the by-elections were to be held. In the first town the struggle over nomination took place between candidates nominated by the protest leadership, and candidates regarded as representatives of the old guard against whom they were pitted in struggle. In the most intensely contested ward branch both sides recruited new members in an effort to swing the vote, and each vote was challenged on the grounds that new members can only vote three months after joining the organisation. Three nomination meetings had to be aborted. Eventually the protesters' candidates were nominated in all the wards. On the election day large crowds turned out to vote, and the protest leadership articulated a sense of excitement and triumph:

> Look there, look that side. It is early, but the people are already queueing. This is massive, Comrade. . . . The masses have spoken through their mass action last year

The Sociological Review, 62:S2, pp. 129–151 (2014), DOI: 10.1111/1467-954X.12196

and now they'll exercise their democratic right to vote for their leader. . . . Today it is like 27 April 1994. The people are happy to come and vote for their leaders. This is the democracy that we fought for.

The by-election gains its meaning from the mass action, including violence, of the protest movement. The democratic right to vote is directly related to the mass action which toppled the previously elected councillors. The analogy is explicitly drawn with the first national democratic elections in 1994, understood as the democracy that was fought for through the mass anti-apartheid struggle and intense violence of the 1980s. In this narrative democracy does not replace the violent conflicts of the 1980s – the fight for democracy is continuous, and its promise remains dependent on the ability of the people to insert themselves forcefully into the institutions of democracy, such as elections. As the protesters said about one of the new councillors:

> He knows the process, he was part of the march. If he does not deliver we will also remove him like the former mayor. It is not guaranteed that violence would not happen again.

The symbolic power of elections is directly related to the symbolic power of popular mobilization (Von Holdt *et al.*, 2011). The legitimacy of electoral processes and results is always provisional, and can be trumped by direct action when necessary.

In the second town the by-election did not symbolize the power of the people. The overarching demand of the protesters was that the provincial boundary should be redrawn so that the town could be incorporated into the better-resourced neighbouring province where, they believed, state services would be better. The ANC refused this demand, and demonstrated its support for the local ANC leadership. Here two nomination meetings in the ward branch were disrupted by ANC members who did not want the elections to proceed until re-demarcation had taken place. Eventually a candidate was nominated by the regional executive of the ANC. Some ANC activists who had been involved in the protests put out a pamphlet urging the community not to vote for the ANC, but for a small opposition party that also had liberation movement credentials, the PAC: 'We must vote PAC to show the ANC that we will not vote for ANC until we are incorporated into Gauteng', read the pamphlet. Many of the protesters, however, adopted a strategy of boycotting the elections with the slogan, 'No Gauteng, no elections'. There was a strong sense that the election lacked credibility among residents; as one said, 'I will not vote for someone to drive an expensive car, while I still live in a shack.' In the end, the ANC candidate narrowly won the ward on a very low voter turnout (Langa, 2010; Von Holdt *et al.*, 2011).

In this case the by-election symbolizes the indifference of authority and the ANC (the two are conflated), rather than the power of the people and so it becomes dis-articulated from democracy. The boycott of elections is a continuation of protest, a new way of sending a message to the ANC; and those who advocated voting for an alternative party did so not in order to support an alternative policy position, but also, and explicitly, to send a signal to the ANC.

In both these cases, the elections gain their symbolic power from their relation to mass action, which includes violence: in the first, the election symbolizes the triumph of mass action on the analogy of the 1994 elections, whereas in the second it symbolizes the indifference of authority in the face of mass action, and becomes an occasion for further symbolic protest. These cases reveal a complex relation between collective violence and the democratic institution of elections. Formal democratic processes do not reign supreme. Collective violence may annul the results of previous elections, and elections gain their symbolic power not only from the tally of citizen votes but also from their relation to popular protest, including violence. Elections are not so much an occasion for choosing between political parties and their policies, but for communicating with the ANC as political authority. While this argument is consistent with that of Booysen's (2009), it differs with the emphasis placed by Alexander (2012) on the significance of relatively small-scale and local electoral alternatives – though such an alternative did emerge in the second of the case studies mentioned here, and may constitute an important trend in future.

The state, patronage and violence

The case studies of protest and collective violence discussed in the previous section concentrated on the relation of citizens in poor communities to elections. However, as has already been noted, community protests tend to have a dual character reflecting not only popular grievances, but also the interests of local elite factions in shifting the configurations of power in the local ANC. Given the role that collective violence plays in these protests, this suggests that some elites are willing to use violence to gain power within the ANC.

Intra-elite conflict is related to access to state resources, the allocation of tenders, and the allocation of jobs within the state. This reality drives intra-elite conflict over patronage and access to economic opportunities within the ANC, shaping its intra-organizational dynamics. Violence is increasingly a factor in these conflicts. One form that such violence takes is the collective violence that emerges during episodes of community protest, as described above. But violence is taking other forms as well, including collective violence at organizational meetings, and targeted assassinations.

As with collective violence in community protests discussed above, these forms of violence are closely entwined with democratic institutions and processes in the broader polity. The ANC is a political party, and its domination in elected assemblies and over the state depends on its performance in national, provincial and local elections. At the same time, success in internal organizational elections at different levels determines the power of individuals and factions and their access to positions in the state, or ability to command influence over state decisions. In particular, control of branches and higher structures means influence over who gets nominated to candidate lists for national elections.

Thus the Secretary General reported in 2010 that a 'General collapse of discipline has characterised the period under review [the previous two years]. Disruption of ANC meetings, assault of members in ANC meetings and taking the ANC to court without exhausting the internal processes are widespread' (ANC, 2010: para. 4.23) and that the leadership had to oversee 'many rowdy provincial conferences'(ANC, 2010: para. 4.20). This 'alien culture' (para. 4.20) started in the North-West Province, at the first provincial conference held after the bitterly divided Polokwane National Conference of the ANC, that 'ushered in a new culture of open physical fights in ANC meetings' (para. 8.110). In the same year violent conflict at a regional conference in the Northern Cape led to one death (para. 8.13).

The run-up to the 2011 local government elections was characterized by bitter conflicts, membership protests, and allegations of fraudulent behaviour in branches over the nomination of candidates. The ANC was only able to restore some kind of internal order by promising to establish a commission that would investigate all allegations after the elections, and that where candidates were found to have benefited from manipulation they would be removed from office, precipitating fresh nominations and a by-election. Over the following year, the commission investigated disputes in 419 wards, finding numerous irregularities, manipulation and fraud, and recommending that 125 selection processes should be re-run, and that disciplinary action should be taken against leaders and members 'who were responsible for gross violation and manipulation of the guidelines' (ANC, 2012: 61–64). According to press reports, the commission found that the votes of ANC members were being bought and traded, gate-keepers were controlling who could attend meetings, and membership lists were manipulated. Intimidation, threats, assaults and shootings were also reported by the commission. The general secretary condemned 'the determination by some members of our movement to destabilise organisation and disrupt meetings as a tactic to get what they want . . .' (*BD live*, 16 January 2013; *City Press*, 17 November 2012; *Mail & Guardian*, 8 February 2013).

In the run-up to the 2012 ANC congress in Mangaung, meetings were disrupted by brawls, armed men threatening violence, gunshots, assaults, stabbings, burning down of opponents' houses, and the aborting of meetings (*The Star*, 16 November 2012; *Business Day*, 7 August 2012, 19 November 2012). Again, access to state power is an important asset, as the police are frequently called in to monitor such meetings and restore 'order' in the case of disruption. For example, in the run-up to Mangaung, a Limpopo provincial general council was 'stormed' by a group of Zuma supporters who hurled bricks and stones, and kidnapped, assaulted and threatened to 'kill' a key supporter of expelled ANCYL leader Julius Malema. Instead of protecting the meeting, the police withdrew, 'allegedly at the instruction of police top brass', after which 'pandemonium erupted' (*The Sunday Independent*, 2 December 2012).

In parallel to these displays of public and collective violence, assassinations of ANC office bearers and representatives have become increasingly visible over the past few years. For example, in one of our research sites in Mpumalanga both the first mayor elected under democracy and the man chosen to replace him were assassinated, and its two subsequent mayors claim to have been victims of assassination attempts (Langa and Von Holdt, 2012). In July 2012 the mayor of Rustenburg in North West province was found guilty, together with his bodyguard, of arranging the murder of a rival councillor who had submitted a dossier of evidence about the mayor's corrupt dealings to the police, while rival ANC factions faced off outside the courtroom (*The Star*, 17 and 18 July 2012). The case was dismissed on appeal, as a key witness recanted his evidence, claiming to have been bribed by the police (*Business Day*, 22 July 2014). Early in 2013, an MEC and deputy chairperson of the ANC in North West Province was arrested together with the provincial chair of the ANC Youth League, a councillor and a ward secretary, for the shooting of a district secretary on the eve of the Mangaung national conference of ANC (*Business Day*, 26 February 2013).

But it is in KwaZulu-Natal, previously the site of high levels of political violence between the ANC and Gatsha Buthelezi's Zulu ethnic political party, Inkatha, that the greatest increase in intra-ANC assassination seems to have taken place. As Inkatha's fortunes have waned, and the ANC has come to dominate the province, political violence has come to characterize internal conflict over power and access to state resources. At the same time, Inkatha-linked violence continues, seemingly focused on the rivalry between it and a breakaway, the National Freedom Party, with the latter claiming 27 of its members had been killed since the party's formation in 2010. Thirty-eight ANC members were killed in KwaZulu-Natal between February 2011 and October 2012, compared to 10 politically linked murders in the previous three years. A journalist was told by one informant that all the 'comrades' now found it necessary to carry guns (*Business Day*, 17 October 2012; *Mail & Guardian*, 20–26 July 2012).

These killings are closely linked to rivalry for positions in the ANC, and local and provincial government, which provide access to state resources and patronage. The *Mail & Guardian* reporter was told violence in the ANC was linked to 'city contracts, ranging from the building of low-cost housing to waste collection, [that] were awarded to influential business associates, who would channel money back to the ANC for its operations, or to small and medium-sized businesses connected to the ANC at ward level' (*Mail & Guardian*, 20–26 July 2012). An ANC NEC member told the *Business Day* reporter that:

> Having ANC membership is the best CV in town. The higher you go in the party, the more you can dish out patronage. It's about taking care of yourself and those close to you. . . . People are reducing the ANC to their personal kitty and are prepared to kill to get their slice of the wealth (*Business Day*, 17 October 2012).

The Sociological Review, 62:S2, pp. 129–151 (2014), DOI: 10.1111/1467-954X.12196

Regarding the murder of Mthembeni Shezi, a local councillor gunned down by two men in a public meeting, his fiancée claimed people hated him because he was fighting corruption, while an ANC official said:

> There are as many bad things to say about Shezi as there are good. People look at his lifestyle and ask, 'how does a herd boy from Nkandla go from having absolutely nothing to a fancy 4x4 and several houses?' People start to see that being a local councillor can be a means to acquire wealth.

Assassination as a form of political violence is not limited to struggles within the dominant political party and between political parties. In the vortex of different forms of violence that characterized the wave of strikes in the platinum mining sector in 2012, culminating in the Marikana massacre in which police shot and killed 34 striking miners, targeted assassination of local trade union leaders has emerged as a new phenomenon. Violence directed against strike breakers, including assaults and killings, have been a recurring feature of militant and protracted strikes in South Africa and were repeated in the platinum strikes (Chinguno, 2013; von Holdt, 2010), but targeted assassinations as a feature of intra- and interunion rivalry have been extremely rare. Since the strikes, though, nine trade union shop stewards and officials have been shot and killed.

The central feature of the strike wave was the rejection of the established National Union of Mineworkers (NUM) by striking workers, and the emergence of a new union, the Amalgamated Mining and Construction Workers Union (AMCU). Since the strikes the latter has consolidated its position in this sector. Of the assassination victims, one was a key AMCU activist, and eight were NUM shop stewards and officials, while a ninth was critically injured. All the victims were shot, and all worked at Lonmin, the mine at the centre of the massacre. On the face of it these killings are motivated by union rivalry, and AMCU is the aggressor union. However, interviews with mine workers suggest that this pattern of shootings represents a continuation and intensification of an already existing tradition of intra-worker struggles at Lonmin mine, but that prior to the emergence of AMCU this took the form of intra-union struggle within the NUM. Indeed, two of the victims had themselves opened fire on strikers when they marched to the NUM office early on in the strike, and according to workers the NUM local leadership had only gained office because 'they lived by the gun'.[2]

There is a direct analogy between this violence and assassination within the ANC. Union office in the mining sector comes with numerous perks negotiated between companies and the NUM – a higher salary, escape from arduous underground work to an office desk, and numerous opportunities for self-enrichment and patronage – which substantially raise the stakes in the battle for election as shop steward or branch official. While this violence may be localized at this point, it shows similarities to the use of assassination in the ANC in the same province (North-West Province), and there is a strong possibility that it may spread, whether through political networks or through the hit squads of professional assassins that undertake this form of violence.

The forms of violence discussed in this section – collective violence and assassination within the dominant political party, the ANC, between political parties, and within trade union structures, are shaped by the opportunities and processes provided by democratic institutions. Political parties are designed to mobilize votes in national elections, and to manage government. Violence is directly related to disputes over who controls party structures and candidate lists, and who therefore gets political office and power over assets and patronage. Likewise, industrial relations in a democratic system provides for a greater degree of interaction and cooperation between trade unions and managers, hence opening a variety of opportunities for trade unionists to benefit personally and in fact to migrate into management, thus raising the stakes in the internal democratic procedures that generally characterize trade unions. Violence in both cases is occasioned by democratic procedures and opportunities, but at the same time is a strategy for limiting their reach and accessibility and controlling their outcomes. Violence, in other words, is produced by democratic institutions and at the same time constrains their democratic potential. Democracy and violence are entangled and mutually shaping processes.

The violence of the democratic state

In this section we will consider two forms of violence practised by the democratic state – the violence directed by state agencies against subaltern movements and protesters, and the internal struggles over the control and deployment of the coercive agencies of the state.

Using deaths of protesters at the hands of police as the key indicator of police violence, independent researcher David Bruce shows a pattern of escalation in the use of lethal violence against protesters and strikers from 2009 to 2011, and correlates this with organizational changes within the police service. Between 2006 and 2009 three people were killed by the police during collective protests, three people were killed in 2010 alone, and nine were killed in 2011 – an escalation which culminated in the Marikana massacre of 34 striking mine workers in 2012. The increase in police killings lagged the increase in collective violence during protests and strikes, which began an upward trend in 2004 continuing into the present. Drawing on his analysis of press reports of these incidents, Bruce concludes that there was a shift by the police to 'brutal new methods for dealing with public protests', including the use of live ammunition, the firing of rubber bullets directly at crowds – which strongly increases the likelihood of lethal outcomes, as well as assaults and other abuses of community members (Bruce, 2012a).

While there is evidence of the new tactics from 2009, the dramatic increase in violence in 2011 coincides with the elevation of the police Operational Response

Services as a full division under new leadership – including paramilitary units such as the Special Task Force, National Intervention Unit and Tactical Response Teams. These units were active in many of the more repressive actions by the police, and they were directly involved in the Marikana massacre (Bruce, 2012a). This kind of violent policing is highly reminiscent of the policing methods used by the apartheid regime. The transformation of repressive police agencies after transitions to democracy is notoriously difficult, but the ANC government elected after 1994 devoted considerable resources and energy to doing just that. With international support, the apartheid 'riot police' were transformed into public order policing units with new management and command structures, intensive training in public order policing, and an empha-sis on the role of the police in supporting the right of the public to assemble and demonstrate (Bruce, 2012a; Marks, 2005). However, over the following decade public demonstrations were generally peaceful, and public order units were redeployed to normal crime combating operations. Their re-emergence as spe-cialists in policing protests has been accompanied by methods that suggest order is more important than rights, and that whenever they have a pretext 'they could dispense with principles of minimum force, and use as much force as they wanted' (Bruce, 2012a).

Our research on protest and violence took place in 2009–10, before the formation of the new police division, but in each case study police action was heavy-handed and violent, and was frequently described as provoking the vio-lence of protesters. Police violence took the form of tear gassing protesters, firing rubber bullets at them and at times quite randomly into crowds of bystanders, and assaulting and beating protesters. In one small town the police acted with particular brutality both in attempting to quell collective action and in pursuing individuals they suspected to be leaders, including violent incursions into their homes and assaulting family members, and detaining and torturing suspects. Since this was the only research site in which protests involved an opposition political party (together with a section of the local ANC) with substantial black support that could conceivably pose an electoral challenge to the ANC, the harshness of police action may well have been motivated by this (Von Holdt *et al.*, 2011; Langa, 2010).

The kind of violent policing described here is antithetical to the provisions of the post-apartheid constitution which lays out the rights, values and institutions of democratic government in South Africa, and is also in several respects illegal. What is its relation to democracy? Is it simply an aberration, a leftover from the pre-democratic period?

As sketched at the beginning of this article, democracy in South Africa is characterized by profound material inequalities and deep levels of unemploy-ment and poverty, strongly shaped by racial factors. Democracy founded on this kind of material base is unlikely to be stable, and indeed the increasing levels of protest violence are linked to frustration about the responsiveness of democratic institutions and elected representatives to the plight of citizens; often this is blamed on incompetence, indifference or corruption – but it is not clear at all that even a more competent or dedicated administration would be able to solve the problems of poverty and inequality within the current economic structures largely inherited intact from apartheid. Democracy in South Africa, in other words, is characterized by a profound contradiction between inclusive political institutions and an exclusionary economic structure. It promises the equality of citizenship and the responsiveness of government, but cannot deliver on this. Structurally unable to accommodate the needs of the poor, democracy produces another language through which the poor communicate their grievances – the language of violence. Democratic government, alarmed, frustrated and affronted that citizens' protests show no sign of subsiding, but instead expand and deploy force outside of the procedures of democracy, respond in the same language – that of violence.

While this language may be regarded as an *element* of democracy through which the poor can supplement their votes by demanding responsiveness from authority, it undermines the processes of public deliberation, election and civility on which democracy depends. In turn, democracy becomes increasingly repressive, diminishing the rights of citizens, eroding the mechanisms through which policing is made accountable, and undermining the rule of law. Relations between citizens and government are regulated by a combination of democratic processes and coercive institutions – constituting violent democracy.

To this general picture of the intersection between violence and democracy in a highly unequal society, must be added evidence of a closer role played by police violence in the struggles over electoral processes described in the previous section. Allegations have emerged that police violence against protesters in the township of Wesselton outside Ermelo in the province of Mpumalanga in early 2011 was directly related to the struggles between different factions of the ANC in the province over the candidate list for local government elections. The protests started when a residents' committee complained that a local ANC strongman had imposed his preferred candidates in the compiling of the election lists, but received no response. Not only did the police respond brutally to the protests, killing two, they were alleged to have subjected those arrested to torture, including electric shocks, suffocation with plastic bags, and immersion under water. According to detainees, the objective was to obtain confessions that the protests had been instigated by political opponents of the Mpumalanga Premier. As Bruce points out, something very similar happened after the Marikana massacre, when large numbers of survivors were arrested and allegedly tortured with the objective of obtaining confessions that Julius Malema, the populist ANC Youth League leader who had been expelled from the organization and was seeking to build a constituency among striking mine workers, had instigated the confrontations with authority (Bruce, 2012b).

It is apparent that there is a short step between more general repression of protest in a violent democracy, and police involvement in more selective and directly political repression of opponents of a democratically elected regime – ranging from opposing factions in the governing party, to opposition political parties such as the PAC or political movements such as Malema's. As with popular protests, the forms of coercion and repression are entwined with the political processes and institutions of democracy and deeply shaped by them. In turn, the democratic rights of association and electoral participation are constrained by the violent practices of state agencies.

The rule of law is a foundational institution of democratic regimes, designed to ensure that all citizens are equal before the law and that the coercive agencies of the state are bound by and accountable to the law. The examples above indicate a drift away from the rule of law. But violent democracy is not only marked by the kind of extralegal violence deployed by protesters or police discussed so far – it is marked as well by institutional struggles for control over the instruments of law, that is to say, the instruments of institutionalized coercion over which the Weberian state is supposed to hold a monopoly. This is precisely to *avert* the equal application of the law to all citizens and the accountability of the state's coercive agencies.

In a society where patronage is central to elite formation, accumulation strategies, and the survival of the marginalized and the poor, it necessarily shapes democratic processes and institutions to its logic and its requirements. The mechanisms for controlling, organizing and dispensing patronage are variously defined by the law as corruption, fraud and theft; hence, whoever controls the various institutions of law is able to decide who should be prosecuted and who protected from prosecution. Over the two decades since democracy was inaugurated in South Africa the struggle for control over these institutions has intensified and ramified through the state. Victims have included commissioners of police, heads of the National Prosecuting Authority (NPA), senior ANC officials, and numerous functionaries beneath them.

The paradigm case for these practices was the arms deal of the 1990s, both because of its scale and the way it has continued to ramify through the ANC and the state. Efforts to contain the damage included executive intimidation of Parliament, curbing the involvement of the auditor general and the public protector, disbanding the Scorpions,[3] political interference with the National Prosecuting Authority (NPA) to protect then-Deputy President Jacob Zuma from prosecution, and selective leaks and disinformation from state intelligence agencies. The intense struggles within state institutions over the arms deal were linked to the battles between then-President Thabo Mbeki and Zuma for leadership within the ANC (Plaut and Holden, 2012).

By their nature many of these struggles are hidden from public view, and when they do surface the media becomes simply one resource among many others for the contesting parties – selective leaks and disinformation campaigns making it extremely difficult to untangle the interests and actions involved. One such struggle involves the head of crime intelligence, General Richard Mdluli, and a senior prosecutor, Glynnis Breytenbach. Mdluli appears to have the support of senior political leaders, including the Minister of Police, and when he was arrested on murder and corruption charges and suspended he wrote a letter to the president claiming that senior police officers were conspiring against him, and that if he was reinstated he would assist the president in his campaign for re-election as president of the ANC. It is widely believed that Mdluli is a key element in the plan of the president's faction within the ANC to ensure that the president and his allies are protected from investigations for corruption.

Breytenbach led the prosecution of Mdluli, refused to withdraw charges when instructed to do so by her superiors, and was then suspended and brought before a disciplinary enquiry. While she claimed that her suspension was because of the Mdluli case, the NPA claimed it was because of misconduct in another high-profile case she was prosecuting against a company owned by figures close to President Zuma, including his son, which was alleged to have connived with government officials to defraud a mining corporation of its mining rights (the company has subsequently been found guilty). All 15 charges were dismissed by the disciplinary enquiry and Breytenbach was reluctantly reinstated, but removed from both cases. Mdluli then laid a charge of intimidation against Breytenbach while a judge instructed the NPA to reinstate charges against Mdluli, currently under appeal (Plaut and Holden, 2012; *Mail & Guardian*, 4–10 May 2012; 8–14 June, 2012; 1–7 February 2013; 8–14 February 2013; 31 May–6 June 2013; 6–12 December 2013).

This case suggests something of what is at stake in the struggle for control of the police and the prosecuting authority: whether and how the law will be applied in cases of fraud and corruption involving figures in the leading faction of the ANC, including those close to the president. As another example, until recently it appeared that Julius Malema, referred to above, who was at the time close to the president, was protected from investigation of the several allegations of fraud levelled against him; this changed when he turned on the president and was eventually expelled from the ANC – he now faces charges of corruption. Similar contestations have surfaced at other levels in the coercive apparatus of the state as well (Von Holdt, 2013b).

These cases demonstrate how the central institutions of democracy – in this instance, institutions of the rule of law – are subjected to processes of contestation and control, and ultimately reconfigured by the forces of factionalism and patronage within a democracy such as South Africa's. This is not to say that such processes are uncontested – there are institutions and officials within the state, as well as public voices in civil society, which challenge and mobilize against the capturing of state institutions and subversion of the rule of law; the result is a kind of war of attrition which rages back and forth across the institutions of state and civil society as first one side and then another appears to gain the upper hand. In the process, though, institutions are destabilized and lose credibility. These institutional battles entail violence. Although their institutional nature, and the legal terrain on which many are fought, tend to mask this, ultimately the law is an instrument of coercion, and where it is applied unequally and as an instrument in political and factional struggles, it constitutes the application of violence to political and economic foes.

The Sociological Review, 62:S2, pp. 129–151 (2014), DOI: 10.1111/1467-954X.12196

Conclusion: violent democracy

In this article I have explored the ways in which institutions and processes of democracy in South Africa provide the occasion for violence and shape its forms. It is important to reiterate that the democracy we are exploring is characterized by political inclusion and high levels of socio-economic exclusion which continue to be shaped by the racial structuring of more than 300 years of colonialism and apartheid. The consequence, as argued earlier in this article, is the recourse by both elites and subalterns to using the resources of the state and the politics of patronage to effect a degree of accumulation and redistribution for the formerly oppressed black majority. Patterns of violence are closely shaped by this reality.

Our examination of local government elections reveals a complex interplay between the institution of elections – the defining feature of democracy – and collective violence. In these communities formal democratic processes do not reign supreme but gain their symbolic power from their relation to popular protest which derives its potency from the mass struggles that ended apartheid and delivered democracy, and elections are not so much an occasion for choosing between political parties and policies, but for communicating with political authority in the form of the ANC. Violence is another way of communicating with political authority when elections fail to bring results. Political parties and elections provide the institutional forms through which patronage politics necessarily works in a democracy. This heightens the stakes for those contesting elections, which explains the resort to manipulation and collective violence in organizational processes, meetings and elections, as well as the escalation of political assassination within and between political parties and to settle trade union rivalries. Finally, the article examined the violence of the state. On the one hand is the growing level of violence with which police are responding to collective protest. On the other are the battles within the state for the control of the institutions of the rule of law, so that coercion can be applied or withheld selectively in the struggles between factions for control of the sources of patronage. The result is an erosion of the rights of citizens, the rule of law, and the accountability of state officials and political representatives.

This nexus of democracy, patronage and violence constitutes what I think can be called *violent democracy*. The concept of violent democracy provides *an analytic category* which can be used to explore the concrete dynamics of this nexus. Democratic institutions and processes generate violence as disputes and conflicts are mediated both within and outside of them, and the forms that violence takes are shaped by these institutions and processes, differing from the forms it takes in authoritarian regimes. At the same time, violence constrains and subverts the workings of democracy, eroding the effectiveness of these institutions and limiting the democratic rights of citizens and the rule of law. Thus violent democracy produces O'Donnell's (1993) 'low intensity citizenship'.

This does not mean that the democracy of violent democracy is an empty term. On the one hand, as argued above, democracy shapes the forms that violence takes, but on the other it also constrains violence and provides new means in the struggle to curb and hold accountable the purveyors of violence, as argued by Holston (2008). In the case of the Marikana massacre, the existence of an independent judiciary, a free press, and civil society organizations, has ensured that considerable evidence incriminating the police has entered the public arena, and it is difficult to imagine that there will not be serious consequences for them. There is a specificity, then, to the violence of violent democracy which differs from the kinds of violence that take place in authoritarian regimes.

This suggests that the line of argument implied by Arias and Goldstein (2010b) and put forward by North *et al.* (2013b) that the institutions of democracy are more or less irrelevant to the workings of violence is wrong. While there certainly are democracies which are so limited that they have little effect on violence, many of the democracies with which we are concerned not only produce and shape violence, but also tend to constrain it. In this sense violence and democracy are simultaneously mutually constitutive and contradictory or 'disjunctive', as Holston (2008) puts it.

Large theoretical questions come into play here. How do we think about the relationship between democracy and social order? And under what conditions does violence come into play? Democracy constitutes a system of power which structures social order and hierarchy in particular ways determined in part by the ways in which it regulates the use of violence. While it claims to empower all citizens equally, in practice it is a system of differential power (or, in Holston's terminology, differential citizenship). But it is not the only system of power – another resides in the shape of the economy. Others are constituted by the system of multiple violent actors operating across and beyond the state – the 'violent pluralism' identified by Arias and Goldstein (2010b) – and a key set of these consists of the various elite factions and coalitions and the dynamics of rent seeking and patronage that are the subject of analysis by North *et al.* (2013b).

Violence, or rather the capability for violence, is a form of power which can be deployed to maintain a particular social order or disrupt it. Where the prevailing political form – in this case democracy – has insufficient capability to sustain or regulate the given social order, violence comes into play. Where the economic structure and its power are grossly inequitable, democracy necessarily becomes unresponsive to the plight of the poor, and cannot sustain order without violence, while the clash between inclusion and exclusion produces the violence of the poor. Where democracy clashes with the system of power through which the order of patronage is organized, violence comes into play. Order is produced and challenged in multiple different sites by multiple different agents with violent capability, not only by the state, as Arias and Goldstein (2010b) point out. People move between these orders depending on circumstances and issues; at times they articulate their concerns and aspirations as citizens, at other times as clients of powerful patrons, and at other times as participants in a local symbolic order with only a tenuous relation to the state.

Here we are just as far from a social order held in place by the internalized processes of Foucault's governmentality or Bourdieu's symbolic violence as we are from the Weberian state and its monopoly of coercion. A sociology that restricts itself to such notions of power, fabricated in the crucible of Western modernity, will not be adequate to the demands of analysing violent democracies in the post-colonial world; and a sociology that is forged in *this* crucible may help to refresh our perspectives on democracy and violence in the West, particularly in this era of savage rollbacks of stable work and social protection.

Western democracy cannot be taken as the paradigm of democracy towards which societies of the post-colonial world are or should be moving – not least because of the role Western democracies have played and continue to play in the formation of violent democracies. But nor can violent democracy in the post-colonial world be regarded as just a variant on democracy: violence constrains democracy and the rights of citizens, as this article has shown. An urgent question facing sociology is how to imagine paths towards democracy which are less violent and more deeply empowering than that of either the West or the post-colonial world – how, in other words, to keep the dream of democracy alive.

Notes

1 The study was jointly undertaken by the Centre for the Study of Violence and Reconciliation (CSVR) and the Society Work and Development Institute (SWOP) at the University of the Witwatersrand, of which I am the director, and funded by the Royal Norwegian Embassy and the CS Mott Foundation.
2 This information was collected by Crispen Chinguno as part of his PhD thesis on strike violence, which I am supervising.
3 An elite prosecution-driven investigating unit located within the NPA.

References

Alexander, P., (2012), 'Barricades, ballots and experimentation: making sense of the 2011 local government elections with a social movement lens', in M. Dawson and L. Sinwell (eds), *Contesting Transformation: Popular Resistance in Twenty-First Century South Africa*, 63–79, London: Pluto Press.
ANC, (2010), 'NGC 2010: Report on the State of the Organisation by ANC Secretary General Gwede Mantashe', available at: http://www.anc.org.za/show.php?id=5946 (accessed 6 July 2013).
ANC, (2012), 'Organisational report of the National Executive Committee of the ANC to the 53rd National Conference by the Secretary General, Gwede Mantashe', Mangaung, 16–20 December.
Arias, E. D., (2006), 'The dynamics of criminal governance: networks and social order in Rio de Janeiro', *Journal of Latin American Studies*, 38 (2): 293–325.
Arias, E. D. and Goldstein, D. M., (2010b), 'Violence pluralism: understanding the new democracies of Latin America', in E. D. Arias and D. M. Goldstein (eds), *Violent democracies in Latin America*, 1–34, Durham, NC: Duke University Press.

Auyero, J., (2007), *Routine Politics and Violence in Argentina: The Gray Zone of State Power*, Cambridge: Cambridge University Press.

Auyero, J., (2010), 'Clandestine connections: the political and relational makings of collective violence', in E. D. Arias and D. M. Goldstein (eds), *Violent Democracies in Latin America*, 108–132, Durham, NC: Duke University Press.

Booysen, S., (2009), 'Beyond the ballot and the brick: continuous dual repertoires in the politics of attaining service delivery in South Africa' in A. McLennan and B. Munslow (eds), *The Politics of Service Delivery*, Johannesburg: Wits University Press.

Bruce, D., (2012a), 'The road to Marikana: abuses of force during public order policing operations', 12 October, SACSIS, available at: http://www.sacsis.org.za/site/article/1455 (accessed 6 December 2013).

Bruce, D., (2012b), 'A template for Marikana was made in Ermelo a year ago', 5 November, Business Day Live, http://www.bdlive.co.za/opinion/2012/11/05/A-template-for-Marikana-was-made-in-Ermelo (accessed 6 December 2013).

Burawoy, M. and Von Holdt, K., (2012), *Conversations with Bourdieu: The Johannesburg Moment*, Johannesburg: Wits University Press.

Chinguno, C., (2013), 'Marikana and the post-apartheid workplace order', SWOP Working Paper 1, Johannesburg.

Holston, J., (2008), *Insurgent Citizenship: Disjunctions of Democracy and Modernity in Brazil*, Princeton, NJ and Oxford: Princeton University Press.

Khan, M., (2005), 'Markets, states and democracy: patron-client networks and the case for democracy in developing countries', *Democratization*, 12 (5): 704–724.

Langa, M., (2010), 'Research Report: protest and collective violence: Case study 3: "Violence is the only language that this government knows" ', Unpublished research report, SWOP/CSVR.

Langa, M. and von Holdt, K., (2012), 'Insurgent citizenship, class formation and the dual nature of community protest: a case study of "kungcatsha" ', in M. Dawson and L. Sinwell (eds), *Contesting Transformation: Popular Resistance in Twenty-First Century South Africa*, 80–100, London: Pluto Press.

Marks, M., (2005), *Transforming the Robocops: Changing Police in South Africa*, Scottsville: University of KwaZulu-Natal Press.

Ndletyana, M., Makhalemele, P., and Mathekga, R., (2013), *Patronage Politics Divides Us: A Study of Poverty, Patronage and Inequality in South Africa*, Johannesburg: Mapungubwe Institute for Strategic Reflection.

NDP, (2012), *National Development Plan 2030: Our Future – Make it Work*, Pretoria: National Planning Commission, The Presidency.

North, D. C., Wallis, J. J., Webb, S. B. and Weingast, P. R., (2013a), 'Limited access orders: an introduction to the conceptual framework', in D. C. North, J. J. Wallis, S. B. Webb and P. R. Weingast (eds), *In the Shadow of Violence: Politics, Economics, and the Problems of Development*, Cambridge: Cambridge University Press.

North, D. C., Wallis, J. J., Webb, S. B. and Weingast, P. R., (2013b), 'Lessons: in the shadow of violence', in D. C. North, J. J. Wallis, S. B. Webb and P. R. Weingast (eds), *In the Shadow of Violence: Politics, Economics, and the Problems of Development*, Cambridge: Cambridge University Press.

North, D. C., Wallis, J. J. and Weingast, B. R., (2009), *Violence and Social Orders: A Conceptual Framework for Interpreting Recorded Human History*, Cambridge: Cambridge University Press.

NPC, (2011), *Diagnostic Overview*, Pretoria: National Planning Commission, The Presidency.

O'Donnell, G., (1993), 'On the state, democratisation and some conceptual problems: a Latin American view with glances at some post-communist countries', *World Development*, 21 (8): 1355–1369.

Plaut, M. and Holden, P., (2012), *Who Rules South Africa? Pulling the Strings in the Battle for Power*, Johannesburg and Cape Town: Jonathan Ball Publishers.

The Sociological Review, 62:S2, pp. 129–151 (2014), DOI: 10.1111/1467-954X.12196

Von Holdt, K., (2010), 'Institutionalisation, strike violence and local moral orders', *Transformation: Critical Perspectives on Southern Africa*, 72/73: 127–151.

Von Holdt, K., (2013a), 'The violence of order, orders of violence: between Fanon and Bourdieu', *Current Sociology*, 61 (2) Monograph 1: *Violence and Society*, 112–131.

Von Holdt, K., (2013b), 'The transition to violent democracy in South Africa', *Review of African Political Economy*, 138: 589–604.

Von Holdt, K., Langa, M., Molapo, S., Mogapi, N., Ngubeni, K., Dlamini, J. and Kirsten, A., (2011), 'The smoke that calls: insurgent citizenship, collective violence and the struggle for a place in the new South Africa: seven case studies of community protests and xenophobic violence', Research report. Johannesburg: CSVR and SWOP.

Walby, S., (2013), 'Violence and society: introduction to an emerging field of sociology', *Current Sociology*, 61 (2) Monograph 1: *Violence and Society*, 95–111.

Violence before identity: an analysis of identity politics

Glenn Bowman

Abstract: Violence is a force for creating integrities as well as one that violates, pollutes and destroys already existing entities. In this paper I address the role of what Ariella Azoulay terms the 'political imagination' in constituting social aggregates committed to the defence of a community itself brought into being by the imagining of a force dedicated to its destruction. Such a group's perception of what Laclau and Mouffe call an 'antagonism' spurs it to mark out and defend its boundaries with violence – a violence often manifested aggressively (pre-emptively). Collective perceptions of an other's antagonism are often overdetermined, either by historical memory or political manipulation, and it is often the case that an enemy is sited and a programme of 'defensive' violence inaugurated without any 'real' justification. Here I demonstrate, using events drawn from the formation of the State of Israel and the collapse of what is now 'Former Yugoslavia', that it is in designating an other against which destructive violence must be mobilized that an entity realizes – through the negation of that it would negate – what it is it fights to defend.

Keywords: political imagination, antagonism, constituent/constitutive violence, defensive violence, interpellation, Israel, former Yugoslavia

Introduction: fantasy and the making of political identities

In the following text I will explore what, borrowing a title from Ernesto Laclau's 1994 edited volume, I call 'the making of political identities' (Laclau, 1994). Violence, or more to the point the imagining of violence, plays a central role in this 'making' insofar as a political identity is an identity mobilized against a perceived threat.

Identity, in everyday civil life, is a relatively unfixed orientation which shifts according to the social setting in which those who express it are engaged.[1] The situatedness of such identity articulations allows us to understand the ways numerous linkages can be made between diverse persons within a community, and the ways in which persons can assert a multitude of occasionally incommensurate identities in the course of moving through the various contexts of everyday life. Political identity, in the way I will use it in the following pages, is

The Sociological Review, 62:S2, pp. 152–165 (2014), DOI: 10.1111/1467-954X.12195

a particular form of identity that can, in contexts marked by the imagining of a serious endangerment to self and others, subsume quotidian identities, forcing to the fore a specific sense of self and community mobilized against that threat. I argue in the following that that threat, which reconfigures and at times even invents a *community against*, need not be real to have that identity structuring effect. It is, in fact, often more effective in so doing if it is a fantasy.

Imagining a 'war of annihilation'

Ariella Azoulay, in recent writings (2011, 2012, 2013), distinguishes between 'civil imagination' and 'political imagination'. For her civil imagination is an imaging of community incorporating a range of persons and groups connected by the contiguity of everyday life. While differential identities are inevitably involved in such networks, these are situational and rarely more than temporarily divisive. The political imagination is a very different construct through which the persons and groups conjoined in civil imagination are bifurcated, producing distinct communities discursively – and practically – deemed mutually antagonistic. Focusing on the process of the establishing of the Israeli state on Palestinian territory, Azoulay writes

> Viewing the late 1940s . . . from a perspective of national sovereignty, it displays a series of events connected to the Zionist phantasm of establishing a national home for one people in an area occupied by a mixed population, and situates two sides at the drama's center: two mutually hostile nations fighting to the death in a conflict only one can survive. These two perspectives bury the question of whether these two sides – 'Jews' and 'Arabs' – in fact existed as separate, hostile parties prior to the war. . . . The unproblematic adoption of the term 'war' to describe the period establishes it at the apex of the 'Israel-Palestine conflict' in a manner that eliminates the complex variety of exchange and interaction between Jews and Arabs, replacing it with a narrow conception of 'national conflict' that justifies an anachronistic reading of the past in which 'war' between them was unavoidable. The term 'war' assumes as self-evident the existence of two hostile sides which fought one another. (Azoulay, 2011: 7)

Via the 'constituent violence' of this act of bifurcation 'nonviolent options for sharing life were constantly eliminated [and] the simple fact that they had existed earlier became inconceivable' (Azoulay, 2013: 551).[2] For Azoulay this cataclysmic shift from civil identity to political identities is an artifice imposed by the machinery of state or state formation; she refers to the events as a 'regime-made disaster' (Azoulay, 2012: 2 and passim) effected by 'an organized, regulated and motivated system of power' (Azoulay, 2012: 2).

Insofar as Azoulay focuses on the Zionist project of state formation, she locates the source of this discourse-changing constituent violence in the machineries of the state in waiting; the *Palmach,* the *Haganah,* the Stern Gang (*Lehi*) and other military and paramilitary forces. *From Palestine to Israel* thus highlights a series of actions – the imposition of military rule over Arab communities, the destruction and expropriation of Arab properties by soldiers and paramilitaries, deportation of populations, and the establishment and enforcement of new borders – that both define and defeat an enemy. The text, and its photographs, also attends to the ways a newly instituted Jewish citizenry accommodated itself to this state of 'war' by adopting the identity of the community at war with the Arab other. It was thus able to sever its ties with the local Arabs, expropriating Arab properties (both immovable and moveable) while legitimating that expropriation through the acceptance of a discourse on 'Absentee Properties', moving into Jewish settlements built over emptied Arab villages, and accepting that the catastrophe which tore the communities apart was simultaneously 'their' *Nakba* (disaster) and 'our' liberation.

Insofar as the construction of a state of war was 'carried out by the Jewish military and political leadership' (Azoulay, 2011: 7), the question has to be asked of how a Jewish population which had for the most part previously cohabited with its Arab neighbours was mobilized to take part in that war. Azoulay, in a rather Foucauldian manner, answers that

> Military force was needed to overcome the opposition of the majority of the land's inhabitants [Jews and Arabs alike] and to realize the plan. In order to produce such military force, the civil population had to be recruited and made submissive. The might of war as an existential threat had to be imposed on the population; the dividing line between Jews and Arabs had to be constituted as essential, that is, as absolute. (Azoulay, 2011: 8)

There appears to be an ambiguity in this articulation; it is not clear whether the 'military force' of the militias and political leadership – what Azoulay terms 'military governmentality' (Azoulay, 2011: 20 and passim) – imposed conditions on the Jewish civilian population which dragooned them into the 'regime-made disaster' or whether rapidly changing events on the ground in the wake of the approval of United Nations Resolution 181 on partition (29 November 1947), and the way these events were described by the Zionist leadership, convinced Jews to take up arms to defend themselves against an 'existential threat'. Ilan Pappé strongly implies the latter in his description of the wave of violence (much of it local rioting initiated by Arabs but responded to with assaults by the *Hagana*) which swept Mandate Palestine from the morning of the resolution through to early January. He notes that the first day of clashes resulted in 'the death of seven Jews and a few burnt down buildings and businesses in Jerusalem, and an equal number of Arabs killed in the wake of Jewish retaliation the morning after' (Pappé, 1992: 77).

> Was this the beginnings of a 'Palestinian onslaught on the Jewish community' in Palestine? Sir Alan Cunningham – the last High Commissioner in Palestine – did not think so. He reported to London that the 'riots in Jerusalem were not the onset of an orchestrated offensive against the Jews, but rather spontaneous demonstrations against the partition resolution'. Cunningham's analysis is shared by Palestinian historians who regard the violence as a natural consequence of the many

The Sociological Review, 62:S2, pp. 152–165 (2014), DOI: 10.1111/1467-954X.12195

demonstrations held in those days. This was in contrast, however, to the view taken by the Jewish leaders, who declared to the world at large that a war of annihilation had begun. (Pappé, 1992: 77)

Pappé describes what one might term a feedback loop operating between assertions by the Jewish leaders that Jews in Palestine faced extermination at the hands of a committed Arab enemy and a number of well-publicized events across what had been Mandate Palestine in which Jews were killed by Arabs (he also chronicles a number of retaliatory operations by *Hagana* forces which provoked further randomly directed reprisals by Arabs against Jews – 1992: 77–78). In that loop, the generalized assertion that all Jews in Palestine faced a lethal organized enemy – an enemy that had until that moment disguised itself in the shapes of neighbours, co-workers and friends – received confirmation from bloody incidents in which Jews were killed *as* Jews. This conjunction of images, rather than a prolonged and carefully planned process of recruiting and subjecting a resistant Jewish population to an acceptance of the necessity of war against neighbours, produced a radical and rapid reconfiguration of quotidian discourse. In a sense it is true that, as Azoulay asserts, 'military force' was needed to impose a sense of 'existential threat' on the Jewish population, but this force served only to ensure that sustained Arab anti-Jewish violence would confirm to those Jews who resisted discursive mobilization that a war of annihilation was in the offing. A series of conjoined acts of violence and counter-violence[3] took place over the following months, ensuring the circulation of a body of stories of inter-communal hostility that divided the population of Mandate Palestine into two armies at war. On 15 May 1948 what is now referred to as the 'civil war' was concluded when the armies of the Arab Leagues invaded the region initiating what history records as the 'Arab–Israeli War'.

'Addressed' by violence

It is the preceding 'discursive shift' and the role of perceived violence in initiating it that concerns me in this paper. Here, by a process analogous to what Louis Althusser terms 'interpellation' (Althusser, 1971), individuals and collectivities perceive themselves as 'addressed' by an act of violence and, in recognizing themselves (or perhaps rather misrecognizing [*méconnaissent*] themselves) as its intended recipient not only mobilize towards a 'defensive' reciprocation but also, via a process analogous to their own generic identification with the actual victims of violence, deindividuate the agency of the literal agents of violence so as to make it the violence of a collectivized 'Other' – in this case the 'Arab'. There is a powerful element of fantasy in operation in this process, reshaping not only the identity of the individual engaging with it but also his or her perception of the community he or she belongs to and the 'other' which is perceived as intending the destruction of that community.

It is important to stress here that the motor of this reconfiguration is not actual violence inflicted on those mobilizing for battle but a perception of a possible violence which is likely to be suffered if it is not pre-emptively countered. This is not to say that there is not a potentiality of attack at hand and that the 'fantasy' which calls one to arms is delusionary; it was quite possible, in the 1947 scenario discussed above, that a Jew minding his or her own business might be attacked and killed by an Arab responding to his or her perceptions of the threat posed by Jews. What needs, however, to be stressed is that the construction of a state of war was one among a number of options posed to those faced with the withdrawal of the British military and the proposed partition scheme. As Azoulay points out above there were multiple civil alliances between Jews and Arabs that refused the conclusion that division and war was the only option the situation posed, and the work of revisionist historians such as Joel Beinin on Arab Jewish labour confederations (Beinin, 1990) and Zachary Lockman on the relations of Arab and Jewish workers between 1906 and 1948 (Lockman, 1996) shows that, notwithstanding class and residential differences, 'intercommunal' collaboration both in production and in union activity was the norm. Once, however, stories of killings and atrocities had started to circulate, and had been accepted as verisimilitudinous by their audiences, it was virtually impossible either to return to the previous state or choose alternative options to war.[4]

For narratives of violent acts to induce changes in existing discourses on identity it is necessary for those acts to pose what Laclau and Mouffe term an 'antagonism' (Laclau and Mouffe, 1985: 93–148, esp. 122–127). For Laclau and Mouffe 'society' is a discursive construct, and an antagonism constitutes the limits of that discourse, that is, reveals the impossibility of its realization. In an example posed by them – 'it is because a peasant *cannot be* a peasant that an antagonism exists with the landowner expelling him from his land' (1985: 125) – we can see the move from 'civil imagination' to 'political imagination' clearly sketched out. The 'peasant' on his or her land inhabits a number of situational identities during his or her traversing of kin, religious, economic and other situated networks. The threat of dislocation that promises to obliterate the connection to site threatens all those roles with impossibility and, in so doing, constitutes the peasant as a self-conscious political entity organized to oppose that antagonism. In this sense the 'peasant' did not exist as a discursively constituted subject prior to its coming into being as the agent of the negation of its own negation (apologies to Hegel), that is, as a political subject.

'Recognizing' the past in the present

In the situation of Israel/Palestine discussed above, as in many others, the creation of political identity is not so *sui generis*. While it is conceivable (but unlikely) that a peasantry threatened with disinheritance might not have a history of previous expulsions to draw upon in its understanding of the situation that both antagonizes and creates it as a political force, in other situations an antagonism is likely to be 'recognized' as a contemporary manifestation of

The Sociological Review, 62:S2, pp. 152–165 (2014), DOI: 10.1111/1467-954X.12195

threats to identity and/or survival drawn from the past. Through that 'recognition' the person or community facing an antagonism is provided with an identification enabling it to 'take up' an identity that is a variant of that which challenged the earlier antagonism. In the case of mobilizing the Jewish population of what was soon to become Israel, there was an extensive repertoire of previous attempts to annihilate the Jewish people to draw upon, ranging from the Babylonian exiles and the Jewish Wars of the Roman Period, through the massacres and expulsions carried out in Medieval Europe and the more recent pogroms of Russia and the East, to, of course, the recently terminated Holocaust. The relatively short history of cohabitation of Jews and Arabs in Palestine offered little in the way of counter-histories to oppose the political construction of the Arab response to the Partition Plan as yet another antagonistic assault on Jewish existence, and the militant Jewish identity constructed against this new attempt to annihilate Jewish existence mirrored the violence it imaged as mobilized against it.

The figure of the antagonist, or antagonism, is a terrifying congeries of all of the possible ways the destruction of the subject, and his or her community, can be imagined:

> Insofar as there is antagonism I cannot be a full presence for myself. But nor is the force that antagonises me such a presence; its objective being is a symbol of my non-being and, in this way, it is overflowed by a plurality of meanings. (Laclau & Mouffe, 1985: 125)

This fantastical enemy is, simply, the negation of all that makes up the being of those who imagine it. Even for the newly self-constituted 'peasant', threatened with expulsion from his land by the figure of the landlord, the landlord is not simply a man or woman driven by economic considerations but an amalgam of forces which would dissolve kinship and neighbourhood networks, impose homelessness and starvation, and even break off the relationship of the peasant with the divine powers which maintain life.

De-federating the SFRY

The polyvalence of the figure of the antagonist, as well as the openness of the category of those politically constituted to oppose it, is evident in the processes generating radical identity shifts amongst the populations of the then Socialist Federal Republic of Yugoslavia in the late 1980s. In the decade leading up to that time, a decade initiated by the death of Marshall Tito in May 1980, the Yugoslav economy had effectively collapsed as international debts were called in and a harsh IMF regime was imposed on the country. Tito, in the popular imagination, had symbolized a 'Yugoslav style that had less to do with socialism, self-management and non-alignment than with freedom of movement, the advent of the consumer society, and fending for oneself' (Pavlowitch, 1988: 27), but in the years following his death, as unemployment surged, inflation sky-rocketed and the standard of living plummeted (Pavlowitch, 1988; and Mencinger, 1991) that ideal image of Yugoslav identity seemed to be under attack by the clumsy attempts of a crumbling federal state to repressively enforce cultural and economic hegemony (Bowman, 1994: 152–59; 2003: 328–35):

> A general disgruntlement . . . set in throughout the country as state policies began to be seen not to defend the people and their standard of living but to be attacking them; in the early eighties a wide range of assertions – expressed in idioms ranging from the economic and political to those of art and culture – began to articulate perceptions of the antagonism of *the state* to *its people.* (Bowman, 2001: 39)

These expressions did not, however, fall 'naturally' into a nationalist idiom. Tito's anti-nationalist policies and the modernization processes which had accompanied them had to a large extent submerged the idiom of national identity beneath a flood of contending discourses on selfhood.[5] Thus initially the violence of the state was not perceived as inflicted upon one's national being but appeared to attack people regardless of nationality in their abilities to earn and save money, to play or listen to rock music, to call for greater representation in political forums, to travel and so on.

Specific activities by political elites, simultaneously conjuring up resurgent antagonisms and reinvigorating ethno-national identity categories in which to shelter from them, worked to reconfigure people's identities as virulently opposed either to the state in general or to neighbouring communities figured as allied with that antagonistic state.

Most famously Slobodan Milošević used a media campaign to alert Serbs to the danger posed to their well-being and rights by the presence of Kosovans (ethnic Albanians who made up 90 per cent of the population of the autonomous region of Kosovo) within the borders of the Republic of Serbia. Not only were they accused of draining Serbia's wealth through the financial support granted Kosovo by the Yugoslav state, but they were portrayed as blood enemies of the Serbian people who raped Serbian girls and nuns in the Orthodox monasteries of Kosovo (monasteries which stand in the Serbian imaginary as monuments to a Greater Serbia destroyed by the late 14th-century Ottoman invasion), who razed and desecrated those Orthodox holy places, and who drove Serbs living in Kosovo out of their homes so as to provide housing for the fast-breeding Kosovan population as well as for the illegal Albanian immigrants they encouraged. Through evoking Kosovan violence towards Serbian attempts to inscribe a Serbian identity on Kosovo, an autonomous region imaged as Serbia's historic heartland, Milošević reconstituted 'Serbia' as a locus of identity and 'Serbian interests' as a focus of concern. At *Kosovo Polje* (the Field of Blackbirds) Milošević gave an impassioned speech on 28 June 1989, the occasion of the 600th anniversary of the defeat and destruction of the medieval Serbian kingdom by the forces of the Ottoman Empire, announcing a call for Serbs to unite – as they had failed to do six centuries earlier – in the face of a mortal threat posed to Serbian well-being and to Serbia's ability to 'function as a

The Sociological Review, 62:S2, pp. 152–165 (2014), DOI: 10.1111/1467-954X.12195

successful state' (Krieger, 2001: 11) by Muslim Kosovans, the disintegrating Yugoslav state which fostered them, and Albanian (and other) external allies.

'This is what they did to us'

I observed a similar process of what Azoulay terms 'constitutive violence' (Azoulay, 2013) in Ljubljana in April 1990 during campaigning for the federal elections which preceded the Wars of Succession. Anti-communist parties, vying for political power while lacking any platform other than opposition to the communist federal state, had set up campaign booths along the main thorough-fares which were bedecked with pictures of caves (*foibe*) filled with the bones of persons allegedly killed by the partisan forces that took place at the close of the Second World War (Ballinger, 2003). The captions on the photographs said simply 'This is what They did to Us'. The assertion was direct – 'they (the communist partisans) killed "us" (Slovenes) *en masse* as they came to power' – and the implication needed no further elaboration – 'and subsequent policies from the communist state towards the Slovenes has been a continuation of national genocide by other means'. This rhetoric, which called on people as Slovenes to recognize that communist violence towards Slovenes in the past was the same as the state's violence towards them in the present, was grounded in a substantial series of misrepresentations.

The corpses found in the depths of the limestone caves of the Istrian Penninsula could not, after 45 years of rot, be authoritatively identified either individually or collectively. Records and memoirs indicate that they are variously made up of 1) ethnic Italians and Slovenes killed by German and Italian soldiers during their occupation and 2) an amalgam of those captured and executed by the victorious partisans at the close of the war, including members of German and Italian fascist units, Croatian Ustaše, Serbian Cetniks, Slovene 'Home Guard' militias as well as camp followers and Italians and Slovenes deemed anti-communist. Only a minority of the corpses are likely to have been those of Slovenes, and there are strong indications that those that were had either been affiliated to pro-Axis parties or killed by Fascist or Nazi forces before the advent of the partisans. The equations of the 'they' with the partisans who went on to establish the Socialist Federal Republic was thus not fully viable, while the identification of the dead with Slovenes was even more untenable. Nonetheless, mute bodies could provide no evident resistance to their discursive consolidation into a 'we' standing in for the Slovene population as a whole, while the brutal deindividuation of their deaths and the sense of loss the bone-filled holes evoked figured forth the genocidal image of an antagonism.[6] Only a minority of the corpses are likely to have been those of Slovenes, and there are strong indications that those that were were either affiliated to pro-Axis parties or had been killed by Fascist or Nazi forces before the advent of the partisans. The equations of the 'they' with the partisans who went on to establish the Socialist Federative Republic was thus not fully viable, while the identification of the dead with Slovenes was even more untenable.

The Sociological Review, 62:S2, pp. 152–165 (2014), DOI: 10.1111/1467-954X.12195
© 2014 The Author. Editorial organisation © 2014 The Editorial Board of the Sociological Review

Nonetheless, mute bodies could evidence no resistance to their discursive consolidation into a 'we' standing in for the Slovene population as a whole, while the brutal deindividuation of their deaths and the sense of loss the bone-filled holes evoked figured forth the genocidal image of an antagonism. All that remained for the circuit of interpellation to work was for contemporary Slovenes, the intended audience of the campaign discourse, to see themselves as the intended victims of a communist state whose founders had once tried to exterminate them as a people and which had been, since that time, working to complete the job.

I am not trying here to offer a history of the break-up of the Yugoslav federation and the rise of the successor states,[7] but instead to provide examples of the ways in which rhetorics of the political imagination employ constitutive violence to forge identities mobilized against figures of antagonism. Serbia and Slovenia, like Israel, emerged from the constitutive violence which accompanied their births as contemporary states different from what had preceded them and populated by a 'rebadged' citizenry politically mobilized towards their defence from the assaults of enemies themselves either invented or reconfigured.

Differential responses

In the cases I have described, persons' investments in the political imaginary are far from uniform and as a consequence not only will there be a diversity of responses to its appeal in particular situations but communities as aggregates of persons will prove more or less responsive to such calls, depending on their histories and the ways the individuals which make them up perceive risks posed by contemporary situations. Insofar as one cannot argue for a group psychology (if there is statistically a set of symptoms collectively evidenced, these can only be an aggregation of individual responses rendered 'equivalent' by the perceived antagonism) then one must, in approaching processes such as those I've discussed above, locate the resultant interpellations in individual psychologies. Some, such as those discussed by Azoulay who refused to see their Arab neighbours as enemies, are resistant to calls to recognize, and oppose, an antagonist whereas others are predisposed to recognize a threat to their being and mobilizing to oppose that threat.

Julia Borossa and Caroline Rooney engage psychoanalytical concepts in examining what they term 'fortress hypochondria' (Borossa and Rooney, 2014) which they trace to 'the real and frightening helplessness of being faced [in childhood] with the sufferings of loved others [that] leads to a heightened consciousness of ontological security' (Borossa and Rooney, 2014: 6).[8] The sense of ontological *insecurity* that drives individual needs to render the self impossibly safe is, the authors point out, gathered in, bolstered and collectivized by 'sociopolitical agendas [that promote] . . . a biopolitics in which the social body has to defend its health from the fear of proximate but different bodies' (2014: 13). These agendas, which employ the fantasy of 'sustaining an invulnerable body' (2014: 12) in the face of a threat to that body – or to bodies the subjects addressed can empathize with – produce 'a fear of contagion that is a contagious fear' (2014: 13) that, depending on historically constructed individual vulnerabilities to 'hypochondria', can spread widely, but irregularly, within a community.

In Israel in the 1947–1948 period the sensed immediacy of the 'Arab threat' was reinforced both by the proximity of violence and the broadcasting of its presence by word of mouth and media channels. In the two Yugoslav instances a widespread sense of the failure of the state to protect and prosper its citizenry had to be both differentiated (in ethno-national terms) and amplified by means of a 'making real' of narratives of earlier threats (whether historical or mythical).[9] In all three instances the violence initially amplified and then produced by these discourses worked to guarantee that further violences would erupt, bringing about war and thus consolidating the grip of the new identities and the 'defensive violences' that were needed to protect them.

The concept of the 'political imaginary' drawn from Ariella Azoulay's recent work suggests that a perceived antagonism stimulates the emergence of an identity constituted precisely by the need to defend itself against that enemy. Political identities generated by discourse-changing eruptions of antagonisms are clearly bounded by a frontier that marks off 'we' from 'them', even when the space of those constituted as the same ('we') by the shared perception of their common enemy is permeated by the presence of those labelled as antagonistic. While this identity is undeniably political, those who embrace it are not necessarily themselves involved in the counter-violence directed towards that antagonism; many, perhaps the majority, take refuge in knowing that others of their community actively oppose the perceived threat. The structure of the societies which emerge from such situations is characterized, as long as the sense of the antagonism threatening them remains powerful, by an aggressive military component aligned with a strong leadership defending a population not itself actively involved in attacking the antagonism but unified in its opposition to it.

Conclusion: aggregation and disaggregation of consensus

Solidarity *against* a perceived antagonism is tenuous, and depends on the continuation of a majority consensus that the threat offered is both shared and significant. As that consensus disaggregates, so too does the popular mandate which supports both the leadership and the military. In Slovenia the DEMOS coalition, voted into power to prepare for independence and organize military resistance to the Jugoslav National Army (JNA), disintegrated within nine months of the conclusion of the Ten-Day War (26 June–7 July 1991) in which Slovenia gained its independence and the JNA, under Serbian control, made manifest its disinterest in keeping Slovenia within Yugoslavia. The withdrawal of the 'external' enemy, as well as the relative absence of ethnic others within Slovenia,[10] meant that subsequent political struggles were internal to the Slovene community. In 1992 the Liberal Democrat party, the successor to the youth fraction of the Communist Party of Slovenia, won the parliamentary elections against the opposition of former members of the DEMOS coalition who, among other things, lost substantial support from women and others by campaigning against abortion on the grounds that 'Slovenia is a small country surrounded by big enemies, and every aborted foetus is a soldier lost to its future defence' (see Salecl, 1993). Milošević's programme of mobilizing Serbs on the grounds that 'Serbia's enemies outside the country are plotting against it, along with those in[side] the country' (speech in Belgrade 19 November 1988, quoted in Ramet 2006: 348) never interpellated the whole of the Serb population, but his mobilization for war against both external and internal enemies called on popular support for the building up of a very substantial police force as well as the establishment and funding of militias to supplement a Serb-controlled JNA. The resultant corruption and internal repression in turn generated internal opposition leading to mass popular demonstrations against the regime in 1991 and 1996–7 and, although there was a period of renewed nationalist mobilization against the Kosovans and their NATO allies between 1998 and 1999, mass dissent re-erupted in 2000, forcing Milošević's resignation and his subsequent arrest, charged with corruption, embezzlement and abuse of power. In both instances the invocation of an antagonism was only temporarily successful in generating national solidarity and legitimating 'defensive aggression'.

After 1948 Israel not only faced the problem of how to establish itself on the previously shared terrain of Mandate Palestine but also that of maintaining its cohesion when its Jewish population was made up of a multitude of immigrant communities often sharing little other than their Jewishness. Certainly, in the early days of state formation and consolidation, war with the local Arabs and the surrounding Arab countries worked to promote a strong national identity *against* the antagonism those posed. Subsequently the drive to recruit Jews from a multitude of countries brought Sephardi and Mizrahi Jews into a national demographic previously constituted for the most part by Ashkenazim. This admixture has generated substantial problems of class and cultural difference, as well as of mutual intolerance and perceived disenfranchisement, that have challenged, and continue to challenge, national unity (see Giladi, 1990; Swirski, 1989; Shenhav, 2006). What has counteracted this threat of intra-communal factionalization is Israel's continuous war footing, a stance towards perceived external and internal threats which maintains much of its population in constant anxiety about both its physical annihilation by external and internal enemies as well as the destruction of the Jewishness of the Jewish state by the demographic threat posed by the Palestinians (backed by 'hostile' foreign advocates of Palestinian rights). This aggregated anxiety about both physical survival and identity survival ensures both defensive national solidarity and near universal support for an intransigent state backed by a powerful military.

Notes

1 'Situational identity' is a concept generally assumed to have been generated by, if not specifically used in, Erving Goffman's theory of the dramaturgical construction of social identity developed

The Sociological Review, 62:S2, pp. 152–165 (2014), DOI: 10.1111/1467-954X.12195

in *The Presentation of Self in Everyday Life* (1959). Max Gluckman, however, elaborated the concept of 'situational selection' in 1940 to characterize how individuals shape their behaviours in different social contexts to conform to the values and practices of groups they there associate with: 'the shifting membership of groups in different situations is the functioning of the structure, for an individual's membership of a particular group in a particular situation is determined by the motives and values influencing him in that situation. Individuals can thus live coherent lives by situational selection from a medley of contradictory values, ill-assorted beliefs, and varied interests and techniques' (Gluckman, 1958 [1940]).

2 Azoulay's research for a film on this 'moment' uncovered 'no less than one hundred local civil alliances that Jews and Arabs tried to achieve from early 1947 until close to the declaration of the State of Israel in May 1948. . . . However, the results of constituent violence condemned most of their content to a chronicle of collaboration, the *co-laboring* of which made it disgraceful. . . . The mere joint action with individuals of the 'other side' was considered treasonous, and whoever refused to be differentiated from others on a national basis was doomed to be declared as an enemy collaborator' (2013: 553–554).

3 What David Ben-Gurion referred to in the 1 January 1948 entry of his diaries as the 'vicious cycle . . . [of] reprisal and counter-reprisal' (Rivlin and Orren, 1982: 99 quoted by Pappé, 1992: 77) initiated by *Hagana* attacks on Arab individuals and villages. Pappé argues that without provocations such as the unprovoked assault on Silwan, the Arab population 'might have [been] left . . . largely indifferent to the developing conflict' (1992: 77).

4 Lockman, in closing his study of Jewish–Arab collaboration (Lockman, 1996: 351–355), chronicles an operation by ETZEL (also known as *Irgun*, the militia led by Menachim Begin) in which operatives threw a bomb from a speeding car into a crowd of several hundred day labourers queuing for work outside of main gate of the Haifa oil refinery (6 were killed and 42 wounded). Outraged survivors rushed into the refinery where Jews and Arabs were working and killed 41 Jews, injuring 49. The next day *Palmach* attacked the village of Balad al-Shaykh, where many of the Arab refinery workers lived, killing 60 men, women and children and levelling a substantial number of the houses, despite recognition, confirmed by a committee of inquiry appointed by Haifa's Jewish community, that 'a significant number of the workers and employees did not participate in [the rampage at the refinery and that in fact] . . . there were isolated incidents of Arab workers and [white collar] employees who in various ways warned and even succeeded in saving a number of Jews, their coworkers' (Histradut Archives, Tel Aviv, AA 250/403-9, quoted in Lockman, 1996: 353–354). Lockman comments that 'the Arab unionist's' effective intervention to prevent violence against Jews at the railway workshops received little public attention. Not surprisingly the Yishuv focused on the massacre of Jews at the refinery, while the Arab community preferred to dwell on the preceding bomb attacks by Jews and the Hagana's subsequent retaliatory raid . . .' (1996: 354).

5 In addition to direct political suppression of nationalisms (Allcock, 2000; Andjelic, 2003), Tito constitutionally broke up the power blocs of the dominant republics (in particular Serbia) by the creation of new republics (Macedonia and Montenegro), the invention of a territorially dispersed Muslim nationality, and the devolution of authority to autonomous regions (Vojvodina and Kosovo). Other forces – *gasterbeiter* labour, migration to cities, mixed marriages, military service – all worked to dissolve national identifications. 'National' identities were thus maintained but drained of significance; 'nationalist' identities were violently extirpated.

6 Katia Pizzi, in an article whose title translates as 'The Silent Speak', discusses the multiple readings which can be imposed on mute corpses, and demonstrates the ways the existence of the dead of the *foibe* has been mobilized by numerous parties – right and left – as 'speaking' in support of their identity agendas (Pizzi, 1998). Ironically in light of the Slovene use of the *foibe* Pizzi shows that for the most part Italians use the *foibe's* dead to illustrate Slav brutality.

7 See Silber and Little (1995), Meier (1999), and Hudson and Bowman (2012).

8 Borossa and Rooney note that the ontological insecurity which founds fortress hypochondria might not simply come from direct experience of others' sufferings (those, for instance, of family

members' pains or deaths encountered in childhood – 2004: 6) but can also be 'directly trans-mitted by identifiable sources' (2004:11). Schwab (2010) examines 'transgenerational trauma' and notes that this can be relayed by stories that suffering persons can empathize with but it can also travel more insidiously through those experiences – near or distant – that, while untold, uncannily destabilize a collective world (see also Caruth, 1996). Elizabeth Cowie, building on Jean Laplanche's theory of *nachträglichlekeit* or 'afterwardness' (Laplanche, 1999) points out that the ontological insecurity generating trauma is itself enigmatic, only taking on meaning as memory when adult experiences write over it (Cowie, 2011).

9 In Serbia in late June–early July 1991, as the war was breaking out, I observed in bookshop windows all over Belgrade a proliferation of copiously illustrated books produced by Serbian state publishing houses chronicling the lethal atrocities imposed on Bosnian Serbs by Croat *Ustaše* in concentration camps such as those of the Jasenovac complex, Gospič, and Pag. These worked to equate Bosnian Serbs as past victims of the *Ustaše* with Serbs in Serbia as future victims of the Croats who were themselves *the same as* the *Ustaše* (Denich, 1991: 11 and *passim*).

10 In 1991 88.3 per cent of the population of Slovenia was ethnically Slovene with no other ethnic group constituting more that 2.8 per cent of the population (Statistical Office of the Republic of Slovenia, Census of population, households and housing 2002, available at: http://www.stat.si/popis2002/en/rezultati/rezultati_red.asp?ter=SLO&st=7 (accessed 27 January 2014).

References

Allcock, John, (2000), *Explaining Yugoslavia*, London: C. Hurst & Co.

Althusser, Louis, (1971), 'Ideology and ideological state apparatuses (notes towards an investiga-tion)', in *Lenin and Philosophy and Other Essays* (trans. Ben Brewster), 121–173, London: Verso.

Andjelic, Neven, (2003), *Bosnia-Herzegovina: The End of a Legacy*, London: Frank Cass.

Azoulay, Ariella, (2011), *From Palestine to Israel: A Photographic Record of Destruction and State Formation, 1947–1950*, London: Pluto Press.

Azoulay, Ariella, (2012 [2010 in Hebrew]). *Civil Imagination: A Political Ontology of Photography* (trans. L. Bethlehen), London: Verso.

Azoulay, Ariella, (2013), 'Potential history: thinking through violence', *Critical Inquiry*, 39: 548–574.

Ballinger, Pamela, (2003), *History in Exile: Memory and Identity at the Borders of the Balkans*, Princeton, NJ: Princeton University Press.

Beinin, Joel, (1990), *Was the Red Flag Flying There? Marxist Politics and the Arab-Israeli Conflict in Eqypt and Israel 1948–1965*, Berkeley, CA: University of California Press.

Borossa, Julia and Rooney, Caroline, (2014), 'Fortress hypochondria: health and safety', in Lene Auestad (ed.), *Nationalism and the Body Politic: Psychoanalysis and the Rise of Ethnocentricism and Xenophobia*, 5–19. London: Karnak Books.

Bowman, Glenn, (1994), 'Xenophobia, fantasy and the nation: the logic of ethnic violence in Former Yugoslavia', in Victoria Goddard, Llobera Josep and Chris Shore (eds), *Anthropology of Europe: Identity and Boundaries in Conflict*, 143–171, Oxford: Berg Press.

Bowman, Glenn, (2001), 'The violence in identity', in Bettina Schmidt and Ingo Schroeder (eds), *Anthropology of Violence and Conflict*, 25–46, London: Routledge.

Bowman, Glenn, (2003), 'Constitutive violence and the nationalist imaginary: antagonism and defensive solidarity in "Palestine" and "Former Yugoslavia" ', *Social Anthropology*, XI: 319–340.

Caruth, Cathy, (1996), *Unclaimed Experience: Trauma, Narrative and History*, Baltimore, MD: Johns Hopkins University Press.

Cowie, Elizabeth, (2011), *Recording Reality, Desiring the Real*, Minneapolis: University of Minne-sota Press.

Denich, Bette, (1991), 'Unbury the victims: rival exhumations and nationalist revivals in Yugosla-via', in *American Anthropological Association Annual Meeting*, 1–14, Chicago: Manuscript copy.

Giladi, Gideon, (1990 [in Arabic, 1988]), *Discord in Zion: Conflict between Ashkenazi and Sephardi Jews in Israel* (trans. R. Harris), London: Scorpion.

The Sociological Review, 62:S2, pp. 152–165 (2014), DOI: 10.1111/1467-954X.12195

Gluckman, Max, (1958 [1940]), *The Analysis of a Social Situation in Modern Zululand* (Rhodes Livingston Paper No. 28 [originally in *Bantu Studies* 14 (1940): 1–30]), Manchester: Manchester University Press.

Goffman, Erving, (1959), *The Presentation of Self in Everyday Life*, Garden City, NJ: Doubleday Anchor.

Hudson, Robert and Glenn Bowman (eds.), (2012), *After Yugoslavia: Identities and Politics within the Successor States*, London: Palgrave Macmillan.

Krieger, Heike (ed.), (2001), *The Kosovo Conflict and International Law: An Analytical Documentation 1974–1999*, Cambridge: Cambridge University Press.

Laclau, Ernesto (ed.), (1994), *The Making of Political Identities*, London: Verso.

Laclau, Ernesto and Mouffe, Chantal, (1985), *Hegemony and Socialist Strategy: Towards a Radical Democratic Politics* (trans. Winston Moore and Paul Cammack), London: Verso.

Laplanche, Jean, (1999), 'Notes on Afterwardness', in *Essays on Otherness*, 260–265, London: Routledge.

Lockman, Zachary, (1996), *Comrades and Enemies: Arab and Jewish Workers in Palestine, 1906–1948*, Berkeley, CA: University of California Press.

Meier, Viktor, (1999), *Yugoslavia: A History of its Demise* (trans. Sabrina Ramet), London: Routledge.

Mencinger, Joze, (1991), 'From a capitalist to a capitalist economy?' in James Simmie and Joze Dekleve (eds), *Yugoslavia in Turmoil: After Self-Management?*, 71–86, London: Pinter Publishers.

Pappé, Ilan, (1992), *The Making of the Arab-Israeli Conflict, 1947–1951*, London: I. B. Tauris.

Pavlowitch, Stevan, (1988), *The Improbable Survivor: Yugoslavia and its Problems, 1918–1988*, London: C. Hurst and Co.

Pizzi, Katia, (1998), ' "Silentes loquimur": *foibe* and border anxiety in post-war literature from Trieste', *Journal of European Studies*, 28: 217–229.

Ramet, Sabrina, (2006), *The Three Yugoslavias: State-building and Legitimation, 1918–2005*, Bloomington, IN: Indiana University Press.

Rivlin, Gershon and Orren, Elhanan (eds.), (1982), *Yoman Hamilhama-Tashah, 1948–1949 (Ben-Gurion's War Diary)*, Tel Aviv: Ministry of Defence Publishing House.

Salecl, Renata, (1993), 'Nationalism, anti-semitism and anti-feminism in Eastern Europe', *Journal of Area Studies*, 78–90.

Schwab, Gabriele, (2010), *Haunting Legacies: Violent Histories and Transgenerational Trauma*, New York: Columbia University Press.

Shenhav, Yehouda, (2006), *The Arab Jews: A Postcolonial Reading of Nationalism, Religion and Ethnicity*, Stanford, CA: Stanford University Press.

Silber, Laura and Little, Allan, (1995), *The Death of Yugoslavia*, London: Penguin and BBC Books.

Swirski, Shlomo, (1989), *Israel: The Oriental Majority* (trans. Barbara Swirski), London: Zed Books.

Competitive violence and the micro-politics of the fight label

Curtis Jackson-Jacobs

Abstract: Although physical fighting is a common theme in research on youth, crime, and schools, social scientists have only rarely confronted a basic question: What makes a fight a 'fight'? The label and its application are highly consequential for violent actors and social control agencies. Based on several years of longitudinal ethnographic fieldwork with several dozen American youth involved in violence (including a qualitative dataset of 189 violent encounters), the analysis documents the meaning of physical fights as a distinctive form of violent interaction. First, a definition of a 'fight' from the sample members' perspective is presented: *a stretch of serious, competitive, hand-to-hand violence.* Next, the article turns to the 'micro-politics' of labelling violence by institutions of discipline and control. By treating violence as a mutual fight, social control agents implicitly deny the roles of 'victim' and 'perpetrator'. Police and school officials may creatively invoke the fight label either to avoid taking action or to punish all parties involved in violence on the street, in the home or at school. Finally, the discussion concludes by addressing variations in how violence is labelled across social ecologies and socioeconomic contexts, and the interrelated nature of the 'fight', 'violence' and 'victim' labels.

Keywords: physical fighting, definitions, ethnography, American youth, micro-politics, labelling violence

Introduction

What makes a fight a 'fight'? The question of the 'fight label' is not merely one of words. Calling violence a fight – rather than, say, an assault or a beating – is both highly consequential and contingent. It is a deeply 'micro-political' matter (Emerson, 1994; Emerson and Messinger, 1977). Within sociology, actions and the labelling process are often analysed as separate phenomena. Yet it is a fundamental premise of interactionist theory that people construct action according to how they define situations and how they anticipate others will do so (Becker, 1963; Blumer, 1969; Holstein and Miller, 1990; Katz, 1988).

To the extent that violence is a dramatic performance, the actor is trying to shape how others will interpret and categorize it (Goffman, 1967; Sacks, 1992). Violent actors not only try to influence the outcome of the immediate situation,

The Sociological Review, 62:S2, pp. 166–186 (2014), DOI: 10.1111/1467-954X.12197

but also to prospectively shape how it will be labelled by witnesses, peers, agents of control – and, indeed, by themselves (Jackson-Jacobs, 2004, 2013; Collins, 2008). In fights, they are trying to convey the impression of *competitive violence.*

The label matters, in the first instance, to those involved – to how they understand and talk about what has happened to them or what they have witnessed (Becker, 1963). It also matters to various third parties (Black, 1983; Emerson and Messinger, 1977). Of special interest are agents of formal social control who rely on shorthand categorizations of persons and situations to perform routine work activities and make discretionary decisions (Lipsky, 1980; Sacks, 1992). In the case of violence, a label can mean the difference between arrest and freedom for disputants, determine whether bureaucratic workers have paperwork to complete and other professional obligations, and shape official agency records, potentially affecting social research and policy decisions (see, eg, Meehan, 2000). Thus, it is important for sociologists to understand the fight, both as a form of interpersonal violence and a label, from the perspective of its principals, its audiences, and others affected by its 'downstream consequences' (Emerson and Paley, 1992).

Based on several years of ethnographic research in a novel field site and a dataset of 240 confrontations (189 violent, 51 'near-violent'), this article focuses on the how the sample members defined a 'fight' and what it meant in their culture. To address the contingencies and consequences of labelling violence, I supplement my ethnographic findings with evidence drawn from popular culture, news reports, and published research. Throughout, I relate how these meanings diverge from or correspond with social control agents' use of the fight label. Finally, by way of comparison to research on youth violence in low-income contexts, I suggest how my sample members' social position may have shaped the process of official labelling.

Sample, setting and data

My sample members were overwhelmingly white and from the same affluent suburban neighbourhood where I grew up, on the outskirts of Tucson, Arizona – a metropolitan area in the southwestern United States with a population of just under one million.[1] After beginning my doctoral studies in sociology at the University of California, Los Angeles, I returned in late 1999 to begin conducting a study of youth violence, having maintained contact with local friends and acquaintances. At that time, the sample members were 18 to 22 years old. To construct a descriptive dataset on violent interactions, I gathered multiple forms of data over the course of more than four years.

First, I created a preliminary set of *retrospective observations.* As a high school and college student, I had witnessed several dozen violent conflicts on or around campus and at bars, parties, and other informal gatherings. In October 1999, before beginning fieldwork, I wrote descriptive accounts of as many violent events as I could recall witnessing over the previous seven years. I included 21 retrospective observations in the final dataset – those which had the highest degree of interactional detail and/or could be used to corroborate or 'triangulate' interview data (Webb *et al.*, 1966).

Second, between December 1999 and June 2004, I travelled to Tucson for fieldwork outings during breaks in the academic calendar and over weekends. I began by asking contacts if they would participate in a study of youth violence and introduce me to others. As I found, virtually all were eager to do so. I focused particularly on a 'core group' of 35 sample members, most of whom had known each other since adolescence. I spent time at their homes, eating with them at restaurants, and going to 'house parties', bars and nightclubs, where most of their violent confrontations took place.

To add variation to the sample, I sought out members of overlapping friend-ship networks, including (by their definitions) current and former members of 'tagger crews' (ie, graffiti artists), youth street gangs and anti-racist skinheads.[2]

Despite the members' routines of frequent carousing and 'looking for trouble', I witnessed serious violence only occasionally. I directly observed many more 'near-fights' than 'real' fights during the fieldwork (Collins, 2008; Grazian. 2003). When fights did happen, the scene was oftentimes so chaotic that it was difficult to catch more than glimpses of action (see also Prus, 1978). Conse-quently, for the present analysis, I rely more heavily on interview accounts and retrospective observations than notes taken in the field.

Third, I conducted both life-history interviews and open-ended interviews about violence, asking for sequential accounts of what the interviewees actually saw, felt and did. My interviews covered experiences from adolescence until the members' late twenties. I continued interviewing until I had amassed a dataset that represented a diverse range of violent experiences. My strategy was to perform preliminary analysis while still collecting data, and then stop gathering new cases unless they were somehow novel or strategically useful for refining my hypotheses (Glaser and Strauss, 1967). Including all members who participated in at least one interview or fieldwork outing, the sample size was 86 (another 45 were described only in retrospective observations).

Interaction level dataset

Many research paradigms advise strictly defining one's terms before collecting data, especially if the goal is to test existing hypotheses. However, my purpose was exploratory, the goal to develop new findings and theories about fighting. Thus, reaching a grounded definition of a 'fight' became a process of data analysis (Katz, 2001).

I defined the unit of analysis as the 'focused encounter' (or series of encounters) over which conflict unfolded (Goffman, 1971). I constructed a dataset of 240 cases that contributed to the analysis below. In order to explain how some interactions became violent and others did not, I included 51 cases of 'near-fights' and

The Sociological Review, 62:S2, pp. 166–186 (2014), DOI: 10.1111/1467-954X.12197

'near-violence'. When relying on interviews alone, I included a case only if I had gathered at least one firsthand account of direct involvement.

I created a file containing separate records for all cases. Each record contained fields for descriptive notes about the setting, the participants, estimated ages, injuries, weapons, third-party involvement, and the date and type of each account. Since members oftentimes witnessed each others' violence, engaged in collective violence, or used violence against one another, many cases contain multiple accounts (including perspectives of opponents, attackers, victims and audience members).

Indeed, by constructing the dataset and defining temporal boundaries for each case, I had already begun to analyse the data (Glaser and Strauss, 1967; Katz, 2001). I next sought to find distinctions between types of cases. Since fighting was central to members' identities, and trying to get into fights was a frequent activity, I first sought to reach a grounded definition of a fight.

I grouped all cases in my dataset according to whether sample members indicated they were clearly 'fights', clearly not fights (including both 'near-fights' and violence besides fighting), and ambiguous or borderline cases.

I then noted descriptive details that appeared regularly in the fight category, but not in the others, and abstracted them into a list of generalized qualitative characteristics. I applied different combinations of these characteristics to the dataset until I reached the most parsimonious set possible (Ragin, 1987). I found a set of four qualities that applied to all clear-cut fights in my dataset but, collectively, did not apply to any of the non-fight interactions.

Finally, I tested my definition against several dozen interview accounts of fighting and other violence provided by undergraduate students in course papers, and published accounts of violence in a diverse range of geographies, historical periods, social ecologies, and institutional contexts.[3]

Importantly, unlike institutional practices of recording violence, my method allowed for the meaning to change over the course of an interaction, consistent with the phenomenology of violent situations (Collins, 2008; Katz, 1988). For instance, an interaction that began with a one-on-one 'fair fight' might conclude with a group beating (referred to as a 'jumping') if partisan audience members started attacking one of the fighters.

Of 189 violent interactions, I coded 122 'fights' (including 44 'group fights', involving between three and dozens of combatants) and 94 stretches of 'other violence' (eg beatings, jumpings, shootings and robberies) – 27 cases involved both a fight and other, non-fight violence.

The simplest adequate definition

To the original question: *What makes a fight a 'fight'?* I base the definition below on the term's practical meaning – on how people use the concept in interaction (Becker, 1963; Blumer, 1969; Emerson and Messinger, 1977; Glaser and Strauss, 1967; Katz, 1988; Matza, 1969). Individual and cultural definitions must always vary to some degree, but to make empirical headway, I highlight the shared meaning in my field setting and, at times, contemporary popular culture.

The simplest adequate definition of a fight is: *a stretch of competitive, serious, hand-to-hand violence*. Each of the four criteria (stretch, competition, seriousness and hand-to-hand violence) serves to distinguish the category 'fight' from other kinds of social interaction, so each requires a brief explanation. Members may have debated amongst themselves how to categorize specific cases, but when disagreement occurred, it rested on these criteria.

In the next pages, I highlight the ambiguous nature of some events in order to emphasize the concept's specific meaning. As such cases illustrate, the definitional criteria themselves are socially constructed, organized in interaction, and subject to interpretation. Thus, unlike a classic 'ideal-type' with sharp boundaries defined by necessary and sufficient conditions, I analyse the 'fight' as a 'fuzzy set' with 'prototypical' qualities – that is, empirically derived 'family resemblances' (Labov, 1973; Ragin, 2000; Rosch, 1973).

Indeed, members recognize this aspect of violence and, as I explain below, may exploit the 'fight label' for various purposes, such as pressuring unwilling opponents into violence or rhetorically neutralizing the potential culpability of performing violence. Likewise, institutional actors may use their discretionary powers to define cases in ways meant to shape their own professional obligations, often with fateful consequences for the actors involved in violence.

(1) Stretch

The word 'stretch' denotes a single course of continuous face-to-face interaction. As members see it, the fight proper begins only after violence has been exchanged between opponents and ends when one or both stop trying to attack the other. The preceding dispute is considered only a prelude to the actual fight. Members define the fight as lasting as long as opponents share a continuous focus on mutual combat, ending when a victory or draw is established, third parties 'break it up', or the fight transforms into another kind of violence. As the final possibility indicates, the end of the fight need not mean an end to the violence. There is a constant threat that fights will 'turn into' something else, usually a more dangerous style of violent attack. This danger adds an extra element of thrill for many people who fight, but is a powerful deterrent for others who do not.

Occasionally, one fight at a social gathering will be followed a few hours or minutes later by a second. If the original 'focused interaction' has ended and the opponents have dispersed, if only temporarily, these are considered multiple, separate fights – even if they involve the same actors (Goffman, 1963). *Group fights*, however, are considered single, collective interactions. Several fighters collectively focus their attention on a continuous stretch of time and space. Audiences corroborate and contribute to this interpretation by circling the 'attention space', forming a single arena (Collins, 2008). Group fights were

The Sociological Review, 62:S2, pp. 166–186 (2014), DOI: 10.1111/1467-954X.12197

relished by my sample members for the *esprit de corps* they made possible, should everyone demonstrate solidarity (Jackson-Jacobs, 2004, 2013).

(2) Competitive

The qualifier 'competitive' excludes violence that seeks only unilateral dominance or purely instrumental ends, and includes only violence undertaken at least partly for the sake of *trying to win* a contest. This criterion not only implies mutuality, but also adds a motivational element to the definition: both sides are trying to win over the opponent's violent resistance. Popular culture provides evidence that this perspective on fighting is widely shared, as when a character in the 2007 film *Eastern Promises* remarks: 'It's not a fight if one of you doesn't fight back, right?' Thus, the competitive criterion rules various forms of assault-style attacks and beatings, rebellions and riots, and most violence in military and law enforcement contexts (cf. Toch, 1969).

The degree to which fights are recognizably competitive does vary. In the clearest cases, often referred to as 'fair fights' (Collins, 2008), opponents may extensively negotiate the details of who will fight, where, when, and how (eg which weapons are allowed). Negotiation is not only a way of establishing ground rules, but also dramatizing that the violence will be competitive.

In the following case, Aaron – who styled himself as a 'punk rocker' – recounts negotiating to fight a rival high school classmate while off campus with his friend Brett:

#68. Aaron vs. The Cowboy.

Aaron: I see two of the cowboys in their car, and this big, big Mexican guy. . . . flipping us off and stuff. So me and Brett followed them into this Taco Bell. . . . sat next to them and were just staring at them. . . . this huge Mexican looked at me and goes, 'What are you fucking looking at? You got a problem?' And I go, 'Yeah, I got a problem!' And he's like, 'Well, why don't we go out behind the Safeway . . .' we drove around to the back. And I had the spikes on [ie a spiked ring]. And he was like, 'You better take those off.' And I'm like, 'No, fuck you!' And he goes and grabs a bottle and smashes it. . . . 'All right! I'll take them off!'

Curtis: And did he put the bottle down?

Aaron: Yeah. . . . he threw the first punch . . . Brett's sitting there like my trainer. Like Mick from *Rocky*: 'C'mon Aaron!' So I got a couple good, like, Karate kicks in . . . but he probably landed more, and his punches were probably a lot harder than mine. . . .

Curtis: Who broke it up?

Aaron: Brett and this guy's friends.

As the fight illustrates, third parties also contribute to defining a fight through spectatorship, coaching and enforcing resolutions.

Certain other forms of violence share common features, or 'family resemblances', with fights but mean something quite different (Rosch, 1973).

'Jumpings' are distinct from fights, though they happen in many of the same kinds of social gatherings, among the same kinds of people, and sometimes immediately following a fight. 'Jumping' can be a noun or verb, meaning a collective beating of an individual or weaker group. Members of the dominant group feel a thrill of ritual solidarity in sacrificing a victim who has somehow challenged the group's symbolic boundaries, thus dramatizing that they are within (Collins, 2008; Jackson-Jacobs, 2013; see also Erikson, 1966; Katz, 1988).

In the extremes 'fair fights' and 'jumpings' look quite different. Consider a violent interaction in which Brad and Freddie (both 22 years old) were attacked but did not counterattack. They were at a drunken house party when Freddie started mocking a young, Latino, anti-racist skinhead. Several other skinheads then attacked Freddie. When Brad came to Freddie's aid, both were knocked to the ground, punched, kicked and stomped. A few days later I met Brad at a bowling alley:

#163. Freddie and Brad Get Jumped by Skinheads.[4]

Fieldnotes: I asked Brad if he was hurt and turned his hands over to look for swelling around the knuckles. Brad told me that he and Freddie 'weren't fighting' – they just kept saying they didn't want to fight. At first, Brad said, the skinheads were all hitting Freddie 'one at a time' – even as he kept saying he didn't want to fight. Brad eventually 'tried to get in the middle,' at which point he started to get hit as well. He summarized, 'Neither of us were fighting back, though.'

By hitting Freddie 'one at a time', it would appear, they meant to provoke him into fighting back. Though Freddie may have instigated the violence, he then dramatized that he 'didn't want to fight'. If they wanted to beat him, in other words, they would have to do it in a jumping.

Brad's account raises an important complexity. There is a distinction between the noun a 'fight' and the verb 'to fight'. Victims of unilateral violence (eg robberies, assaults, domestic abuse) may 'fight back' *defensively*, but typically not *competitively* – that is, in order to 'win'. As I explain, this distinction has historically been of great consequence, particularly in the discretionary response of police to domestic violence (Davis, 1983; Ferraro, 1989; Smith and Klein, 1984).

(3) Serious

The qualification of emotional seriousness distinguishes what members consider 'real' fights and violent contests that are playful or athletic. Play-fighting, boxing and various other kinds of sparring are only 'fights' in a figurative sense: They are simulations of the 'real' thing (Hoffman, 2006).

However, given the competitive quality of fights, there is no hard-and-fast line between 'play' and 'real' fights. My dataset includes six fights following 'rough play out of hand' and several others following similar scenarios (eg food fights that turned violent). Indeed, part of the excitement and challenge of play-fighting is to test one's composure or ability to maintain the state of relaxed play (Anderson, 1999).

The Sociological Review, 62:S2, pp. 166–186 (2014), DOI: 10.1111/1467-954X.12197

Ambiguous events illustrate the importance of the distinction. When play fights become rough, it may not be clear whether either side was actually serious. In fact, whether to consider it a real fight depends precisely on imputations of emotional seriousness. The meaning could be ambiguous, for instance, if one opponent considered the fight 'real' but the other considered it a play fight. This seems to have happened only once in my dataset:

#39. Walter and Skyler on the Bus.

Retrospective Observation: Walter (age 14) was sitting in the back of the school bus with KJ, a popular older boy. Both played football and had reputations for being tough and 'bad.' Walter began wrestling – playfully at first – with another teammate, Skyler (15), who had a more studious reputation. After Skyler scratched Walter's ear, causing it to bleed, Walter growled angrily and tried to throttle Skyler. Skyler forced Walter's head out of the window. The altercation ended abruptly when Skyler freed Walter, who quickly moved to the back of the bus. Walter shouted that he would put Skyler in the hospital. Skyler never seemed upset or particularly scared, commenting in a friendly tone that they both 'got in some good moves.' He stopped talking when KJ warned him to drop it.

Whether, or when, Skyler recognized that Walter was 'serious' was unclear. But this level of uncertainty is highly uncharacteristic. Fighters usually try to avoid that predicament by dramatizing that 'this is a real fight', much as robbers do by explicitly announcing, 'This is a stickup' (Katz, 1988; Luckenbill, 1981; Wright and Decker, 1997). A few minutes after having a food fight at school, Kenny approached Hippie before gym class:

#49. Kenny v 'Hippie.'

Kenny: He was like, 'You want to fight?' Put his arms up and . . . went to push me. And I went to push him away . . . I just started punching him in the head.

Note that the fight proper begins, in this case, only after an explicit verbal proposal 'to fight'. Importantly, the opponents agree not only to exchange violence, but establish that they will do so in the form of a fight.

(4) Hand-to-hand violence[5]

From members' perspectives, 'real' fights involve 'real' violence. What counts as real, however, can be open to disagreement and depends on qualities of the situation. Fights frequently begin with aggressive invasions like 'accidental' bumps or hard stares, and may progress to threats, intimidating postures, and shoving. Such acts are viewed as aggressive proposals to fight, but as long as the dispute does not escalate further, members will not define the event as an actual fight:

#195. Near-Fight Playing Pool.

Lonnie: . . .we'd almost gotten in a fight earlier that night. With a group of people. . . . We just exchanged words. . . . I walked up and [my friend] just pushed the guy. Then mostly bystanders broke it up.

'Just' arguing and 'just' pushing constitute 'almost' fights – or *near-fights*, as I call them.

The violence required to establish a 'real', authentic fight radically transforms the situation. Once 'real' violence begins, verbal disputes are abandoned and, typically, both sides attack each other at a dramatically faster pace and with qualitatively greater intensity. Techniques of 'real' violence include punching, kicking, choking, or striking with hand-held weapons. Most fights in my dataset were unarmed, though members did sometimes fight with weapons, especially 'handy weapons' – ordinary objects like bottles and billiard balls. It was rare to fight with manufactured weapons (however, there were robberies and unilateral attacks with guns and knives, and a few occasions when someone pulled or fired a gun at the end of a fight).

The cultural meaning of fights

Most members of the culture I studied specialized in fighting, purposely refraining from openly predatory violence. This choice was motivated by the cultural meaning of fights. They were attracted to 'toughness' and competitive fighting, not violence for its own sake. In the following sections I describe three ways they understood fighting: (1) through the metaphor of the 'fight-as-athletic contest', (2) as a form of thrilling 'action', and (3) as a 'victimless crime'.

The fight-as-athletic contest metaphor

A central theme in the meaning and experience of fighting is the metaphor of the fight as an athletic contest. Despite the literal differences, there is considerable overlap between the sequential, narrative structures of athletic matches and physical fights. Two opposing sides confront each other face-to-face. There are stretches of physically creative action, organized by each side's focus on achieving reciprocal outcomes. Each has an offensive and defensive aim. In fighting – as in sports like soccer, hockey, and basketball – defence and offence must be played simultaneously in continuous stretches of emotionally intense action. Every move requires an awareness of the field's creative possibilities for attack and simultaneous sensitivity to one's own vulnerabilities. Part of the thrill of fighting is the opportunity to spontaneously try out fantastic possibilities, as when a skinhead reportedly leaped into the air to jump-kick an opponent with both heels, or when Rick (an accomplished martial artist) claimed to have kicked a bottle off a table at an opponent's head just to see if he could do it. Even if fantasy, such accounts illustrate fighters' athletic aspirations.

Literal athletic matches conclude differently than fights. Time runs out or a certain number of points are achieved. But, for each, the narrative is organized to conclude with victory and defeat, with 'winners' and 'losers' or in 'draws'. Fighters try to 'beat' each other in two senses of the word – not only by

The Sociological Review, 62:S2, pp. 166–186 (2014), DOI: 10.1111/1467-954X.12197

'attacking', but also by 'defeating' the opponent. The idea is not simply to injure, but to overcome the opponent's active resistance, and to do so by creative feats of athleticism under pressure.

During group fights there are also strong parallels with the idea of teams in sport. In Europe, groups or 'firms' of so-called 'football hooligans' are fighting teams loyal to particular football clubs. They may spend match days trying to fight the groups loyal to their club's current opponent (Armstrong, 1998; Buford, 1990; Collins, 2008; Marsh *et al.*, 1978). In fighting groups, different members may be known for playing different positions on the team, and even 'coaches' (see Case #63, above; cf. Athens, 1992). In my field site, Bob and Powel were known for playing the role of 'instigator'. Neither was very skilful at the technical side of fighting, but both had a special talent for inciting strangers to attack them during group drinking outings. At that point, their friends would come to their aid, then friends on the other side would 'jump in', and, finally, some star slugger like Chad would stroll through the crowd, levelling opponents with monstrous right-handed 'haymakers'.

The athletic metaphor is strong for observers as well. Witnesses become audiences, forming circles or semi-circles around the fighters, constructing impromptu arenas for the bout. On American high school campuses there is a familiar routine (eg portrayed in the film *Three O'Clock High* [Universal Pictures 1987]; see also Collins, 2008). During the day a rumour spreads that 'so-and-so' and 'so-and-so' are going to meet 'at the wall' or 'in the pit' or some such secluded place when the day ends. Throngs of classmates gather at the appointed location at three o'clock, standing around, talking in anticipation and reckoning the outcome. As in most spectator gatherings there are vocal displays of approval or displeasure.

I witnessed such a fight between high school classmates in about 1996. Notice how the audience, myself included, treated the fight as a spectator event:

#33. Brady and Anthony Showdown.

Retrospective Observation: A large crowd of about forty high school students followed a junior, Brady, and a freshman, Anthony, out into the desert after school. We had been talking about the fight all afternoon. The two squared off and pushed each other several times. Mostly they just stared at each other. After about five minutes the crowd was jeering the two. . . . Brady threw a punch at Anthony. I commented to Perry that it looked like a painful punch. He agreed, noting that it hit Anthony's temple. I heard Marshal say, 'Let's see some elbows and knees.' Both boys punched each other in the face several times, stopping for as much as several minutes between exchanges. . . . The next day people commented at school that the fight was 'weak.' They said that Anthony and Brady were 'pussies' because they took breaks and didn't fight continuously.

Bars and other carousing scenes provide ready-made audiences of drunken acquaintances and strangers, should the spectacle of violence arise (Collins, 2008; Tomsen, 1997; Winlow and Hall, 2006). Rick used the language of spectator sports to recount watching a nightclub brawl between his military friends and a group of men from another branch of the military (Case #15). His team was 'winning', so Rick felt he was not needed. Instead, he recounted, 'I was just kind of like sitting on the sidelines, drinking my beer, watching.'

The metaphorical relationship between athletics and fighting works in both directions and holds in a diverse range of cultures. Sports are often a form of violent spectacle (eg Mayan and Roman death sports; Elias and Dunning, 1986). Historically, American football has been a self-conscious training field for developing manly toughness, aggression and violent skill. Fighting sports like professional boxing liberally allude to the disputatious character of 'real fights'. To cultivate an audience, boxing promoters often establish an atmosphere of personal conflict between opponents. Boxers and their entourages occasionally attack one another in staged press conferences (eg Mike Tyson v Lennox Lewis, 2002).

The metaphor of a fight-as-athletic contest suggests motivations to fight, including, first of all, to put one's self publicly on the line in a high stakes, unpredictable competition. Committed fighters repeatedly tell stories of these events to peers, narratively constructing their biographies so as to demonstrate 'strong character' (Collins, 2008; Goffman, 1967; Jackson-Jacobs, 2004). Successful fighters often report feeling a sense of gloried celebrity among their peers, especially while they are still attending high school, much like athletes in the literal sense (Adler and Adler, 1989).

Fighting as 'action'

Like all sports, fighting is a form of 'action' in Erving Goffman's (1967) sense of the term (see also Lyng, 1990). In this special sense, action has two qualities: It presents fateful risks to the actor, and the actor enters it voluntarily for the sake of taking the risk – or, in some cases, for the sake of *having* taken it (see also Schinkel, 2010). Goffman's archetype was an episode of high-stakes casino gambling. He noted the sub-category of 'interpersonal action', or contests, including fights, arguments, ritualized verbal aggression, and other challenges consisting of face-to-face competition (see, eg, Labov, 1972; Lee, 2009).

To be precise, people do not undertake action only 'for its own sake', but instead for its variety of experiential and symbolic attractions. In particular, action is thrilling. Thrill itself can be understood as an emotional appreciation of a situation's potential damages and payoffs. Borrowing Jeremy Bentham's term, Geertz (1973) described the Balinese cockfight as a form of 'deep play', meaning that the stakes were too high to be rational by utilitarian standards. The Balinese men Geertz observed bet huge sums on cockfights – more than they could afford to lose – in order to put on the line 'one's pride, one's poise, one's dispassion, one's masculinity', to experience 'the thrill of risk, the despair of loss, the pleasure of triumph' (1973: 434).

Certain outcomes depend on the specific kind of action – financial ruin or hitting it big in gambling, humiliating rebuff or a self-affirming encounter in seeking out sex partners. But others are present in all action situations, including, most importantly, the potential to demonstrate 'character', especially the masculine version of character.

Fighting as a 'victimless crime'

To say that members consider fighting a 'victimless crime' is not to make a judgement that there are not, in fact, victims. Nor is it to say that some do not feel privately victimized before, during, or after a fight (some do), nor claim that the combatants are truly 'consenting'. It is to say that members *interpret* fights as a collaborative activity between voluntary opponents, rather than an act perpetrated against a victim.

They view fighting as a form of 'action' in a class with, and often performed in the same scenes as, many of the traditionally dubbed 'victimless crimes', such as drug use and prostitution. They view the difference between fights and beatings as analogous to consensual sex and rape. Furthermore, they may use the fight label itself as a rhetorical device for denying that those involved were victims (Sykes and Matza, 1957; see also Holstein and Miller, 1990).

The language we use reveals clues about what a concept means to us, often at a level beneath our conscious recognition (Pinker, 2007). Consider how we talk about fights. One cannot fight 'at', 'on' or 'to' someone. Instead, one must fight 'with' someone, implying a quality of cooperation or competition. (People sometimes use the preposition 'against', also implying competition.) In order for one to fight with another, the other must also fight.

Compare this to other kinds of violence. In abuse, 'X beat Y'. The verb construction is revealing. The violent actor X is the only active agent in the statement, while the victim Y is only the passive object of the action. Note that it is possible to use the verb 'to fight' without a preposition ('A fought B'), but the statement implies the reciprocal ('B fought A'). The meaning is virtually identical, a symmetrical quality absent in the use of verbs such as 'to beat'. To make Y the subject of a statement on beating requires a passive verb construction: 'Y was beaten by X'. The same applies to bullying, attacking, robbing, raping, shooting and other unilateral violent acts.

The unilateral direction of action is found not only in language but also in the actual practices of predatory violence. Robberies and violent attacks on romantic partners typically rely on stealth, overwhelming force, or a history of 'intimate terrorism' to discourage resistance (Dobash and Dobash, 1979; Gelles and Straus, 1988; Johnson, 1995; Luckenbill, 1981; Wright and Decker, 1997). Fighters, by contrast, routinely issue challenges and insults to provoke their opponents into mutual combat. If an instigator fails to secure an apparently authentic counterattack from his opponent, then he must choose between aborting the fight-attempt or committing an act of bullying, assault, or abuse – unilateral violent acts that some people find attractive in certain situations, but which conferred minimal or negative prestige in the culture I studied. Thus, when someone tries to start a fight, he or she must *orient to mutual combat* – that is, orient to his opponent as a *partner in competition* – or risk coming off as a predator or sadist.

'Fight' is a normative as well as descriptive concept. Characterizing violence as a fight can be a rhetorical device for neutralizing the potential culpability of committing violence or even to deny the shame of being passively victimized (Goffman, 1971; Scott and Lyman, 1968; Sykes and Matza, 1957). My sample members usually preferred to see themselves as 'winners' rather than 'perpetrators', and even as 'losers' rather than 'victims'. In other words, the morality of fighting is a concern for fighters themselves in many of the same ways that it is for outsiders.

Some situations are easy to construct as 'fights', especially when both sides appear to be motivated by a spirit of thrill-seeking and voluntarily escalating a conflict. Others are more difficult. The following case illustrates the extent of interactional work that actors may employ to convey the impression of a fight.

Below, Tim, a 21-year-old skinhead, describes a violent exchange that he and his friends initiated against several men he characterized as 'drug-dealing bums'. It is worth noting that Tim's network used unilateral violence in a wider range of contexts than most of my other sample members. Nonetheless, he performs considerable interactional work to deflect the impression of a one-sided assault:

#120. Tim v 'The Bums.'

Tim: Well, the sad thing is, we get in the occasional fight with bums . . . Just being drunken idiots . . . Probably wasn't the last fight I been in. But we got into it. . . . We're like, 'You know what? We need to fuck with some drug-dealing bums.'. . .

Curtis: Cause they were drug dealers or what?

Tim: Yeah . . . I don't tend to like the scum of society. . . . And occasionally it's justified. . . . It's like, 'Get a job. We're all working to survive.'. . . I really wouldn't do it . . . But the fact is we're drunk. . . . 'We're gonna take care of,' you know, 'cure society's ills by walking to the park.' . . . So we were walking around and we found this guy. And, fucking, Moreno walks up to him. . . . 'Hey, man, you got some fucking rock [crack-cocaine]?' And this guy's like, 'Man, what you need, man?' . . . Moreno's like, 'Are you a fucking crack dealer?!'. . . Moreno with a fucking set of brass knuckles just – *Boom!* Just plows this guy right in the face. . . . he fucking takes off running and he goes into an alley. . . . And this guy comes back out with a fucking two-by-four. . . . hits Moreno between the neck and the shoulder . . . It's the crack dealer and this new bum who just came up out of nowhere. And he's talking shit to us. . . . I got a big ass rock in my hand ready to fucking smash his head. . . . So the crack dealer took off and the bum is still there. . . . And he starts heaving rocks at us. And we're going after him, trying to get him. . . . The crack-head comes back . . . with a huge-ass knife. . . . We back up. All of a sudden the ghetto bird [police helicopter] is above, like right on us. . . . Anyway, so the cops come over. . . . and we're like, 'It was the bum. He started it.' So they hit the bum with a ticket. And they found the crack-head at [a gas station]. They let us go scot-free.

Not only does Tim preface the account by specifically characterizing the event as a 'fight', but he expresses shame or embarrassment (eg 'sad . . . drunken idiots'), dramatizes that the other men fought back with comparable weapons, and emphasizes that the police sided with his group. He uses a variety of rhetorical devices to symbolically transform what might be viewed as an unprovoked assault – perhaps even a 'hate crime' – into either a 'fight' or a 'justified' effort to 'cure society' of 'scum' (in Sykes and Matza's, 1957, terminology, 'denying the victim' and 'appealing to higher loyalties'). Moreover, according to Tim's version of events, his group strategically organized the violence itself (selecting disreputable, potentially violent targets and provoking a vigorous counterattack) in ways meant to prospectively encourage the 'fight' label and minimize predatory interpretations.

Since men in violent cultures and certain contexts (eg some schools, jails, and 'the streets') feel obligated to accept challenges and vigorously participate in battle, aggressors may try to mitigate their potential culpability by exploiting that obligation (Anderson, 1999; Nisbett and Cohen, 1996). Especially during adolescence, the youth I spoke with frequently felt coerced into publicly demonstrating willingness to fight even while privately wishing they could escape. From the instigator's perspective: *Why simply bully a victim when you can goad him into fighting and then beat him up anyway?* That is, in order to construct a fight – to organize violence without an apparent 'victim' – one's opponent must *seem to be* a voluntary, mutual combatant.

Institutional responses

Fighters are not the only ones who frequently treat fights as 'victimless crimes'. The normative consequences of labelling a 'fight' are also reflected in the administrative practices of institutions that respond to and classify cases of violence.

Organizations such as schools, prisons, and police departments have obligations to victims within their jurisdictions – namely, protection and justice. Claiming or applying the label 'victim' constitutes violence as a unilateral violation and *not* a fight (Emerson, 1994; Holstein and Miller, 1990). Labelling someone a victim exonerates them and entitles them to special privileges. But sorting out the details of violence can be complicated and organizationally costly, and it often violates the sensibilities of social control agents.

For agents of formal control, it is oftentimes more expedient and morally palatable to simply classify violence as a 'fight' and punish each party equally (or not at all) than to sort out perpetrators and victims (eg Garot, 2010; Hagedorn, 2011). Historically, American police officers routinely opted for this solution by applying the label 'family fight' to cross-sex domestic violence calls. There are certainly mutual fights within families and between men and women (see Johnson, 1995). Yet sociological fieldwork indicates that police frequently applied the fight label to unilateral attacks in order to avoid making arrests and to justify treating violence as 'conflict' rather than 'crime' (Davis, 1983; Ferraro, 1989; Smith and Klein, 1984).

After a social movement to criminalize family violence, American lawmakers expanded the powers of police to make arrests in misdemeanour domestic violence, imposing so-called 'must arrest' legislation (Ferraro, 1989). Though such laws were meant to eliminate officers' discretion to treat violence as non-criminal conflict, police initially resisted. They only reframed domestic violence as criminal assault in response to a growing perception of their own civil liability, following high-profile lawsuits in the 1980s and 1990s.

As sociological fieldworkers have repeatedly found, police officers display a *preference for non-arrest* in cases they view as fights or interpersonal conflicts. In the written decision to *Watson v Kansas City* (857 F. 2d 690, 696 [10th Cir. 1988]), the court noted that law enforcement 'training encourages officers to attempt to "defuse" the situation and to use arrest as a last resort', particularly in cases of domestic violence (see also Emerson, 1981; Hawkins, 2003). Alternatively, when criminal justice workers are motivated to pursue official action (rather than avoid it), they may do so by specifically denying that an event was a 'fight' (Emerson, 1994).

To illustrate how the 'fight label' can be consequential to the administration of justice, consider the case of Luis Noriega, an Illinois bartender, beaten to death by three men and one woman in 2007. Initially, some members of the community and its news media referred to the event as a fatal 'fight'. The State's Attorney held a press conference intended to assign a label to the violence:

> There were some early reports that Mr. Noriega's death was a result of a fight. . . . The use of the word 'fight' would imply that the confrontation was mutual. In making the charging decision in this case, we believe this was an attack against Mr. Noriega where he was badly outnumbered and was struck by an individual who was superior in size. . . . (*Daily Chronicle* [DeKalb, IL], 21 April 2007)

The deceased's girlfriend also emphasized the normative consequences of labelling it an 'attack' rather than a 'fight': 'I think it's a great thing that the (state's) attorney changed the wording from "fight." It was not; it was an attack. . . . Luis had no chance.'

Louisiana Circuit Court Judge J.P. Mauffray invoked similar themes in his decision to uphold the high-profile battery conviction of so-called 'Jena Six' member Mychal Bell:

> The victim was 'sucker punched' and knocked immediately unconscious before being stomped and kicked. . . . There was no credible evidence . . . that the victim had provoked the attack by word or gesture. The evidence showed that this was an attack, not a fight. (*Associated Press*, 14 September 2007)

Mauffray not only dismissed the 'fight' label directly. He also indirectly supported the 'attack' categorization by emphasizing the 'victim' label and denying any precipitating provocation (see Holstein and Miller, 1990). More broadly,

American and British jurisprudence have long upheld 'fairness' as an essential normative principle of 'mutual combat' – a mitigating factor in violence – including 'comparable tools and capabilities' (*Harvard Law Review* 2005: 2437).

Indeed, 'mutual combat' is official criminal justice terminology. It can be used to warrant arrests for 'disorderly conduct/fighting', but it can also be used to justify informal practices of *not* making arrests for assault or battery. As one Illinois police officer told me, judges had criticized him for bringing 'mutual combat' cases to court (personal communication, 2006). In actual practice, if not written law, the justice system often treats fights as do members of the broader culture – a 'victimless crime'.

Discussion: variations

When official social control agents intervene in disputes and 'troubles', as Emerson and Messinger (1977: 128–131) noted, a critical contingency is whether or not they align with one party over the other.[6] In *symmetrical* interventions, the agent does not side with either party, defining the situation as 'conflict'. By intervening *asymmetrically*, the agent treats one party as 'victim' and the other as 'wrongdoer' framing the situation as 'deviance'.

Examining fights and other disturbances across contexts, however, suggests an additional mode of intervention: agents may, on occasion, intervene symmetrically by labelling *both sides* culpable.[7] In the US, the most conspicuous variation may be across social ecologies and socioeconomic contexts, although situational factors are also consequential.

When law enforcement officers arrived on the scene of violence in my fieldwork, they virtually always appeared oriented to 'restoring order'. If they did make arrests, it was rarely for fighting or any kind of personal violence, but instead for incidental misdemeanours (eg alcohol-related charges, damaging property).

In lower income contexts, social control agents may be more inclined to respond punitively toward all parties (Black, 1982, 1983; Smith and Klein, 1984). Researchers have reported that, when public fights or domestic disturbances occur among non-white or lower-income actors, police have historically either ignored the complaint entirely, or responded in particularly punitive fashion, charging all parties with some form 'assault', 'battery' and, in cases involving youth, applying 'gang'-related labels (Anderson, 1999; Black, 1982; Chambliss, 1973; Jackson and Rudman, 1993; Klein, 1995; Meehan, 2000; Sanders, 1994).

It is worth noting that control agents tend to classify particular cases in ways that correspond to whether certain forms of violence – and, indeed, certain kinds of people and places – have already been defined as 'social problems'. During periods of high-intensity 'gang' policing, youth who are non-white and live in low-income neighbourhoods may be treated especially punitively (Katz and Jackson-Jacobs, 2004).

Likewise, after the rampage shooting at Columbine High School in Littleton, Colorado, schools across the US began imposing strict punitive policies for even minor acts of violence, in which any infraction deemed violent may result in suspension or expulsion (see, eg, Adams, 2000; Lyons and Drew, 2006; Garot, 2010; Muschert and Peguero, 2010; Newman, 2004; Skiba *et al.*, 2002). Ironically, it was higher-income suburban and rural white youth who committed the crimes that inspired increased social control; yet so-called 'zero-tolerance' policies in schools have had especially dire consequences for lower-income and non-white youth (Adams, 2000; Farmer, 2010; Hirschfield, 2008; Skiba *et al.*, 2002; Verdugo, 2002; Welch and Payne, 2010).

The meaning and practices of labelling fights challenge a number of widely held notions about violence. While outsiders may view fighting as an aggressive, fundamental breach of order, fighters themselves view their action as competitive and even 'recreational' (Conley, 1999). Though technically criminal, law enforcement agents themselves may not treat 'mutual combat/fights' as criminal in practice.

Some may question whether competitive fights of the type I describe are violence at all. Perhaps what is most important is exactly this ambiguity: agents of control may choose to label a fight as an exchange in mutual combat and ignore it or, alternatively, define it as a violent episode requiring discipline. Likewise, social control agents may strategically decline to recognize or report an assault, but instead treat it as a fight.

Central to contemporary conceptions of violence are the roles of victim and culprit. Yet, from the members' perspective, fights are symmetrical violent contests between 'opponents'. It is not for the sociologist to settle these divergent perspectives, but instead to explore the ambiguities and variations surrounding interpersonal conflict and violence. Understanding how bureaucratic actors creatively employ 'fight', 'violence' and 'victim' labels highlights the complex relationship between violent encounters, local contexts and formal social control. Ultimately, for the sociologist, recognizing the phenomenon of competitive violence not only helps to explain what makes a fight a 'fight', but comparatively illuminates the entire spectrum of violence in social life.

Acknowledgements

This research received generous funding from the Harry Frank Guggenheim Foundation. Robert Emerson, Robert Garot, Jack Katz, Mark Kleiman, and Calvin Morrill provided invaluable guidance during the research process.

Notes

1 The population was about 844,000 when I began the study (United States Census Bureau, 2000, 2010).

The Sociological Review, 62:S2, pp. 166–186 (2014), DOI: 10.1111/1467-954X.12197

2 Different skinhead groups define themselves around various competing identities, ideologies, and symbols: racist, anti-racist, anti-drug, and so on. Those I knew were vehemently antagonistic toward racist groups (several were Latino and at least one was black). They defined themselves around a politically conservative, anti-drug, blue collar ideology.

3 Anderson (1999); Athens (1979); Collins (2008); Conley (1999); Farrington *et al.* (1982); Garot (2007, 2010); Gorn (1985); Horowitz and Schwartz (1974); Jones (2004, 2009); Labov (1982); Luckenbill (1977); Marsh *et al.* (1978); Morrill *et al.* (2000); Polk (1999); Prus (1978); Sanders (1994); Short and Strodtbeck (1968); Toch (1969); Tomsen (1997); Winlow (2001); Winlow and Hall (2006).

4 Fieldnotes: 20 December 2000. The account was corroborated by three witnesses (one female, two male) who were friends with both parties.

5 'Hand-to-hand' does not necessarily mean 'unarmed'. By 'hand-to-hand' I mean close-quarters fighting – opponents within reach, able to touch one another – rather than exclusively throwing objects or discharging firearms. Knife-, sword-, and gunfights might be considered subtypes in other settings, but in my dataset there were too few to say with any confidence. (It is worth noting that it appears, compared to the US, fights in the UK more frequently involve sharp-edged, penetrating weapons – a phenomenon sometimes dubbed Britain's 'blade culture'.)

6 Elaborating Aubert (1965).

7 This mode of intervention implicitly rejects the 'victimless crime' interpretation. The agent effectively treats both parties as having victimized 'the public' by violating 'moral order' or breaching 'peace'.

References

Adams, T., (2000), 'The status of school discipline and violence', *The Annals*, 567: 140–156.

Adler, P. and Adler, P., (1989), 'The gloried self', *Social Psychology Quarterly*, 52 (4): 299–310.

Anderson, E., (1999), *Code of the Street*, New York: W. W. Norton.

Armstrong, G., (1998), *Football Hooligans*, Oxford: Berg.

Athens, L., (1979), *Violent Criminal Acts and Actors*, Champaign, IL: University of Illinois Press.

Athens, L., (1992), *The Creation of Dangerous Violent Criminals*, Champaign, IL: University of Illinois Press.

Aubert, V., (1965), *The Hidden Society*, Totowa, NJ: Bedminster Press.

Becker, H., (1963), *Outsiders: Studies in the Sociology of Deviance*, New York: Free Press.

Black, D., (1982), *The Manners and Customs of the Police*, New York: Academic Press.

Black, D., (1983), 'Crime as social control', *American Sociological Review*, 48 (1): 34–45.

Blumer, H., (1969), *Symbolic Interactionism*, Englewood Cliffs, NJ: Prentice-Hall.

Buford, B., (1990), *Among the Thugs: The Experience, and the Seduction, of Crowd Violence*, New York: W. W. Norton & Company.

Chambliss, W., (1973), 'The roughnecks and the saints', *Society*, 11 (1): 24–31.

Collins, R., (2008), *Violent Conflict: A Micro-Sociological Theory*, Princeton, NJ: Princeton University Press.

Conley, C., (1999), 'The agreeable recreation of fighting', *Journal of Social History*, 33 (1): 57–72.

Davis, P., (1983), 'Restoring the semblance of order: police strategies in the domestic disturbance', *Symbolic Interaction*, 6: 261–278.

Dobash, R. and Dobash, R., (1979), *Violence against Wives: A Case against the Patriarchy*, New York: Free Press.

Elias, N. and Dunning, E., (1986), *The Quest for Excitement: Sport and Leisure in the Civilizing Process*, Oxford: Basil Blackwell.

Emerson, R., (1981), 'On last resorts', *American Journal of Sociology*, 87: 1–20.

Emerson, R., (1994), 'Constructing serious violence and its victims: processing a domestic violence restraining order', in G. Miller and J. Holstein (eds), *Perspectives on Social Problems: A Research Annual*, vol. 6, New York: JAI Press.

183

Emerson, R. and Messinger, S., (1977), 'The micro-politics of trouble', *Social Problems*, 25 (1): 121–134.

Emerson, R. and Paley, B., (1992), 'Organization horizons in complaint-filing', in K. Hawkins (ed.), *The Uses of Discretion*, Oxford: Oxford University Press.

Erikson, K., (1966), *Wayward Puritans*, New York: Wiley & Sons.

Farmer, S., (2010), 'Criminality of black youth in inner-city schools: "moral panic," moral imagination, and moral formation', *Race, Ethnicity and Education*, 13 (3): 367–381.

Farrington, D., Berkowitz, L. and West, D., (1982), 'Differences between individual and group fights', *British Journal of Social Psychology*, 21: 323–333.

Ferraro, K., (1989), 'Policing woman battering', *Social Problems*, 36: 61–74.

Garot, R., (2007), ' "Where you from": gang indentity as performance', *Journal of Contemporary Ethnography*, 36: 50–84.

Garot, R., (2010), *Who You Claim: Performing Gang Identity in School and on the Street*, New York: New York University Press.

Geertz, C., (1973), *The Interpretation of Cultures*, New York: Basic Books.

Gelles, R. and Straus, M., (1988), *Intimate Violence*, New York: Simon and Schuster.

Glaser, B. and Strauss, A., (1967), *The Discovery of Grounded Theory: Strategies for Qualitative Research*, Chicago: Aldine de Gruyter.

Goffman, E., (1963), *Behavior in Public Places*, Glencoe, IL: The Free Press.

Goffman, E., (1967), *Interaction Ritual*, New York: Anchor Books.

Goffman, E., (1971), *Asylums*, Garden City, NY: Anchor Books.

Gorn, E., (1985), ' "Gouge and bite, pull hair and scratch": the social significance of fighting in the Southern Backcountry', *American Historical Review*, 90 (1): 18–43.

Grazian, D., (2003), *Blue Chicago: The Search for Authenticity in Urban Blues Clubs*, Chicago: University of Chicago Press.

Hagedorn. J., (2011), 'Reframing gangs: the case of Jacqueline Montanez', presentation to the *International Crime, Media and Popular Culture Studies Conference*, Terre Haute, IN, 27 September.

Harvard Law Review (2005), 'Criminal law – mutual combat mitigation – Appellate Court of Illinois holds that disproportionate reaction to provocation negates mutual combat mitigation', 118: 2437–2444.

Hawkins, K., (2003), *Law as a Last Resort: Prosecution Decision-Making in a Regulating Agency*, New York: Oxford University Press.

Hirschfield, P., (2008), 'Preparing for prison? The criminalization of school discipline in the USA', *Theoretical Criminology*, 12 (1): 79–101.

Hoffman, S., (2006), 'How to punch someone and stay friends: an inductive theory of simulation', *Sociological Theory*, 24 (2): 170–193.

Holstein, J. and Miller, G., (1990), 'Rethinking victimization: an interactional approach to victimology', *Symbolic Interaction*, 13:103–122.

Horowitz, R. and Schwartz, G., (1974), 'Honor, normative ambiguity and gang violence', *American Sociological Review*, 39 (2): 238–251.

Jackson-Jacobs, C., (2004), 'Taking a beating: the narrative gratifications of fighting as an underdog', in K. Hayward, J. Ferrell, W. Morrison and W. Presdee (eds), *Cultural Criminology Unleashed*, London: Glasshouse Press.

Jackson-Jacobs, C., (2013), 'Constructing physical fights: an interactionist analysis of violence among affluent, suburban youth', *Qualitative Sociology*, 36: 23–52.

Jackson, P. and Rudman, C., (1993), 'Moral panic and the response to gangs in California', in S. Cummings and D. Monti (eds), *Gangs: The Origins and Impact of Contemporary Youth Gangs in the United States*, Albany, NY: SUNY Press.

Johnson, M., (1995), 'Patriarchal terrorism and common couple violence: two forms of violence against women', *Journal of Marriage and the Family*, 57: 283–294.

Jones, N., (2004), ' "It's not where you live, it's how you live': how women negotiate conflict and violence in the inner city', *The Annals*, 595: 49–62.

The Sociological Review, 62:S2, pp. 166–186 (2014), DOI: 10.1111/1467-954X.12197

Jones, N., (2009), *Between Good and Ghetto: African American Girls and Inner City Violence,* New Brunswick, NJ: Rutgers University Press.

Katz, J., (1988), *Seductions of Crime,* New York: Basic Books.

Katz, J., (2001), 'Analytic induction', in N. Smelser and P. Baltes (eds), *International Encyclopedia of the Social Sciences,* New York: Elsevier.

Katz, J. and Jackson-Jacobs, C., (2004), 'The criminologists' gang', in C. Sumner (ed.), *The Blackwell Companion to Criminology,* Oxford: Blackwell.

Klein, M., (1995), *The American Street Gang: Its Nature, Prevalence, and Control,* New York: Oxford University Press.

Labov, W., (1972), *Language in the Inner-City: Studies in the Black English Vernacular,* Philadelphia, PA: University of Pennsylvania Press.

Labov, W., (1973), 'The boundaries of words and their meanings', in C. Bailey and R. Shuy (eds), *New Ways of Analyzing Variation in English,* Washington, DC: George Washington University.

Labov, W., (1982), 'Speech actions and reactions in personal narrative', in D. Tannen (ed.), *Georgetown University Round Table on Language and Linguistics 1981,* Washington, DC: Georgetown University Press.

Lee, J., (2009), 'Battlin' on the corner: techniques for sustaining play', *Social Problem,* 56 (3): 578–598.

Lipsky, M., (1980), *Street-Level Bureaucracy: Dilemmas of the Individual Public Services,* New York: Russell Sage Foundation.

Luckenbill, D., (1977), 'Criminal homicide as a situated transaction', *Social Problems,* 25 (3): 176–186.

Luckenbill, D., (1981), 'Generating compliance: the case of robbery', *Urban Life,* 10 (1): 25–46.

Lyng, S., (1990), 'Edgework: a social-psychological analysis of voluntary risk taking', *American Journal of Sociology,* 95 (4): 851–886.

Lyons, W. and Drew, J., (2006), *Punishing Schools: Fear and Citizenship in American Public Education,* Ann Arbor, MI: University of Michigan Press.

Marsh, P., Rosser, E. and Harré, R., (1978), *The Rules of Disorder,* London: Routledge & Kegan Paul.

Matza, D., (1969), *Becoming Deviant,* Englewood Cliffs, NJ: Prentice-Hall.

Meehan, A., (2000), 'The organizational career of gang statistics: the politics of policing gangs', *The Sociological Quarterly,* 41 (3): 337–370.

Morrill, C., Yalda, C., Musheno, M. and Bejarano, C., (2000), 'Telling tales in school: youth culture and conflict narratives', *Law and Society Review,* 34 (1): 101–144.

Muschert, G. and Peguero, A., (2010), 'The Columbine effect and school antiviolence policy', *Research in Social Problems and Public Policy,* 17: 117–148.

Newman, K. 2004. *Rampage: The Social Roots of School Shootings.* New York: Basic Books.

Nisbett, R. and Cohen, D., (1996), *Culture of Honor: The Psychology of Violence in the South,* Boulder, CO: Westview Press.

Pinker, S., (2007), *The Stuff of Thought: Language as a Window into Human Nature,* New York: Viking Books.

Polk, K., (1999), 'Males and honor contest violence', *Homicide Studies,* 3: 6–29.

Prus, R., (1978), 'From barrooms to bedrooms: towards a theory of interpersonal violence', in M. Gammon (ed.), *Violence in Canada,* Toronto: Methuen.

Ragin, C., (1987), *The Comparative Method: Moving Beyond Qualitative and Quantitative Strategies,* Berkeley, CA: University of California Press.

Ragin, C., (2000), *Fuzzy-Set Social Science,* Chicago: University of Chicago Press.

Rosch, E., (1973), 'Natural categories', *Cognitive Psychology,* 4 (3): 328–350.

Sacks, H., (1992), *Lectures on Conversation,* (ed. G. Jefferson), Oxford: Blackwell Press.

Sanders, W., (1994), *Gangbangs and Drive-bys: Grounded Culture and Juvenile Gang Violence,* New York: Aldine de Gruyter.

Schinkel, W., (2010), *Aspects of Violence: A Critical Theory,* New York: Palgrave Macmillan.

Scott, M. and Lyman, S., (1968), 'Accounts', *American Sociological Review,* 33: 46–62.

Short, J. and Strodtbeck, F., (1968), 'Why gangs fight', in J. Short (ed.), *Gang Delinquency and Delinquent Subcultures,* New York: Harper & Row.

Skiba, R., Michael, R., Nardo, A. and Peterson, R., (2002), 'The color of discipline: sources of racial and gender disproportionality in school punishment', *The Urban Review,* 34 (4): 317–342.

Smith, D. and Klein, J., (1984), 'Police control of interpersonal disputes', *Social Problems,* 31: 468–481.

Sykes, G. and Matza, D., (1957), 'Techniques of neutralization', *American Sociological Review,* 22 (6): 664–670.

Toch, H., (1969), *Violent Men: An Inquiry into the Psychology of Violence,* Chicago: Aldine de Gruyter.

Tomsen, S., (1997), 'A top night: social protest, masculinity, and the culture of drinking violence', *British Journal of Criminology,* 37: 90–102.

Verdugo, R., (2002), 'Race-ethnicity, social class, and zero-tolerance policies: the cultural and structural wars', *Education and Urban Society,* 35 (1): 50–75.

Webb, E., Campbell, D., Schwartz, R. and Sechrest, L., (1966), *Unobtrusive Measures: Nonreactive Research in the Social Sciences,* Chicago: Rand McNally.

Welch, K. and Payne, A., (2010), 'Racial threat and punitive school discipline', *Social Problems,* 57 (1): 25–48.

Winlow, S., (2001), *Badfellas: Crime, Tradition, and New Masculinities,* Oxford: Berg Press.

Winlow, S. and Hall, S., (2006), *Violent Night: Urban Leisure and Contemporary Culture,* Oxford: Berg.

Wright, R. and Decker, S., (1997), *Armed Robbers in Action: Stickups and Street Culture,* Boston, MA: Northeastern University Press.

The Sociological Review, 62:S2, pp. 166–186 (2014), DOI: 10.1111/1467-954X.12197

Mainstreaming domestic and gender-based violence into sociology and the criminology of violence

Sylvia Walby, Jude Towers and Brian Francis

Abstract: Sociological and criminological views of domestic and gender-based violence generally either dismiss it as not worthy of consideration, or focus on specific groups of offenders and victims (male youth gangs, partner violence victims). In this paper, we take a holistic approach to violence, extending the definition from that commonly in use to encompass domestic violence and sexual violence. We operationalize that definition by using data from the latest sweep of the Crime Survey for England and Wales. By so doing, we identify that violence is currently under-measured and ubiquitous; that it is gendered, and that other forms of violence (family violence, acquaintance violence against women) are equally of concern. We argue that violence studies are an important form of activity for sociologists.

Keywords: violence, domestic violence, crime, victim-offender relationship, gender, measurement, quantitative methods

Introduction

Žižek (2009) is wrong to argue that sociologists should refrain from examining direct violence on the grounds that this distracts from more important matters. Bourdieu (2000 [1997]) is wrong to argue that violence involves the complicity of those who undergo it. These men underestimate the importance of violence in the lives of women; the significance of visceral physical force and the harm that it causes. The scholarly neglect of domestic violence and other forms of violence against women has a long heritage. Weber (1948) thought the modern state had a monopoly of legitimate violence in its territory, even at a time when rape and violence in the domestic sphere were not crimes when committed by husbands against wives. Merton (1938) was one of many sociologists and criminologists to locate violence as the product of socio-economic inequalities, studying young disadvantaged men; but allowed their victims to remain largely invisible.

The Sociological Review, 62:S2, pp. 187–214 (2014), DOI: 10.1111/1467-954X.12198

The mainstream neglect is embedded in the construction of public knowledge. Taking England and Wales as an exemplar, the official count of violent crime, police recorded crimes, has no categories in which to capture domestic violence or gender-based violence (with the exception of some sexual offences); thus violent crime against women is routinely made invisible in the public sphere.

Beyond the analysis of inter-personal violence there is work on other forms of violence – that of violence of states, militaries and political movements (Tilly, 2003; Mann, 1986), but this is beyond the scope of this paper, though see Walby (2009, 2013), Ray (2011), Wieviorka (2009) and Malešević (2010).

There has been a growing challenge to the gendered assumption that domestic violence and gender-based violence against women are not important. There is an emerging epistemic community (Haas, 1992), combining the development of new knowledge and practices, involving feminist activists, service providers, academics and public officials. The violence emerges into public view in the form of 'scandals', when some famous man is accused of perpetrating gendered violence (eg Jimmy Saville, Julian Assange, Strauss-Kahn), or when a particularly horrendous incident stirs public outrage (eg sex abuse of children by Catholic priests; gang rape in India). But this particular knowledge is not yet sedimented into authoritative academic knowledge, although there are significant attempts to achieve this (eg Walklate, 2004). As Sharp (2006: 3) notes, in her editorial on the launch of the journal *Feminist Criminology*, 'the majority of criminological research in the top-tier journals still either ignores women or treats gender as a control variable'.

There is an emerging field at the intersection of and in the interstices between sociology, gender studies, criminology, social policy and social statistics that investigates and analyses domestic and gendered violence. This field includes debates as to the extent to which: domestic violence is gendered (Straus and Gelles, 1990; Dobash *et al.*, 1992; Archer, 2000); domestic abuse is violent (Stark, 2007); and frequent repetitions of domestic violence can be counted (Johnson, 1995, 2008).

Despite its vibrancy, the field of domestic and gendered violence has developed relatively separately from mainstream disciplines. It has developed its own conferences and journals; its own theories, concepts and forms of measurement; its priority fields of enquiry. This separate development has consequences for the integration of the scholarship and research on domestic and gendered violence into mainstream sociology and criminology that are not always positive. The purpose of this paper is to mainstream the analysis of domestic and gendered violence into sociology. This is not merely a one-way impact, but a process of mutual adaptation of these two complex systems of thought.

By mainstreaming violence, this paper is able to pursue a challenge to orthodox views by investigating the extent to which interpersonal violence is domestic and is gendered, using a form of knowledge widely considered to be authoritative: statistics. It rejects the view that official statistics are inevitably part of the dominant order; arguing that instead they can be used to speak 'truth to power'. It contributes to the agenda of making visible this violence by addressing and

The Sociological Review, 62:S2, pp. 187–214 (2014), DOI: 10.1111/1467-954X.12198
© 2014 The Authors. The Sociological Review published by John Wiley & Sons Ltd on behalf of the Editorial Board of The Sociological Review

solving some of the dilemmas and complexities of measurement necessary to identify the violence as a robust object for analysis. It draws on analysis of a range of sources of data including, in particular, the Crime Survey for England and Wales (CSEW), formerly the British Crime Survey.

As part of this mainstreaming, there is also a need for some of the particularities of the challenger field of gendered violence to be modified. This includes reconsideration of concepts and measurements so as to be compatible with the mainstream. There is need to explicitly address the less than full overlap of the violence that is variously 'domestic', 'gender-based' and 'against women'. This includes consideration of violence that is gendered, but not domestic.

In this way, the paper develops further the critique of current theoretical frameworks in which domestic violence and gender-based violence are marginalized; identifies the scale of domestic and gendered violence as a proportion of all violent crime; demonstrates the implications of different definitions of domestic and gendered violence for substantive findings and analysis; and establishes the significance of domestic and gendered violence to social theory.

Review

The neglect of gendered inter-personal violence is widespread in contemporary social theory. This occurs in two main ways. First, violence is defined in such a way as to position its harm as if it derives abstractly from systems of inequality, thereby obscuring physical harms and physical violence from men to women, as illustrated by the work of Žižek and Bourdieu. Second, within the analysis of violence within the field of sociological criminology, there is segregation of mainstream accounts of violence that leave gender out of focus from an emerging specialized school of gender-based violence. Although there are attempts to merge the insights from the specialized analysis of gendered violence into mainstream theory in this area (eg Walklate, 2004; Hearn, 2012), they have had limited impact. We identify some of the reasons for this lack of impact in order to suggest how they may be addressed, thereby offering a route to more successful mainstreaming of the analysis of gendered violence into the analysis of inter-personal violence and into social theory.

Social theory: Žižek and Bourdieu

Žižek (2009: 10) argues that the focus on, the 'fascination' with, direct violence, or 'subjective violence', is a distraction from more important systemic issues. He distinguishes between 'subjective violence – that violence which is enacted by social agents, evil individuals, disciplined repressive apparatuses, fanatical crowds' (2009: 9) and 'the fundamental systemic violence of capitalism . . . that is no longer attributable to concrete individuals and their "evil" intentions, but is purely "objective", systematic, anonymous' (2009: 11). He concludes thus 'to chastise violence outright, to condemn it as 'bad', is an ideological operation par excellence, a mystification which collaborates in rendering invisible the fundamental forms of social violence' (2009: 174).

Žižek is right to note that the prioritization of different forms of violence is not a simple given but is socially variable and influenced by media and other social practices. But his examples of victims, starting with elites who suffer from revolutionary violence, suggest that he is unaware of the actual distribution of victims of violence in unequal societies. His prioritization of the 'objective' wider system is insensitive to these actual patterns in inter-personal violence, in which women and other minoritized groups are further harmed. His ostensibly radical argument that it is important to focus on 'the system' not its immediate victims merely rehearses the same old gender-blind practices of the traditional left.

Bourdieu (2000), like Žižek, also seeks to displace physical violence from the centre of attention of analysis, but by a different theoretical manoeuvre. Bourdieu broadens the concept of violence so that it overlaps with and is indistinguishable from that of power. This might initially appear to expand the scope of analysis, but in fact it merely erodes the specificity and potential for distinctive explanatory power of the concept of violence, since if violence is merely symbolic power, then it is no more than other forms of symbolic power. Indeed, Bourdieu goes further and suggests that victims of violence are complicit in this violence because they have learned their position within the practices of power and these are deeply sedimented in their habitus and embedded in their bodies. Bourdieu (2000: 169–170) writes of

> the inscription of a relation of domination into the body . . . The practical recognition through which the dominated, often unwittingly, contribute to their own domination by tacitly accepting, in advance, the limits imposed on them . . . submitting, however reluctantly, to the dominant judgement, sometimes in internal conflict and 'self-division', the subterranean complicity that a body slipping away from consciousness and will maintains with the violence of the censures inherent in the social structures.

> Symbolic violence is the coercion which is set up only through the consent that the dominated cannot fail to give to the dominator. . . . The effect of symbolic domination (sexual, ethnic, cultural, linguistic, etc) is exerted not in the pure logic of knowing consciousness but in the obscurity of the dispositions of habitus, in which are embedded the schemes of perception and appreciation . . . below the level of the decisions of the conscious mind and the controls of the will.

In consequence, Bourdieu cannot theorize violence as separate from other forms of power; he cannot identify its specific character, rhythms and modalities. The concept of 'symbolic violence' refuses the specificity of the visceral, the particularity of the power that comes from control over physical pain rather than over economic resources. In so doing he is rejecting a conceptual distinction that is relevant to the analysis of the modalities of power. Even more odd is his claim that those who suffer symbolic violence collaborate with and are complicit with their oppressor rather than resist and fight back. Such a position is rejected by

The Sociological Review, 62:S2, pp. 187–214 (2014), DOI: 10.1111/1467-954X.12198

Fanon (1990), who details the ever-present awareness of the oppressed of the risk of violence from the hated colonial oppressor (see also von Holdt, 2013). Bourdieu's position is the opposite of that of Gramsci (1971), for whom coercion made visible the relations of domination that could in less contentious times be disguised by consent.

These critical social theorists, Žižek and Bourdieu, not only marginalize gendered violence, but also inter-personal violence more generally. Žižek argues that the abstract systemic 'violence' of capitalism is more important than the concrete examples of direct violence that are picked up in the media, while Bourdieu refuses the specificity of violence distinct from other forms of symbolic power. If 'theory' is so problematic, will matters improve when looking at the empirical social science closest to violence, criminology?

Criminology

Most of the empirical analysis of inter-personal violence in the social sciences now takes place in the field of criminology, though this overlaps with sociology and other disciplines, and within a relatively segregated field of 'violence against women'. Much, though not all, criminology subsumes violent crime into a general crime category, except where the analyses are more specific to crime type. Criminology is internally diverse, being subdivided into several competing and overlapping schools of thought (Maguire *et al.*, 2012; McLaughlin *et al.*, 2003; Newburn, 2013); hence, the generalizations that are made below come with warnings about the need for caution and caveats. Nevertheless, it is not unreasonable to identify the following schools of thought, theories and paradigms: structural strain theory (Merton, 1938), many times reworked (Agnew, 1992, 1999), which branches into the Chicago school of social disorganization (Shaw and McKay, 1942), the inequality/relative deprivation school (Young, 1999), and related approaches to macro level sources of variation (Pratt and Cullen, 2005); and rational choice theory originating in economics (Becker, 1968), which informs the development of the routine activity paradigm (Cohen and Felson, 1979), the self-control deficit paradigm (Gottfredson and Hirschi, 1990) and the criminal career paradigm (Piquero *et al.*, 2003) as well as economic criminology (Cook *et al.*, 2013). Gender is remarkable by its absence from these schools of thought, appearing instead as a separate field. In textbooks and overviews of criminology gender will often appear as a separate chapter that is ill-integrated into the rest of the text (see, for example, Miller and Mullins, 2008).

In the classic sociological account by Merton, the cause of crime lay in the 'malintegration', or structural strain between 'culturally defined aspirations' and 'socially structured means' of obtaining them (Merton, 1938: 674).

> The fact that actual advance toward desired success symbols through conventional channels is, despite our persisting open-class ideology, relatively rare and difficult with those handicapped by little formal education and few economic resources . . . On the one hand, they are asked to orient their conduct toward the prospect of accumulating

wealth and on the other they are largely denied effective opportunities to do so institutionally. The consequences of such structural inconsistency are psycho-pathological personality, and/or antisocial conduct, and/or revolutionary activities. (Merton, 1938: 679)

Crime is thus one of the outcomes of structural strain between culturally defined aspirations and class-based inequalities in the means to fulfil them. Merton situates the causality of crime at the level of social structure, in the tensions generated by socially structured inequalities. Yet, despite gender relations being deeply structured by inequalities, gender is omitted from this foundational account of crime.

More recent work develops the analysis of the implications of structural inequality for crime, including violent crime, through the route of both inequality and relative deprivation and also that of poverty and social disorganization. The conceptual focus on relative deprivation lends itself to synergy with political economy and left realism (Young, 1999). For example, there are studies that link cross-national rates of homicide with economic inequality and poverty (Cole and Gramajo, 2009; Pridemore, 2008; van Wilsem, 2004), including Fajnzylber *et al.* (2002) who find not only a statistically significant correlation of the link between economic inequality and homicide in a cross-national data set over time, but also evidence that inequality is the cause of changes in its rate. The focus on social disorganization, developed by the 'Chicago school' (Shaw and McKay, 1942), is focused on the social disorganization that can be the consequence of poverty, but which is mediated by the different ways civil society and the social relations within neighbourhoods are constituted (Sampson *et al.*, 2002). There is a very large body of empirical evidence linking economic inequality, variously operationalized as poverty, income inequality, unemployment, poverty and disadvantage, with crime including violent crime, at both individual and macro levels. A very strong correlation is found in several major reviews, including a meta-review of 63 studies by Chiricos (1987), of 34 studies by Hsieh and Pugh (1993), and the meta-analysis of over 200 studies by Pratt and Cullen (2005). The finding across these myriad of studies, methodologies and perspectives is that crime, including violent crime and homicide, is perpetrated by the disadvantaged. Yet, there is little discussion of gender, despite the significance of gender inequalities.

In the work informed by the more individualistic traditions of psychology and economics, such as rational choice theory (eg Becker, 1968), the link between disadvantage and violent crime re-emerges, but is articulated through different causal pathways. In rational choice theory, crime is committed when the benefits of crime outweigh its costs in the sanctions that might be brought to bear on the perpetrator (Becker, 1968) by the state or civil society. In studies within the self-control deficit paradigm (Gottfredson and Hirschi, 1990), the correlation that is discovered between harsh and poor upbringing and later criminality is explained by variations in self-control: poor upbringing in early childhood causes poor self-control, which causes crime because such individuals

The Sociological Review, 62:S2, pp. 187–214 (2014), DOI: 10.1111/1467-954X.12198

find it harder to resist temptation. This paradigm has become one of the most important in contemporary criminology, with a meta-analysis of 21 studies finding that self-control was a strong predictor of crime (Pratt and Cullen, 2000). This paradigm meshes with the criminal career paradigm (Piquero *et al.*, 2003), in which poor upbringing results in a criminal career, and the worse the upbringing the earlier the onset and later the desistance from crime. Although these methodologically individualist approaches might appear to float free from social structurally generated inequalities and disadvantages, in fact this is not entirely the case, since they are brought in by the back door of the social conditions that shape the family circumstances that lead to the development of individuals with low self-control, while the existence of non-linear effects (Mears *et al.*, 2013) suggests the relevance of mediating social institutions. Again women are largely invisible, though with a few exceptions.

Additionally, gang theories of violence have been proposed. For example, there may exist a normative acceptance of violence in some societal groups (Wolfgang and Ferracuti, 1967). Such values are transmitted within the cultural group, and individuals can also be born into such a subculture. The theory has proved controversial as it has become associated with ethnic or black violence, but Wolfgang and Ferracuti also identified social class as a relevant societal group.

There are some specific criminological theories of individualized violence that are not general theories of crime. Such authors turn to psychopathological explanations of violent behaviour such as conduct disorder or sociopathic tendencies. Moffit (1993) identifies brain injury and abnormal brain activity as associated with life-course persistent offending – a small percentage of offenders who are most likely to be involved in violence. However, she goes on to state that social factors such as poverty and childhood upbringing will interact with these biological factors – children can overcome psychological deficit through successful upbringing.

Most criminology, therefore, suggests that violence and crime are generated by the disadvantaged, in one way or another, with many empirical studies consistent with this paradigm. Women appear, if at all, as an absence, as the mother who failed to socialize her children into appropriate levels of self-control. Women as the victims of male violence are rarely visible in mainstream criminology, being treated as a separate field. This is beginning to be seen as a problem. For example, the meta-analysis of studies on self control and victimology notes the absence of studies on intimate partner violence, violence against women, family violence, and child abuse and concluded 'self-control theory cannot assume the flavour of generality for which it was originally intended' until these studies are included (Pratt *et al.*, 2014: 90).

Gender-based violence against women

A specialist sub-field of gender-based violence against women has developed over the last 30 years. It has developed by identifying, naming, describing, documenting, counting, and analysing an increasing range of forms of violence. As part of a wider epistemic community, alongside activists, service providers and policymakers, this academic field has helped to bring the issues of gender-based violence against women into public view, established a field of political activism, steady policy development, and increasingly a field of social scientific enquiry with journals and conferences. Most of the field is self-contained, with only a limited literature that simultaneously addresses the specialist and general analytic fields. There are several theoretical and methodological divergences between the mainstream and gendered fields that are conducive to their continued segregation: first, in theoretical assumptions; second, in definition of violence; third in the significance of the relationship between offender and victim; fourth in whether the extent of the violence concerns the number of violent events or the number of victimized people.

Contrary to much criminology, most of the analysis of gender-based violence treats this violence to be primarily from the advantaged (largely men) and directed primarily towards the disadvantaged (largely women). Gender-based violence against women is commonly seen as both a consequence and a cause of gender inequality (Dobash and Dobash, 1979; Kelly, 1988). The direction of violence, from advantaged to disadvantaged, is different from much mainstream criminology where such directionality of violence is not part of the dominant paradigm. This theoretical divergence hinders the integration of the two fields. An example of such work in the field of domestic violence is that of Kalmuss and Straus (1982) that found the greater were the objective intra-household gender inequalities, the more likely that conflict would lead to violence. Objective dependency was considered to occur when the wife was not employed, when her husband earned more than 75 per cent of the couple's income, and when there were the further constraint of children aged five or younger at home. However, there are both exceptions to this generalization and also multiple ways in which 'gender inequality' is interpreted and operationalized. For example, there is a minority tradition in the field, which argues that domestic violence is perpetrated by women as much as by men; which rejects the claim of the link between gender disadvantage and domestic violence, suggesting instead that women can be as violent as men and that family dysfunction is the main cause of the violence (Straus, 1979). While there are claims that studies support this view (Archer, 2000), the weight of the evidence in the field does not support this view of gender symmetry of the perpetrators of the violence (Dobash *et al.*, 1992; Walby and Allen, 2004). But the issue as to the nature of relative and absolute gender inequalities and ascertaining which of diverse potential causal pathways between inequality and violence are the most important is not yet fully resolved. Vieraitis *et al.* (2007) find that variations in women's absolute status correlate with their risk of being victims of homicide, but not their relative position, in a cross-sectional analysis of US counties in 2000. Pridemore and Freilich (2005) find a positive relationship between gender income equality and women being victims of homicide, in a cross-sectional study in the US, which they interpret as caused by a backlash from conservative men to reductions in gender inequality;

The Sociological Review, 62:S2, pp. 187–214 (2014), DOI: 10.1111/1467-954X.12198
© 2014 The Authors. The Sociological Review published by John Wiley & Sons Ltd on behalf of the Editorial Board of The Sociological Review

though they note caveats and limitations in that there was no correlation with the strength of a masculine subculture. Further, there are complex interactions between different inequalities, including gender and ethnicity as well as those of gender and socio-economic position (Crenshaw, 1991; Burgess-Proctor, 2006; Bernard, 2013). The divergence in the assumptions about the disadvantaged position of perpetrator and victim in the mainstream and specialist field presents challenges to the integration of gender-specific and general theories of violent crime.

The second divergence between the mainstream and gender fields stems from tension between a definition of violence that focuses on criminalized physical actions and another that extends this to encompass many other forms of power, which is reflected in different measures of the nature and severity of the acts in mainstream crime analysis and in the gender violence field (Walby, 2013). This debate has parallels in fields of research on violence (de Haan, 2009). The mainstream crime field deploys a set of specific categories built up over years of development of nationally based criminal law, while the gender violence field, through developments in international policy (UN General Assembly, 1993) and research methodology (Straus, 1979; Dobash *et al.*, 1992) has developed a very broad definition. The UN General Assembly (1993), in its Declaration on the Elimination of Violence against Women, defined violence against women thus:

'For the purposes of this Declaration, the term "violence against women" means any act of gender-based violence that results in, or is likely to result in, physical, sexual or psychological harm or suffering to women, including threats of such acts, coercion or arbitrary deprivation of liberty, whether occurring in public or in private life. Violence against women shall be understood to encompass, but not be limited to, the following: (a) Physical, sexual and psychological violence occurring in the family, including battering, sexual abuse of female children in the household, dowry-related violence, marital rape, female genital mutilation and other traditional practices harmful to women, non-spousal violence and violence related to exploitation; (b) physical, sexual and psychological violence occurring within the general community, including rape, sexual abuse, sexual harassment and intimidation at work, in educational institutions and elsewhere, trafficking in women and forced prostitution; (c) Physical, sexual and psychological violence perpetrated or condoned by the State, wherever it occurs.'

The definition of domestic violence used by the UK government (Home Office, 2013) and its approach to eliminating violence against women and girls (UK Government, 2013) reflects the broad UN definition of gender-based violence against women. There has been discussion in the gender field as to the merits and consequences of restricting the definition of violence to physical actions or extending it to non-physical forms of abuse (DeKeseredy, 2000; Gordon, 2000; Kilpatrick, 2004; Saltzman, 2004). On the one hand are those that argue for a broad definition that includes acts of power that are not crimes so as to build concepts of a 'continuum' of violence (Kelly, 1988) and 'coercive control' (Stark, 2007). On the other are those that note that the consequences of breadth are not always desirable since they draw minor acts into the frame of violence that can obscure the extent of gender inequality found in the more severe acts (Radford, 2003). For example, Steffensmeier *et al.* (2006) find that, between 1980 and 2003 in the US, widening the definition of violent crime so as to include borderline incidents changes the gender composition of perpetrators since these borderline incidents are disproportionately perpetrated by women, thereby leading the official record to show a narrowing of the gender gap in the perpetration of violent crime. A compromise is to collect data on a wide range of forms of abuse that enables definitions data to be drawn at different thresholds to meet different definitions (Saltzman *et al.*, 1999; Walby and Allen, 2004).

The third divergence concerns the importance or otherwise of the relationship between offender and victim. Recorded crime statistics do not treat this relationship as relevant so it is not recorded; but documenting the presence or absence of a domestic relationship is essential to the field of domestic violence. In mainstream crime analysis this is not usually regarded as important, so this information is rarely included in recorded crime statistics. In the gender field the relationship between offender and victim is very important; indeed in the field of domestic violence it is part of the definition, so this information is essential. The near-invisibility of the gendered relationship between offender and victim in police recorded crime statistics, since the relationship between offender and victim is not recorded there, is thus a problem for the gender field. It is certainly possible for the police to collect and record data on the relationship of the perpetrator to the victim. Indeed, there are a few minor examples of such subdivision: the categories of rape and sexual assault are subdivided by whether the victim is female or male; and there is a special category of assault for those instances where it is racially or religiously aggravated. However, in order to achieve a gender division within categories of violence against the person, it would be necessary for statute law to require this. In some countries, for example, Sweden, there is a specific offence of domestic assault against women, but not the UK. The response in the UK, and some other countries, is to find other ways to record the relationship between alleged perpetrator and offender in criminal justice system data, by the use of additional 'flags' but this is usually less reliable than the main statistics produced by the police, since the data collection tends to be less well resourced and the process is less rigorously audited (Walby *et al.*, 2010).

The fourth concerns whether the extent of violence is counted as the number of violent events or as the number of people victimized. In the mainstream, recorded crime statistics usually count the number of offences, while the domestic violence field has tended to count the number of victims. This makes it hard to make even simple calculations such as the percentage of violent crime that is gender-based since in one case the unit is the offence and in the other it is the victim. The repeated nature of domestic violence needs to be taken into account if its nature is to be described and analysed (Farrell *et al.*, 1995). But there is more than one way to do this. On the one hand, there is a call for the development of the concept of 'coercive control' (Stark, 2007; Myhill and Dunne, 2015)

The Sociological Review, 62:S2, pp. 187–214 (2014), DOI: 10.1111/1467-954X.12198

thus privileging the data unit of a 'course of coercive control' rather than of multiple offences. On the other hand, there is a call to increase the sophistication of the counting of frequency so as to be able to investigate whether there is a distinction between types of domestic violence, as in Johnson's (1995, 2008) typology of domestic violence that varies according to the frequency and severity of the violence between 'intimate terrorism' with many incidents and 'situational couple violence' in which there are a very few instances of low levels of violence both ways between the partners; or indeed between a largely non-victimized population and a small chronic sub-population (Hope and Norris, 2013). The way forward is to gather information using both units of measurement, victims and offences, in order to overcome this polarity.

The argument here is that if gender-based violence and domestic violence are to be mainstreamed into criminology and into sociology, then there must be a unified set of categories in which violence, both gender-based and otherwise, is measured. This might be produced in one of four ways. First, the use of mainstream categories by both fields; but this omits data that enables distinctions that are essential to the domestic violence field. Second, the use of the specialized categories by the mainstream; but that neglects the legal distinctions between crimes, so omits data that enables distinctions that are essential to the mainstream. Third, complex ad hoc acts of translation between the measurement typologies used by the two fields; but while this may be expedient on occasion it is not a satisfactory basis in the long run. Fourth, the modification of the mainstream categories in the light of the requirements of the gender violence field so that they can encompass both; which is the best long-term solution, but requires some developmental work.

Methodology

The paper investigates the consequences of mainstreaming domestic and gendered violence for social theory. It takes as its focus to address this question, the investigation of the consequences of including domestic and gendered violence within mainstream measurements of violence and of revising mainstream measurement devices to take better account of gendered concerns. It compares the pattern of violence that is made visible before and after gender mainstreaming. By investigating the extent of domestic and gendered violence as compared with other forms of violent crime, it offers a new perspective on its scale and significance. Using a variety of measurement techniques, we investigate the extent of gender-based and domestic violence relative to other forms of violence; at each step addressing the conceptual and methodological issues in varying the measurement categories. Following the detailed empirical analysis, we address the significance of the gendering of violence for criminological and social theory. We assume that the more gender violence that is made visible by changing the techniques of measurement, then the greater is the challenge to existing theory and the greater need for its revision to be in alignment with evidence about the empirical world. Our hypothesis is that there is sufficient evidence of the large-scale extent of domestic and gendered violence to require the modification of mainstream sociological and criminological theory; however, this requires modification to the traditional categories of measurement in order to make these matters visible.

There are three gendered concepts that need to be disentangled and analysed separately: domestic violence; gender-based violence; and violence against women. So far in the paper the distinction between these terms has followed usage in the specific text under discussion. From this point onwards they are distinguished, and further distinctions are made, although they remain overlapping concepts. Domestic (in England and Wales, at least) can be divided into two further categories: intimate partners, both current and former; family members other than intimate partners. Gender-based violence is violence that is directed against a person on the basis of gender (EIGE, 2014). Violence against women is defined by the UN as 'any act of gender-based violence that results in or is likely to result in physical, sexual or mental harm or suffering to women' (UN General Assembly, 1993). Of course, most of this violence is primarily directed from men to women; but not all of it.

The definition and conceptualization of interpersonal violence is contested. Within mainstream crime categories, the boundary can be drawn either narrowly around the category 'violence against the person' or more widely so as to additionally include 'sexual offences' and perhaps also 'threats'. Within the gender literature, the boundary can be drawn narrowly around acts restricted to unwanted physical and sexual contact, or extended to include threats, and further to emotional and financial abuse. We deploy more than one definition of violence in order to investigate the implications of each.

There are several sources of data that inform social science analyses of violence in the UK. These include: police 'recorded' crime statistics; police and CPS 'flagged' domestic violence; the Crime Survey for England and Wales main questionnaire and self-completion module. These will be addressed in turn using the most recent data sources in England and Wales.

Findings

Police recorded crime

The police produce a set of statistics known in England and Wales as the 'Recorded crime statistics' which record criminal offences that are reported to them and which they have recorded. These statistics do not include the relationship between alleged offender and victim, so it is not possible to construct a category of domestic violence from them. Those forms of domestic violence that are sufficiently serious to cross a criminal threshold are recorded within the crime categories; but they are not separately visible. The only form of gender-based crime that is immediately visible is that of sexual offences, since this is a

Table 1: *Police recorded crimes, England and Wales, 2011/12*

	Number of recorded crimes	Percentage of all crime
Homicide	529	0.01
Of which: female victims	*171*	*<0.01*
Of which: male victims	*358*	*<0.01*
Sexual offences[1]	52,760	1.00
Of which: Sexual offences against women and girls	*34,547*	*0.90*
Of which: Sexual offences against men and boys	*3,548*	*<0.10*
Violence against the person[2]	626,720	16.00
Other crime	3,343,675	83.00
All crimes	4,022,626	100.00

[1] Note that there are additional sexual offences which are not gendered and therefore the two subcategories of sexual offences against females and against males do not sum to the total of sexual offences.

[2] Police recorded crime category of violence against the person includes homicide.

Source: Office for National Statistics (ONS, 2013a) 02. Appendix Tables – Crime Survey for England and Wales Year Ending September 2013: Table A4 Police Recorded Crime by Offence: Office for National Statistics (2013b) *Focus on: Violent Crime and Sexual Offences:* Figure 2.2 Homicide Offences currently recorded by the police in England and Wales by sex of victim 1996/97 to 2012/13.

gender-based group of offences, and moreover, offences in which men usually attack women. The smaller number of sexual attacks on men (usually by men) is separately identified. In addition, the published statistics on homicide are published in gender disaggregated form. Table 1, which lists the main categories of crime, shows when looking through the lens of 'recorded crime', domestic violence is invisible and instances of other forms of gender-based violence appear tiny.

Flagged domestic violence in the criminal justice system

In order to address this invisibility of domestic and gender-based violence in UK official statistics on recorded crime, the police and Crown Prosecution Service (CPS) have started to 'flag' incidents and offences that are 'domestic' in order to ascertain their progress through the criminal justice system. The process of flagging started in 2004 and was extended in 2009. The flags are a way in which police can track the extent to which the events to which they are called out are domestic, by flagging those incidents and offences where the perpetrator was in a domestic relationship with the victim. 'Domestic' includes actions from partner and former partners and also by family members. 'Domestic' 'flags' are applied to both criminal offences and to incidents that do not cross a criminal threshold. A 'domestic incident (non-notifiable crime)' would 'include rowdy/inconsiderate behaviour (raised voices, heated arguments etc) occurring in domestic situations involving partners (including former partners) and/or family members' (National Policing Improvement Agency, 2009: 56). This practice begins to make domestic violence visible in police activity, with 817,000 flagged incidents recorded in 2011/12. But, in 2014, these figures do not have the standing of national statistics, their collection is not on a mandatory statutory basis, not all police forces provide them, and significant inconsistencies remain in the data (Office for National Statistics, 2013b). In addition, every police force has developed its own method of recording, making national analysis problematic.

The Crown Prosecution Service (CPS), like the police, has recently adopted the practice of flagging cases where the alleged offender, the defendant, is in a domestic relationship with the victim. However, there is a discontinuity between the two data systems, since the police count the number of offences and the CPS count the number of defendants, which means that there are no easily available statistics on the attrition of cases of gender-based violence through the criminal justice system (CJS). It is thus necessary to engage in detailed research to ascertain the extent to which the gender-based violent crimes that are recorded by the police lead to convictions in the courts. The CPS presents data on conviction rates of 73 per cent for violence against women flagged crime (CPS, 2013a), which is lower than 86 per cent for all crimes (CPS, 2013b); but these figures only address that small part of the CJS process between prosecution and conviction in courts. When detailed, but rare and ad hoc, research projects address attrition as measured from the point of recording by the police through to conviction, estimates of CJS conviction rates for gender-based violence are much lower, ranging from 6 per cent (Lovett and Kelly, 2009) to 7–8 per cent (Walby *et al.*, 2010) to 12 per cent (Feist *et al.*, 2007) for rape; and 2–6 per cent for domestic violence (Hester *et al.*, 2008). While the use of flags is a major innovation in data collection, there is still no routine presentation of data to make visible the processing of the crimes of domestic and gender-based violence within the CJS as a whole.

Crime Survey for England and Wales, main questionnaire

Many people do not report crimes committed against them to the police, so they cannot be included in the 'police recorded crime' statistics, nor in police flagged statistics, nor in the data of the Crown Prosecution Service, since their cases have not entered into the criminal justice system. This means that a considerable amount of crime is unknown to the administrative data systems of the criminal justice systems.

In response, the UK and some other countries, such as the US, have introduced surveys of their national populations in order to produce more accurate estimates of the extent of crime and changes in it over time. In the UK, a British Crime Survey started in the early 1980s and is now an annual survey, differentiated between 'England and Wales', 'Scotland', and 'Northern Ireland'. The Crime Survey for England and Wales (CSEW) is regarded by the Office for National Statistics (ONS) as the most reliable measure of the extent of crime in its territory. The ONS (2013b: 3) states that: 'For the crime types and population groups it covers, the CSEW provides a better reflection of the true extent of crime and a more reliable measure of trends than police recorded crime statistics. It has a consistent methodology and is unaffected by changes in levels of reporting to the police, recording practice or police activity' (ONS, 2013b: 3). Indeed in 2014, the UK Statistics Authority (2014) temporally deselected police recorded crime statistics from the category of 'national statistic' because of concerns over their quality. This leaves the CSEW as the most authoritative data on crime in the UK.

The CSEW is complicated and there is a range of options for the organization and presentation of the data. We start with an account of the data as presented in official publications, and follow this by our own analysis of the raw data, in which we offer a series of methodological revisions, to better capture the extent of domestic and gendered violence. The extent of violence against the person as reported in official CSEW publications, disaggregated into three categories by the relationship of the perpetrator to the victim. These are: (a) *domestic* (current and former wife/husband/partner/boyfriend or girlfriend; other family members including son/daughter (in law); other relative; or other household member); (b) *acquaintances* (someone known to the victim, at least by sight, including: workmates/colleagues; clients/members of the public met through work; friends/acquaintances; neighbours; youths from the local area; tradesmen/builders/contactors; and (ex) husband/wife/partner of a household member); and *strangers* (c) (someone unknown to the victim). Table 2 shows the violence estimates foe 2011/12. Domestic violence appears to be 17 per cent of violent crime.

We reanalyse the raw data of the CSEW (ONS, 2014) in order to bring its presentation into better alignment with contemporary conceptual and methodological developments. We make two adjustments: including sexual offences; and removing the 'cap' (see following paragraph). We consider that sexual offences should be treated as 'violent crime', even though it is not in the same legal category as 'violence against the person', since this is the dominant understanding in the field. Prior to 2003, the category 'sexual offences' contained 'consensual' crimes of some male homosexual practices, which made its categorization as 'violence against the person' inappropriate. However, the gradual changing of the law (completed by the Sexual Offences Act 2003) to decriminalize most homosexual acts means that most of the remaining offences, rape and sexual assault, are more appropriately included within the category of 'violence'.

We remove the cap on the number of offences reported to the survey that are included in its published findings. The count of the number of incidents are currently 'capped' so that in a 'series' offence, the number of offences is limited to 5 per 'series offence'. A series offence is one in which 'the same thing is done

Table 2: *Violence against the person, by domestic, acquaintance or stranger, Crime Survey for England and Wales, 2011/12, published data*

	Estimated number of offences	Percentage of violent crime	Percentage of all crime
Domestic	308,000	17	3
Acquaintance	731,000	41	8
Stranger	753,000	42	8
All violence against the person[1,2]	1,792,000	100	19
All offences	9,500,000		100

[1] CSEW is a victimization survey and therefore VAP does not include homicide.
[2] Snatch theft and robbery are not included in these figures.
Source: Office for National Statistics (2013a) 02. Appendix Tables – Crime Survey for England and Wales Year Ending September 2013: Table A1 Trends in CSEW Incidents of Crime from 1981 to 2012/13 with Percentage Change and Statistical Significance of Change.

under the same circumstances, probably by the same people', so contains several instances of the same offence (ONS, 2013c: 15). Although the full reported number of instances is still available, when reporting violence, the ONS caps the number of offences at 5 on the grounds that otherwise there is a risk that a small number of respondents reporting a high number of incidents will skew the overall estimates: 'the restriction to the first five incidents in a series has been applied since the CSEW began in order to ensure that estimates are not affected by a very small number of respondents who report an extremely high number of incidents and which are highly variable between survey years . . . This sort of capping is in line with other surveys of crime and other topics' (ONS, 2013c: 15).

The process of capping survey responses has been criticized both in the UK (Farrell and Pease, 2007) and in the US (Planty and Strom, 2007). It skews the estimates in a way that understates the significance of multiple offences in a course of domestic violence (and indeed other forms of violence). Domestic violence in particular is known to be an offence that is marked by repetition (see Farrell *et al.*, 1995), and so, in order to capture its nature, we consider that all the incidents that respondents report to the CSEW and are recorded by the CSEW should be included in findings using CSEW data.

Our re-estimation of the extent of violence when the cap that limits the presentation of data that has been collected has been removed is shown in Table 3. We find that 'uncapping' significantly increases the size of the estimates of violence against the person offences and sexual offences. Thus, for all violence against the person, the ratio of the new uncapped to the old capped estimates is 1.6. This is especially where the perpetrator is known to the victim, not only in a domestic relationship (1.7 times higher for violence against the person) but also as an acquaintance (twice as high for violence against the person). The

Table 3: *Estimated numbers of violence against the person and sexual offences, by domestic, acquaintance or stranger, Crime Survey for England and Wales, 2011/12, revised by 'uncapping' offences*

	Estimated no. of offences 'capped'[1]	Estimated no. of offences 'uncapped'	Ratio of uncapped to capped violence
Domestic	315,000	526,000	1.7
Acquaintance	777,000	1,529,000	2.0
Stranger	797,000	996,000	1.2
All violence against the person	**1,889,000**	**3,051,000**	**1.6**
All sexual offences	*77,000	*120,000	1.6
Violent and sexual offences	**1,966,000**	**3,171,000**	**1.6**

* N (number of cases) is greater than 10 but less than 50 thus caution should be exercised in considering these as national estimates.

[1] Our capped estimates are slightly higher than the published capped estimates because we use an alternative methodology based on prevalence, rather than incident weights. This is necessary to estimate uncapped offences.

Source: ONS (2014): Crime Survey for England and Wales 2011/12 accessed via the UK Data Service.

inclusion of 'sexual offences' in the more general category of violence is justified on conceptual grounds, but does not make a large difference to the estimates of the amount of violence.

We next disaggregate these categories by gender, as shown in Tables 4 and 5. Table 4 shows the gender distribution for each type of perpetrator-victim relationship, (row percentages) whereas Table 5 shows the distribution within each gender for the individual sub-types of relationship making up the three broad categories of "domestic", "acquaintance" and "stranger" (column percentages). The gender disaggregation of the category of 'domestic', which has been a source of dispute in the field, shows the expected gender asymmetry of victims. Most (71 per cent) of the incidents of domestic violence that are severe enough to cross the criminal threshold are perpetrated against women, but a significant minority (29 per cent) are perpetrated against men. While (current and former) intimate partners are, as expected, the largest category of domestic violence perpetrators, that perpetrated by other family members is significant, especially against women: 38 per cent of domestic violence against women is from family members other than the intimate partner; and 28 per cent for men.

The majority (77 per cent) of violence perpetrated by strangers is against men (23 per cent against women), as expected. But, while the amount of violence by strangers is somewhat larger (1,021,000 offences) than that by domestic perpetrators (589,000 offences), it is perhaps surprisingly less than double the amount.

Table 4: *Estimated number of violence offences (including sexual offences) disaggregated by gender and relationship*

	FEMALES		MALES		ALL		Gender ratio (F/M)
	Estimated No.	%	Estimated No.	%	Estimated No.	%	
Domestic	419,000	71.1	170,000	28.9	589,000	100	2.46
Acquaintance	760,000	48.7	801,000	51.3	1,561,000	100	0.94
Total 'known to victim'	1,179,000	54.8	971,000	45.2	2,150,000	100	1.21
Stranger	238,000	23.3	782,000	76.7	1,021,000	100	0.30
Total	**1,417,000**	**44.7**	**1,753,000**	**55.3**	**3,171,000**	**100**	**0.81**

Note: Figures are uncapped estimates from the Crime Survey of England and Wales 2011/12 main survey victim forms. The combined number of VAP and sexual offences may differ slightly to the total number of VAP and sexual offences given in Table 3; this is because the methodology estimates the combined total.
Source: ONS (2014).

The Sociological Review, 62:S2, pp. 187–214 (2014), DOI: 10.1111/1467-954X.12198

Table 5: *Estimated number of violence offences (including sexual offences) in England and Wales 2011/12 by perpetrator relationship and gender*

Perpetrator	FEMALES		MALES		ALL	
	Est. No. (000s)	%	Est. No. (000s)	%	Est. No. (000s)	%
Domestic relationship						
Intimate partners including (ex)husband/(ex)wife/partner/boyfriend/girlfriend	259	61.8	*122	71.8	381	64.7
Family/household members including son or daughter (in law); other relative; other household member	160	38.2	*48	28.2	208	35.3
TOTAL DOMESTIC VIOLENCE	**419**	**100.0**	**170**	**100.0**	**589**	**100.0**
Acquaintance relationship						
Workmate/colleague	*38	5.0	*84	10.5	*122	7.9
Client/member of public contacted through work	265	34.8	*133	16.6	398	25.4
Friend/acquaintance	*59	7.9	124	15.5	183	11.8
Neighbour	*61	8.0	*49	6.1	110	7.0
Young people in local area	*224	29.4	172	21.3	396	25.3
(Ex) husband/wife/partner of someone in the household	*33	4.3	*6	1.0	*39	2.5
Other acquaintance	*80	10.6	*233	29.0	*313	20.1
TOTAL ACQUAINTANCE VIOLENCE	**760**	**100.0**	**801**	**100.0**	**1,561**	**100.0**
Stranger relationship						
Stranger	238	100.0	782	100.0	1,021	100.0
TOTAL STRANGER VIOLENCE	**238**	**100.0**	**782**	**100.0**	**1,021**	**100.0**

* N (number of cases) is greater than 10 but less than 50 thus caution should be exercised in considering these national estimates.

Note: All violence figures include sexual violence.

Source: ONS (2014): Crime Survey of England and Wales 2011/12 main survey victim forms.

The Sociological Review, 62:S2, pp. 187–214 (2014), DOI: 10.1111/1467-954X.12198
© 2014 The Authors. The Sociological Review published by John Wiley & Sons Ltd on behalf of the Editorial Board of The Sociological Review

Violence by acquaintances is more frequent (1,561,000 offences) than either domestic violence (589,000 offences) or by strangers (1,021,000 offences). Violence by acquaintances is very nearly as likely against women (49 per cent) as it is against men (51 per cent). Within the category of acquaintances, women are especially vulnerable to violence from a client or member of the public contacted through work (265,000 offences against women).

In total, there are nearly as many violent offences against women (1,417,000) as there are against men (1,753,000); that is, women were the victims in 45 per cent of violent offences and men in 55 per cent. This challenges the assumption that 'violence' is primarily a matter of men being violent to other men. The challenge to the orthodox view is only partially due to the significance of domestic violence, important as that is; it is also because of the scale of violence by acquaintances in which women are almost as frequently victimized as men.

From the perspective of violence against women, the majority (54 per cent) of the violence experienced by women is from acquaintances; this is more than from those with whom she has current or former domestic relations (30 per cent) and more than from strangers (17 per cent). This is a challenge to the orthodox view in the 'violence against women' field, which assumes that the majority of violence against women is from current or former intimate partners.

Crime Survey for England and Wales, special module on intimate violence

The CSEW has two sets of questions on intimate violence: the main questionnaire where questions are asked face-to-face and entered by the interviewer in a laptop computer; and a self-completion module in which respondents enter their answers to a slightly different set of questions directly into the computer themselves thereby ensuring much greater confidentiality (Walby and Allen, 2004).

The self-completion modality of delivery of the questionnaire produces greater disclosure from victim-survivors of violence. As shown in Table 6, the self-completion module generates a 3.8 times higher rate of disclosure among victims of domestic violence than in the face-to-face questionnaire. Further, among those that answer the question on frequency of domestic abuse, the average number of incidents per victim is 7.7, which is 1.75 times higher than the face to face.[1]

The self-completion module uses a different typology of domestic violence from the face-to-face questionnaire. This is a revised version of the conflict tactics (CT) scale that is widely used in the field (Walby and Myhill, 2001; Johnson, 1996). In addition, the module collects information on injuries from these acts in a graded typology. The CT scale is distinctive to the field of domestic violence, which is different from the conventional crime classifications. However, while the mainstream and specialized typologies appear initially to be incomparable, it is possible to make an approximate translation between the acts of the CT scale and the mainstream crime codes; though an alternative route of translation can be achieved using the injury typology (Walby, 2004). Currently, the main problem in comparing the findings of the self-completion

The Sociological Review, 62:S2, pp. 187–214 (2014), DOI: 10.1111/1467-954X.12198
© 2014 The Authors. The Sociological Review published by John Wiley & Sons Ltd on behalf of the Editorial Board of The Sociological Review

Table 6: *Crime Survey for England and Wales 2011/12, comparing face-to-face and self-completion estimates of victims of domestic violence*

	Face-to-face (F2F) main questionnaire			Self-complete (SC) module		
	DOMESTIC VIOLENCE					
	Females	Males	All	Females	Males	All
VICTIMS: domestic[1] violence[2]	133,000	*52,000	185,000	458,000	244,000	702,000
Ratio: F2F to SC				3.4	4.7	3.8

* N (number of cases) is greater than 10 but less than 50 thus caution should be exercised in considering these as national estimates.
[1] Domestic includes partners/ex-partners and other family members.
[2] The SC uses the CT scale rather than criminal offence categories. VAP from the SC is constructed using the CT scale items: pushed, held down, or slapped; kicked, bit, hit with fist or had something thrown at; choked or tried to strangle; used weapon; used other force; plus sexual assault.
Source: Crime Survey for England and Wales dataset 2011/12.

module with the main questionnaire is lack of robust frequency data in the SC, which in its recent iterations has too limited a set of questions to enable this to be captured with accuracy.

While the limitations to the comparability of the self-completion module to the main questionnaire mean that estimates of the increased proportion of violence that is domestic, against women or sexual must be made with caution, it is reasonable to conclude that this proportion is significantly larger. Nearly four times as many people disclose experience of domestic violence in the last year in the self-completion as compared with the face-to-face questionnaire. The number of incidents that each victim discloses is also much higher in the self-completion than in the face-to-face questionnaire.

Discussion and conclusions

Mainstreaming domestic and gender-based violence into sociology and criminology makes a difference to social theory. In order to achieve this, it is necessary to overcome several major divergences in methodology between the mainstream and gender fields. These include: the definition of violence; the conceptualization and measurement of the repetition of violence; and the making visible the relationship between offender and victim. When these revisions are made, then the scale of violence that is made visible becomes larger, and its distribution is differently gendered.

Violence against women is almost invisible in police recorded crime statistics, which have traditionally been the most authoritative account of crime, since crimes, other than the sub-categories of rape and sexual assault within the Sexual Offences category and homicide, are not disaggregated by the gender of the victim. Innovation in the recording practices in the criminal justice system by the police and prosecutors has begun to address this, but these initiatives, such as 'flagging' are still marginal to the main statistics. Only within the new data collection exercises of the national surveys is there serious possibility of making visible domestic and gender-based violence; but even here the issues are relatively marginalized.

The first methodological difference concerns the breadth of the definition. At one end of the continuum are the crime codes, based on the development of law, which are far behind developments in other domains, and which make violence against women nearly invisible. At the opposing end of the continuum, are definitions of violence against women that extend to almost all forms of power that are detrimental to women's well-being. We argue for the more systematic development and deployment of categories at the centre of this continuum, which would facilitate more comparability. Sexual offences are crimes and should be included within the category of violent crime. Violence against women covers both criminal and non-criminal behaviour, but significant parts of it are crimes. In order to address it as a crime, we need to include similar categories as other crimes, though revised to make gender issues visible. One of the essential revisions is to include data both on the relationships between offender and victims and also on the gender of offenders and victims, since this is necessary if the category of 'domestic' violence is to be made visible, and indeed the further distinctions in the categories of 'acquaintances' and 'strangers'. This is available in the CSEW, but in police recorded data only through the process of flagging, which is not yet sufficiently developed for routine use. A further essential revision is to deploy mechanisms that allow for the counting of crimes that are repeats. This is especially important in the case of domestic violence, which is often a repeat offence. The survey is potentially a productive way of measuring repeated incidents, but this requires the removal of the 'caps' that artificially restrict the analysis of incidents that some report to surveys. These should not be treated as outliers that may be appropriately discarded, but rather an important part of the field. By defining and measuring 'violence' as uncapped offences of violence against the person and sexual offences, we find that the number of violent offences captured by the CSEW increases by 60 per cent compared to the published 'capped' count.

The violence that is made visible by delving into the raw data from the CSEW has implications for theory. We find that violence against women is not a small specialized form of practice, but a significant minority of the violence: 45 per cent of violent offences are committed against women. This is even when the full extent of domestic violence is hard to estimate accurately

The Sociological Review, 62:S2, pp. 187–214 (2014), DOI: 10.1111/1467-954X.12198
© 2014 The Authors. The Sociological Review published by John Wiley & Sons Ltd on behalf of the Editorial Board of The Sociological Review

because of the limited data on frequency in the self-completion module of the CSEW.

The picture of violent crime as primarily constituted by men being violent to other men is wrong. There is almost as much violence against women as there is against men. It is not the case that violence is overwhelmingly from men to men.

We find that violence from strangers is a smaller proportion of violent crime than often assumed – less than a third (32 per cent). The majority of violent crime is perpetrated by someone known to the victim: an intimate partner, other family member, or an acquaintance. This is not only true for women, but also for men. It is not the case that most violence is from male stranger to male stranger: just a quarter of violent offences are committed by strangers against male victims.

Violence against women is not confined to violence from current or former partners, but is also from other family members and also from acquaintances. Violence to women is overwhelmingly from people they know at least slightly (83 per cent of violent offences). The category of 'acquaintance' is underestimated in current theory, which tends to polarize between, on the one hand, conceiving 'gender-based violence against women' as perpetrated by domestic intimates, and on the other hand conceiving of 'violence' as perpetrated by men to other men in public spaces.

The concept of violent crime is differently gendered than usually imagined. Mainstreaming 'domestic violence' into 'violent crime' changes the nature of the category of 'violent crime'. Violent crime ceases to be something that primarily concerns what men do to other men who are strangers. Rather, violent crime is gendered and concerns those who are known to each other either through domestic relations or as acquaintances. This challenges the theoretical assumptions behind leading theories of crime. These are not crimes perpetrated by those who are only disadvantaged. The intersectionality of class and gender is central to the understanding of violent crime.

Hence we argue, contra Bourdieu, that it is important to acknowledge the specificity of physical violence and not to conflate it with other forms of power. And to reject his assumption of complicity, that bodies are so habituated to hierarchy that they oblige power without resistance. Further, we argue contra Žižek, that the analysis of violence is not a distraction from the analysis of more important matters. Violence in society is ubiquitous, not aberrant, with over three million physical attacks in England and Wales over the past year. As part of that, violence from people known to the victim is an important part of the structuring of the lives of many people. And, we argue, against both, that violence cannot be understood outside of its intricate gendering. These are our conclusions for sociological theory.

Our conclusion for the violence against women field starts from the finding that violence against women is more often perpetrated by acquaintances than intimates. This invites a broadening of the relevant domains so as not only to include domestic relations, but a wider range of gendered contexts. Our conclusion for criminology is that gender is more important in the patterning of violence and its theorization than currently occurs. Criminological theory should more systematically address the gendered patterns of violence in which violence against women is nearly as common as violence against men. The gendering of violence is not a marginal special issue, but should be central to the field.

Acknowledgements

This work was supported by the Economic and Social Research Council, grant number ES/K002899/1, as part of the Secondary Data Analysis Initiative.

We thank the ONS for the use of the Crime Survey for England and Wales, and the UK Data Service for its assistance in accessing this data.

We state, as requested, that the original data creators, depositors or copyright holders, the funders of the Data Collections (if different) and the UK Data Service bear no responsibility for their further analysis or interpretation.

Note

1 Frequency of domestic abuse cannot be estimated using 2011/12 data so 2008/9 CSEW data is used for this analysis.

References

Agnew, Robert, (1992), 'Foundation for a general strain theory of crime and delinquency', *Criminology*, 30 (1): 47–87.

Agnew, Robert, (1999), 'A general strain theory of community differences in crime rates', *Journal of Research in Crime and Delinquency*, 36 (2): 123–155.

Archer, John, (2000), 'Sex differences in aggression between heterosexual partners: a meta-analytic review', *Psychological Bulletin*, 126: 651–680.

Becker, Gary, (1968), 'Crime and punishment: an economic approach', *Journal of Political Economy*, 76 (2): 169–217.

Bernard, April, (2013), 'The intersectional alternative: explaining female criminality', *Feminist Criminology*, 8 (1): 3–19.

Bourdieu, Pierre, (2000 [1997]), *Pascalian Meditations*. Cambridge: Polity Press.

Burgess-Proctor, Amanda, (2006), 'Intersections of race, class, gender, and crime: future directions for feminist criminology', *Feminist Criminology*, 1 (1): 27–47.

Chiricos, Theodore, (1987), 'Rates of crime and unemployment: an analysis of aggregate research evidence', *Social Problems*, 34 (2): 187–212.

Cohen, Lawrence and Felson, Marcus, (1979), 'Social change and crime rate trends: a routine activity approach', *American Sociological Review*, 44 (4): 588–608.

Cole, Julio and Gramajo, Andrés M., (2009), 'Homicide rates in a cross-section of countries: evidence and interpretations', *Population and Development Review*, 35 (4): 749–776.

Cook, Philip, Machin, Stephen, Marie, Olivier, and Mastrobuoni, Giovanni (eds), (2013), *Lessons from the Economics of Crime*. Cambridge, MA: MIT Press.

The Sociological Review, 62:S2, pp. 187–214 (2014), DOI: 10.1111/1467-954X.12198
© 2014 The Authors. The Sociological Review published by John Wiley & Sons Ltd on behalf of the Editorial Board of The Sociological Review

Crenshaw, Kimberlé, (1991), 'Mapping the margins: intersectionality and women of color', *Stanford Law Review*, 43 (6): 1241–1299.

Crown Prosecution Service (CPS), (2013a), *Crown Prosecution Data on Violence against Women Strategy*, available at: http://www.cps.gov.uk/publications/docs/vawg_2012_2013_tables.pdf.

Crown Prosecution Service (CPS), (2013b), *Court Outcomes Data*, available at: http://www.cps.gov.uk/data/case_outcomes/index.html.

De Haan, Willem, (2009), 'Violence as an essentially contested concept', in Sophie Body-Gendrot and Pieter Spierenburg (eds), *Violence in Europe*, New York: Springer.

DeKeseredy, Walter, (2000), 'Current controversies on defining nonlethal violence against women in intimate heterosexual relationships', *Violence against Women*, 6 (7): 728–746.

Dobash, Rebecca Emerson and Dobash, Russell P., (1979), *Violence against Wives*, New York: Free Press.

Dobash, Russell P., Dobash, Rebecca Emerson, Wilson, Margo and Daly, M., (1992), 'The myth of symmetry in marital violence', *Social Problems*, 39: 401–421.

EIGE, (2014), *What is gender-based violence?* European Institute for Gender Equality, 28 February, available at: http://eige.europa.eu/content/what-is-gender-based-violence

Fanon, Franz, (1990 [1967]), *The Wretched of the Earth*, London: Penguin.

Farrell, Graham and Pease, Ken, (2007), 'Crime in England and Wales: more violence and more chronic victims', *Civitas Review*, 4 (2): 1–6.

Farrell, Graham, Philips, Coretta and Pease, Ken, (1995), 'Like taking candy: why does repeat victimization occur?' *British Journal of Criminology*, 35 (5): 384–399.

Fajnzylber, Pablo, Lederman, Daniel and Loayza, Norman, (2002), 'Inequality and violent crime', *Journal of Law & Economics*, 45 (1): 1–39.

Feist, Andy, Ashe, Jane, Lawrence, Jane, McPhee, Duncan and Wilson, Rachel, (2007), *Investigating and Detecting Recorded Offences of Rape*. Home Office Online Report 18/07, available at: http://rds.homeoffice.gov.uk/rds/pdfs07/rdsolr1807.pdf

Gordon, Malcolm, (2000), 'Definitional issues in violence against women', *Violence against Women*, 6 (7): 747–783.

Gottfredson, Michael and Hirschi, Travis, (1990), *A General Theory of Crime*, Stanford, CA: Stanford University Press.

Gramsci, Antonio, (1971), *Selections from the Prison Notebooks of Antonio Gramsci*, London: Lawrence and Wishart.

Haas, Peter, (1992), 'Introduction: epistemic communities and international policy coordination', *International Organization*, 46 (1): 1–35.

Hearn, Jeff, (2012), 'A multi-faceted power analysis of men's violence to known women: from hegemonic masculinity to the hegemony of men', *Sociological Review*, 60: 589–610.

Hester, Marianne, Westmarland, Nicole, Pearce, L. and Williamson, Emma, (2008), *Early Evaluation of the Domestic Violence, Crime and Victims Act 2004*. Ministry of Justice Research Series 14/08.

Home Office, (2013), *New Government Domestic Violence and Abuse Definition*, available at: https://www.gov.uk/government/publications/new-government-domestic-violence-and-abuse-definition (accessed 28 February 2014).

Hope, Tim and Norris, Paul, (2013), 'Heterogeneity in the frequency distribution of crime victimization', *Journal of Quantitative Criminology*, 29 (4): 543–578.

Hsieh, Ching-Chi and Pugh, M. D., (1993), 'Poverty, income inequality and violent crime: a meta-analysis of recent aggregate data studies', *Criminal Justice Review*, 18 (2): 182–202.

Johnson, Holly, (1996), *Dangerous Domains: Violence against Women in Canada*, Ontario: Nelson.

Johnson, Michael, (1995), 'Patriarchal terrorism and common couple violence: two forms of violence against women', *Journal of Marriage and the Family*, 57: 283–294.

Johnson, Michael, (2008), *A Typology of Domestic Violence: Intimate Terrorism, Violent Resistance, and Situational Couple Violence*, Boston, MA: Northeastern University Press.

Kalmuss, Debra and Straus, Murray, (1982), 'Wife's marital dependency and wife abuse', *Journal of Marriage and the Family*, 44 (2): 277–286.

Kelly, Liz, (1988), *Surviving Sexual Violence*, Cambridge: Polity Press.

211

Kilpatrick, Dean, (2004), 'What is violence against women? Defining and measuring the problem', *Journal of Interpersonal Violence*, 19 (11): 1209–1234.

Lovett, Jo and Kelly, Liz, (2009), *Different Systems, Similar Outcomes? Tracking Attrition in Reported Rape Cases in Eleven Countries. Country Briefing: England and Wales*. Child and Woman Abuse Studies Unit: London Metropolitan University.

Maguire, Mike, Morgan, Rod and Reiner, Robert (eds), (2012), *The Oxford Handbook of Criminology*, 5th edn, Oxford: Oxford University Press.

Malešević, Siniša, (2010), *The Sociology of War and Peace*, Cambridge: Cambridge University Press.

Mann, Michael, (1986), *The Sources of Social Power. Volume 1. A History of Power from the Beginning to A.D. 1760*, Cambridge: Cambridge University Press.

McLaughlin, Eugene, Muncie, John and Hughes, Gordon (eds), (2003), *Criminological Perspectives: Essential Readings*, 2nd edn, London: Sage.

Mears, Daniel, Cochran, Joshua and Beaver, Kevin, (2013), 'Self-control theory and nonlinear effects on offending', *Journal of Quantitative Criminology*, 29 (3): 447–476.

Merton, Robert, (1938), 'Social structure and anomie', *American Sociological Review*, 3 (5): 672–682.

Miller, Jody and Mullins, Christopher, (2008), 'The status of feminist theories in criminology', in Francis Cullen, John Wright and Kristie Blevins (eds), *Taking Stock: The Status of Criminological Theory*. Advances in Criminological Theory, 15: 217–249, New Brunswick, NJ: Transaction Publishers.

Moffitt, Terrie, (1993), 'Adolescence-limited and life-course-persistent antisocial behavior: a developmental taxonomy', *Psychological Review*, 100 (4): 674–701.

Myhill, Andy and Dunne, Danielle, (2015), 'Measuring coercive control: what can we learn from national population surveys', *Violence against Women*. Forthcoming.

National Policing Improvement Agency (NPIA), (2009), *The National Standard for Incident Recording: Definitions and Guidance*, London: Association of Chief Police Officers, Home Office and Association of Police Authorities, available at: http://www.acpo.police.uk/documents/partnerships/2009/200906LPPNSIR01.pdf (accessed on 25 February 2014).

Newburn, Tim, (2013), *Criminology*. 2nd edn, London: Routledge.

Office for National Statistics (ONS) (2013a), 02. Appendix Tables – Crime Survey for England and Wales Year Ending September 2013, available at: http://www.ons.gov.uk/ons/rel/crime-stats/crime-statistics/period-ending-september-2013/rft-appendix-tables.xls

Office for National Statistics, (2013b), *Focus on: Violence Crime and Sexual Offences 2012/13*, Cardiff: ONS.

Office for National Statistics, (2013c), *User Guide to Crime Statistics for England and Wales*, Cardiff: ONS.

Office for National Statistics, (2014), *Crime Survey for England and Wales, 2011–2012* [computer file]. Colchester, Essex: UK Data Archive [distributor], March 2013. SN: 7252, http://dx.doi.org/10.5255/UKDA-SN-7252-1

Piquero, Alex, Farrington, David and Blumstein, Alfred, (2003), 'The criminal career paradigm', *Crime and Justice*, 30: 359–506.

Planty, Michael and Strom, Kevin, (2007), 'Understanding the role of repeat victims in the production of annual US victimization rates', *Journal of Quantitative Criminology*, 23: 179–200.

Pratt, Travis and Cullen, Francis, (2000), 'The empirical status of Gottredson and Hirchi's general theory of crime: a meta-analysis', *Criminology*, 38 (3): 931–964.

Pratt, Travis and Cullen, Francis, (2005), 'Assessing macro-level predictors and theories of crime: a meta-analysis', *Crime and Justice*, 32: 373–450.

Pratt, Travis, Turanovic, Jullian, Fox, Kathleen and Wright, Kevin, (2014), 'Self-control and victimization: a meta-analysis', *Criminology*, 53 (1): 87–116.

Pridemore, William, (2008), 'A methodological addition to the cross-national empirical literature on social structure and homicide: a first test of the poverty-homicide thesis', *Criminology*, 46 (1): 133–154.

The Sociological Review, 62:S2, pp. 187–214 (2014), DOI: 10.1111/1467-954X.12198

Pridemore, William and Freilich, Joshua, (2005), 'Gender equity, traditional masculine culture, and female homicide victimization', *Journal of Criminal Justice*, 33 (3): 213–223.

Radford, Jill, (2003), 'Professionalising responses to domestic violence in the UK: definitional difficulties', *Safer Communities*, 2 (1): 32–39.

Ray, Larry, (2011), *Violence and Society*, London: Sage.

Saltzman, Linda, (2004), 'Definitional and methodological issues related to transnational research on intimate partner violence', *Violence against Women*, 10 (7): 812–830.

Saltzman, Linda, Fanslow, J., MacMahon, P., and Shelley, G., (1999), *Intimate Partner Violence Surveillance: Uniform Definitions and Recommended Data Elements* (version 1.0). Atlanta: CDC National Center for Injury Prevention and Control.

Sampson, Robert, Morenoff, Jeffrey and Gannon-Rowley, Thomas, (2002), 'Assessing "neighbourhood effects": social processes and new directions in research', *Annual Review of Sociology*, 28: 443–478.

Sharp, Susan, (2006), 'Editorial', *Feminist Criminology*, 1 (1): 3–5.

Shaw, Clifford R. and McKay, Henry D., (1942), *Juvenile Delinquency and Urban Areas*, Chicago: Chicago University Press.

Stark, Evan, (2007), *Coercive Control: How Men Entrap Women in Personal Life*, New York: Oxford University Press.

Statistics Authority, (2014), 'Assessment of compliance with the Code of practice for Official Statistics: Statistics on Crime in England and Wales. Assessment report 268. London: Statistics Authority, available at: http://www.statisticsauthority.gov.uk/assessment/assessment/assessment-reports/assessment-report-268—statistics-on-crime-in-england-and-wales.pdf (accessed 25 February 2014).

Steffensmeier, Darrell, Zhong, Hua, Ackerman, Jeff, Schwartz, Jennifer and Agha, Suzanne, (2006), 'Gender gap trends for violent crimes: a UCR-NCVS Comparison', *Feminist Criminology*, 1 (1): 72–98.

Straus, Murray, (1979), 'Measuring intrafamily conflict and violence: the conflict tactics (CT) scale', *Journal of Marriage and the Family*, 41 (1): 75–88.

Straus, Murray and Gelles, R. J. (eds), (1990), *Physical Violence in American Families*, New Brunswick, NJ: Transaction Publishers.

Tilly, Charles, (2003), *The Politics of Collective Violence*, Cambridge: Cambridge University Press.

UK Government, (2013), *A Call to End Violence against Women and Girls: Action Plan 2013*, available at: https://www.gov.uk/government/uploads/system/uploads/attachment_data/file/181088/vawg-action-plan-2013.pdf (accessed 25 February 2014).

UK Statistics Authority, (2014), *Assessment of Compliance with the Code of Practice for Official Statistics: Statistics on Crime in England and Wales*, Assessment Report 268, London: UK Statistics Authority.

United Nations General Assembly, (1993), *Declaration on the Elimination of Violence against Women*, A/RES/48/104, available at: http://www.un.org/documents/ga/res/48/a48r104.htm (accessed 25 February 2014).

van Wilsem, J., (2004), 'Crime victimization in cross-national perspective', *European Journal of Criminology*, 1: 89–109.

Vieraitis, Lynne, Britto, Sarah and Kovandzic, Tomislav, (2007), 'The impact of women's status and gender inequality on female homicide victimization rates', *Feminist Criminology*, 2 (1): 57–73.

von Holdt, Karl, (2013), 'The violence of order, orders of violence: Between Fanon and Bourdieu', *Current Sociology*, 61 (2): 112–131.

Walby, Sylvia, (2004), *The Cost of Domestic Violence*, London: DTI Women and Equality Unit.

Walby, Sylvia, (2009), *Globalization and Inequalities: Complexity and Contested Modernities*, London: Sage.

Walby, Sylvia, (2013), 'Violence and society: an introduction to an emerging field of Sociology', *Current Sociology*, 61 (2): 95–111.

Walby, Sylvia and Allen, Jonathan, (2004), *Domestic Violence, Sexual Assault and Stalking: Findings from the British Crime Survey*, London: Home Office.

Walby, Sylvia and Myhill, Andy, (2001), 'New survey methodologies in researching violence against women', *British Journal of Criminology*, 41: 502–522.

Walby, Sylvia, Armstrong, Jo and Strid, Sofia, (2010), *Physical and Legal Security and the Criminal Justice System: A Review of Inequalities*, Equality and Human Rights Commission, Available at: http://www.equalityhumanrights.com/uploaded_files/triennial_review/triennial_review_cjs_review.pdf (accessed 25 February 2014).

Walklate, Sandra, (2004), *Gender, Crime and Criminal Justice*, London: Willan Publishing.

Weber, Max, (1948), *From Max Weber: Essays in Sociology* (trans. and edited by H. H. Gerth and C. W. Mills), London: Routledge and Kegan Paul.

Wieviorka, Michel, (2009 [2005]), *Violence: A New Approach*, London: Sage.

Wolfgang, Marvin E., and Ferracuti, F., (1967), *The Subculture of Violence: Towards an Integrated Theory in Criminology*, London: Tavistock Publications.

Young, Jock, (1999), *The Exclusive Society*, London: Sage.

Žižek, Slavoj, (2009 [2008]), *Violence: Six Sideways Reflections*, London: Profile Books.

The Sociological Review, 62:S2, pp. 187–214 (2014), DOI: 10.1111/1467-954X.12198

Notes on contributors

Glenn Bowman is Reader in Social Anthropology at the University of Kent's School of Anthropology and Conservation. His research (1983–present) has predominantly concerned Israel/Palestine (particularly Jerusalem and Bethlehem District) where he has examined topics ranging from pilgrimage and inter-communal shrine sharing to nationalist mobilization and the historic and contemporary practices of structured separation. He has carried out cognate research in Yugoslavia (1990–present) and Divided Cyprus (2009–present). Significant recent publications are 'Israel's Wall and the Logic of Encystation: Sovereign Exception or Wild Sovereignty?' (2009), 'Nationalizing and Denationalizing the Sacred: Shrines and Shifting Identities in the Israeli-Occupied Territories' (2012), 'The Politics of Ownership: State, Governance and the Status Quo in the Anastasis (Holy Sepulchre)' (2014) and, edited with Robert Hudson, *After Yugoslavia: Identities and Politics within the Successor States* (2012). e-mail:g.w.bowman@kent.ac.uk

Mark Cooney is Professor of Sociology and Adjunct Professor of Law at the University of Georgia, USA. Interested in the causes and handling of conflict, he has published work on a variety of topics, including the production of legal evidence, the role of third parties in violent conflict, the historical decline in rates of homicide, everyday discrimination against immigrants in Ireland, and last statement apologies by Texas death row prisoners. He is the author of two books, the most recent being *Is Killing Wrong? A Study in Pure Sociology* (University of Virginia Press). e-mail: mcooney@uga.edu

Brian Francis is Professor of Social Statistics, and a member of the Centre for Law and Society at Lancaster University, UK. He has over 30 years of experience of statistical consultancy and applied statistical research, as well as a substantive interest in criminology. His work has focused recently on the analysis of criminal careers and issues relating to serious crime, including homicide, kidnap, domestic violence and trafficking, as well as organized crime. He is currently co-editing the *Oxford Handbook of Sex Offences and Sex Offending*. His 200 publications span statistics, criminology health, sociology and psychology, developing analytic approaches. Recent work includes papers on football

The Sociological Review, 62:S2, pp. 215–219 (2014), DOI: 10.1111/1467-954X.12217
Editorial organisation © 2014 The Editorial Board of the Sociological Review. Published by John Wiley & Sons Ltd, 9600 Garsington Road, Oxford OX4 2DQ, UK and 350 Main Street, Malden, MA 02148, USA

and domestic violence, the desistance of sex offenders and the statistical modelling of social networks. His methodological interests include quantitative methods in criminology and the social sciences, latent class methods and analysis of preference and ranked data. e-mail: b.francis@lancaster.ac.uk

Steve Hall is Professor of Criminology and Co-director of the Teesside Centre for Realist Criminology, Teesside University, UK. In the 1970s he was a journeyman musician, general labourer and avid reader of anything political or philosophical. In the 1980s he worked with young offenders in the de-industrializing north-east of England, and he was active politically during the steelworks and mine closures in Co. Durham. In 1988 he returned to university, and, after graduating in 1991 began teaching, researching and publishing. Essentially a criminologist, he has also published in the fields of sociology, history and philosophy. He is co-author of *Violent Night* (Berg, 2006), *Criminal Identities and Consumer Culture* (Willan/Routledge, 2008) and *Rethinking Social Exclusion* (Sage, 2013). He is author of *Theorizing Crime and Deviance: A New Perspective* (Sage, 2012) and co-editor of *New Directions in Criminological Theory* (Routledge, 2012). e-mail: steve.hall@tees.ac.uk

Curtis Jackson-Jacobs received his PhD in Sociology from UCLA. His research and teaching has emphasized the interactional dynamics and 'micro-politics' of trouble – both at the level of face-to-face interaction, based on ethnographic research, and at the level of institutional responses, as well as the relationship between individual conduct and institutional contexts. He has conducted in-depth ethnographic research on criminality, conflict, and other troubles, particularly in non-traditional contexts, such as 'hard drugs' on college campuses and violence among socioeconomically privileged youth. His research interests also extend to issues of methodology and the sociology of knowledge in fields related to conflict and deviance. e-mail: curtisjacksonjacobs @gmail.com

Jane Kilby is a Senior Lecturer in English and Cultural Studies at the University of Salford. She is a specialist in violence and the cultural politics of speaking out, with a particular interest in women's experiences and accounts of sexual abuse. *The Future of Testimony* (edited with Antony Rowland, Routledge, 2014) is her latest publication in this area. In a radical departure from her usual, and distinctly conventional, style of academic practice, she is now experimenting with a new form of writing. Ficto-criticism is an approximate but enabling term for this creative enterprise. Planned publications include a ficto-critical reading of the life and death of Aileen Wuornos; and of *Lucky*, Alice Sebold's rape memoir. e-mail: j.e.kilby@salford.ac.uk

Kevin McSorley is Senior Lecturer in Sociology at the University of Portsmouth. His research explores contemporary transformations in violence and warfare in

The Sociological Review, 62:S2, pp. 215–219 (2014), DOI: 10.1111/1467-954X.12217
Editorial organisation © 2014 The Editorial Board of the Sociological Review

terms of the associated modes of embodiment, material cultures and affective regimes. He is the editor, with Sarah Maltby, of *War and the Body: Militarization, Practice and Experience* (Routledge, 2013) and a special issue of the *Journal of War and Culture Studies* on War and Embodiment. He has written widely on the embodied and sensory experiences of war and militarism. He is currently conducting ethnographic research on military fitness regimes and working on the collection *Sensing War*. e-mail: kevin.mcsorley@port.ac.uk

Siniša Malešević is a Professor of Sociology at University College, Dublin and a Visiting Professor (Eric Remacle Chair in Conflict and Peace Studies) at the Université Libre de Bruxelles. He is an elected member of the Royal Irish Academy and Academia Europaea. Previously he held research and teaching appointments at the Institute for International Relations (Zagreb), the Centre for the Study of Nationalism, CEU (Prague), the National University of Ireland, Galway, the London School of Economics and the Institute for Human Sciences (Vienna). His recent books include *Nation-States and Nationalisms: Organisation, Ideology and Solidarity* (Polity Press, 2013; Croatian translation in press); *The Sociology of War and Violence* (Cambridge University Press, 2010; reprinted in 2012; Croatian translation, 2011), *Identity as Ideology* (Palgrave, 2006; Persian translation, 2012), *The Sociology of Ethnicity* (Sage, 2004; Serbian translation, 2009; Persian translation, 2011) and co-edited volumes *Nationalism and War* (Cambridge University Press, 2013) and *Ernest Gellner and Contemporary Social Thought* (Cambridge University Press, 2007). e-mail: sinisa.malesevic @ucd.ie

Larry Ray is Professor of Sociology at the University of Kent. His publications and research include the areas of sociological theory, globalization, post-communism, memory, collective and interpersonal violence. His interests in the sociology of violence include research and publication on civil war and genocide, racist violence and violent crime. In 2011 he published *Violence and Society* (Sage) which develops a wide-ranging and integrated account of the many manifestations of violence in society. This examines violent behaviour and its meanings in contemporary culture and throughout history. He has also recently worked on photography and representations of suffering and on post-Holocaust Jewish identity and memory in the UK and Europe. He is a Fellow of the Academy of Social Sciences. e-mail: l.j.ray@kent.ac.uk

Jude Towers is a Senior Research Associate in the Sociology Department at Lancaster University, UK. She has a PhD in Applied Social Statistics. Her research concentrates on the measurement of gender-based violence and on exploring the relationship between different forms of gender-based violence within varying economic, social and political contexts using large-scale quantitative datasets. She has worked on research projects on gender-based violence funded by the Economic and Social Research Council, the European

Parliament, and the Northern Rock Foundation and Trust for London. She is currently working on the ESRC-funded Secondary Data Analysis Initiative 'Is the rate of domestic violence increasing or decreasing? A re-analysis of the British Crime Survey led by Professor Sylvia Walby and with Professor Brian Francis. Her website is: http://www.lancaster.ac.uk/sociology/profiles/jude -towers. e-mail: j.towers1@lancaster.ac.uk

Karl von Holdt is the Director of the Society Work and Development Institute (SWOP), University of the Witwatersrand, Johannesburg, which he joined as a senior researcher in 2007. Prior to that he was at the Congress of South African Trade Unions (COSATU)-linked policy institute, NALEDI, and before that Editor of the South African Labour Bulletin. He has published *Transition from Below: Forging Trade Unionism and Workplace Change in South Africa* (2003), *Beyond the Apartheid Workplace: Studies in Transition* (2005) co-edited with Eddie Webster, and co-authored with Michael Burawoy, *Conversations with Bourdieu: The Johannesburg Moment* (2012). His current research interests include collective violence and contentious politics, strikes and labour movements, democracy, citizenship and civil society, the functioning of state institutions, and social theory and the global South. e-mail: karl @yeoville.org.za

Sylvia Walby OBE is Distinguished Professor of Sociology and UNESCO Chair in Gender Research, in the Department of Sociology at Lancaster University, UK. She has conducted research on gendered violence for the European Commission, European Parliament, European Institute for Gender Equality, UN Economic Commission for Europe, UN Division for the Advancement of Women, UK Home Office, Women and Equality Unit, and EHRC. Relevant publications include: *Domestic Violence, Sexual Assault and Stalking: Findings from the British Crime Survey* (with J. Allen, Home Office 2004), *The Cost of Domestic Violence* (DTI Women and Equality Unit, 2004); *Globalization and Inequalities* (Sage, 2009), and a special issue of *Current Sociology* on 'Violence and Society' in 2013. She leads the ESRC-funded project 'Is the rate of domestic violence increasing or decreasing? A reanalysis of the British Crime Survey', on which she works with Brian Francis and Jude Towers. Her website is: http:// www.lancaster.ac.uk/fass/sociology/profiles/Sylvia-Walby. e-mail: s.walby @lancaster.ac.uk

Michel Wieviorka is Professor of Sociology at L'Ecole des Hautes Etudes en Sciences Sociales and President of the Fondation de la Maison des Sciences de l'Homme, both located in Paris. He is a member of the scientific board of the European Research Council and has been President of the International Sociological Association (2006–2010). Among his recent books in English are *Evil*, (Polity Press, 2012) and *The Front National* (Counterpoint, 2013). He is the founder of a new journal, *SOCIO*. e-mail: wiev@msh-paris.fr

218

Simon Winlow is Professor of Criminology and the Co-Director of the Teesside Centre for Realist Criminology at Teesside University, UK. He is the author of *Badfellas* (Berg, 2001) and the co-author of *Bouncers* (Oxford University Press, 2003), *Violent Night* (Berg, 2006), *Criminal Identities and Consumer Culture* (Willan, 2008), *Rethinking Social Exclusion* (Sage, 2013) and the forthcoming *Revitalizing Criminological Theory* (Routledge, 2015) and *Riots and Political Protest* (Routledge, 2015). email: s.winlow@tees.ac.uk

Index

Derrida, J., 34
desubjectivation, 62–63
determinism, 51
deterritorialization, 19
DNA testing, 23
domestic violence, 179–180; categories,
198; definition, 195–196;
mainstreaming, 187–214; measurement,
196–197
drones, 79, 82, 120

Egypt, 132
Eichmann, A., 53, 61
Eisner, M., 5, 13, 14, 16
elections, 132, 133; South Africa,
134–138, 147
Elias, N., 5, 6, 14, 15, 16, 69, 100, 123;
see also civilizing process
empires, 72, 73, 75, 80
ethnology, 53, 63
event theories, 90
evil, 2, 60; psychosocial basis, 24–28;
socioeconomic function, 13–31
exclusion, 8, 60, 144, 147, 148
experience, embodied, 107, 108, 113–120
Eyerman, R., 3

family, dissolution, 18–19;
honour-sensitive, 94–95; violence,
179–180
fathers, 40–41, 42, 44, 88, 92, 95
feminism, international relations, 112–115
Fielding, H., 22
fights, as 'action', 176–177; as athletic
contest, 174–176; as 'victimless crime',
177–181; as violence, 166–167; cultural
meaning, 174–179; definition, 169–174;
group fights, 170–171, 175;
institutional responses, 179–181;
interventions, 181; serious, 172–173
financial crisis 2008, 7
football hooligans, 175
Former Yugoslavia, 152, 157–159
Foucault, M., 59, 60, 116, 130, 149
Francis, B., 9, 187–214
Freud, S., 5, 6

gangs, 4, 17, 18, 19, 58, 124, 131, 168,
187

gender, 2, 7, 74; gender-based violence,
187–214; stratification, 94–95, 100
genocide, 4, 7, 8, 66, 68, 91, 102, 103, 159
Gerlach, C., 8–9
Girard, R., 6, 8, 62; mimetic violence, 8;
violent doubles, 8
global South, and violent democracy,
129–151
globalization, 65, 68, 76, 83
Gluckman, M., 163
Goffman, E., 55, 162, 176
Goldstein, D.M., 131–132, 133, 148
Grabowski, J., 9
Gramsci, A., 191
guilt, 32–49; and humiliation, 42–47

habitus, 33, 34, 39, 116
Hall, S., 2, 6, 13–31
Higate, P., 115, 116, 121
historical sociology, and war, 71–82, 111
history, 2, 59; European, 17–21
Hobbes, T., 5
Hockey, J., 116, 124
Holocaust, 157
Holston, J., 131, 132, 148
honour violence, 7, 87–106; abandonment
of culture, 99–100; and gossip, 96;
bridewealth, 97; conflicts, 93; murders,
92
Horkheimer, M., 3
human rights, 51, 69, 70, 88, 135
Human Security Brief, 5–6, 8
humanism, commercial, 20
humiliation, and guilt, 42–47

identity politics, 152–165; in Former
Yugoslavia, 157–159
immigrants, 103, 158
individualism, 24, 38, 41
individualization, 19, 20
industrialization, 21, 23; of warfare, 74
insults, 37, 39, 177
interactions, 52, 55–57, 59, 62, 95, 167,
168, 169, 170, 195
International Centre for Prison Studies, 6
international relations, feminist, 112–115
internet, 3, 54, 77
interpellation, 155, 160
Islam, 54, 60

The Sociological Review, 62:S2, pp. 220–224 (2014), DOI: 10.1111/1467-954X.12225

The Sociological Review, 62:S2, pp. 220–224 (2014). DOI: 10.1111/1467-954X.12225
Editorial organisation © 2014 The Editorial Board of the Sociological Review